# THE STRAIGHT POOP

# THE STRAIGHT POOP

## A Plumber's Tattler

*by Peter A. Hemp*

**TEN SPEED PRESS**

CIP
Library of Congress Cataloging-in-Publication Data

Hemp, Peter A. (Peter Addison)
    The straight poop.
    1. Plumbing—Amateurs' manual. I. Title.
TH 6124.H45  1985    644'.6    85–18367
ISBN 0-89815-146-5

TEN SPEED PRESS
P. O. Box 7123
Berkeley, California 94707

Library of Congress Catalog Number 85-18367
ISBN 0-89815-146-5

Cover design and illustrations by Peter A. Hemp
Printed in the United States of America
10 9 8 7 6 5 4 3 2 1

My Heartfelt Thanks go out to
Danny Cline, Jimmie Kane, Winn Talmon,
Ray Chandler, Mary Webb, Ann Bell,
Irene Hegarty, Mike Prusky, and Katherine Hemp.
AND
Thanks Again! George Inskeep...
Wherever You Are.

Anyone using this book must recognize that the author does not and cannot accept liability from its use. However, much effort has been devoted to making all statements in the book correct.

# Table of Contents

# Part II  Replacing The Offender

## Part III    Toilets

# Plumbing De-mystified
## or
## "You Can Never Go Down The Drain"

Psychologists say that one of the most common childhood fears is that of being swept down the bathtub drain when the stopper is pulled — second only to the fear of being flushed down the toilet. Such fears are so common that Dr. Spock advises parents about them and Mr. Rogers even has an appropriate song ("You Can Never Go Down The Drain"). Well, we grow up and leave such fears behind, or, more accurately, we transform them into a fear of the plumber — that bogeyman who comes and does mysterious things and charges a ransom if we want our house back. This may be why so many otherwise self-sufficient, well-informed adults become helpless children again when confronted with a plumbing problem.

I am a professional plumber practicing a residential and commercial trade, both in repair and in new construction. I've spent many an hour at the drugstore, supermarket and hardware store bookracks waiting for my family to finish shopping. I've read every do-it-yourself plumbing guide available. Most books on do-it-yourself plumbing assume the reader *already knows* what needs to be fixed or replaced, and so merely outline the basic procedures. THIS book assumes the reader does not know an angle stop from a valve stem, and would not recognize a gravity leak if it dripped onto Aunt Clara's cat. More sophisticated readers (plumbing wise) can skip directly to the information they need, but for the first timer I will take the time to explain each step of the process. In particular, I offer the "DIRTY DOZEN," that will help you diagnose what the problem is and what to do about it. The list pretty much covers the kinds of problems homeowners face.

In addition, Part I contains an illustrated list of plumbing tools and parts, a description of how the plumbing system works in your house, and some essential procedures, like how to turn the water off.

If the problem requires more than a fix-it approach, or if you are remodeling, Part II of the book covers the "Ultimate Repair" — replacement of the fixture itself. Each type of installation is described in plain talk, with step-by-step advice and simple drawings to guide the novice.

As a plumber, I have ceased to be amazed at the "Rube Goldberg" combinations of home plumbing remedies that the layperson can devise (like a Ford transmission part in the ballcock). In writing this book, I wanted to reach those who need my help the most. So it was written and illustrated *expressly* for the timid, the cowards, the desperate, the first-time do-it-yourselfer, and those previously scathed but nonetheless surviving veterans of do-it-yourself campaigns.

As you use this book, you will discover that I mention and recommend *specific* brand names. I do so because I want this book to be as much help to you as possible, and so I will give you the same advice I would give a friend. My recommendations may not be exhaustive, and certainly new products are on the market every year, but these are the products I have found to be reliable, well-made, or cost-effective.

So, let's pick up our wrenches and march forward. Fear not: Whatever happens, *you can never go down the drain.*

Peter Addison Hemp

# Part I
# Basic Repairs

## Man's Greatest Luxury: Indoor Plumbing

That title phrase may hold little water with you, until for one or more reasons you find yourself abruptly without your indoor plumbing. Then the true weight of that phrase falls upon you with all the presence of Niagara Falls! Forbearance wears pretty thin after borrowing the use of a neighbor's "potty" or shower for more than twenty-four hours. For those of you who have endured an abrupt, unplanned, and extended absence of a convenient, private plumbing system, you have shared the intrinsic parity of all savages, and all of a sudden civilization takes on new dimensions.

Before you learn basic plumbing repair, it is helpful to understand how the plumbing system works in a house.

In the residential building trade, plumbers are involved with several plumbing systems: heating (gas lines or oil lines, sheet metal ducting and flu venting); cooling (gas lines and condensate lines, ducting and venting); ground water drainage (around the building perimeter water courses) and the last two systems which I wish to discuss here: *fresh water supply*, and *drains, waste and vent* systems.

### Fresh Water Supply

Fresh water (drinking water), whether it is pumped into a building from a private well or a municipal water main, enters the house or building under a pressure usually between 55 to 90 pounds per square inch. The water enters the building cold, usually in the fresh water system's largest diameter pipe. Off this larger cold water pipe, *branch lines* split off and carry water to the hose bibs (outside faucets) at various locations around the building. If you have a rooftop solar water heating system, a branch line will take off to feed that, and if you have a swimming pool or backyard hot tub, the cold water main line will continue on its way to feed that also. Also, off the cold water main line, branch lines split off and proceed to each plumbing location: bathroom, kitchen, laundry and bar sink, if any. Eventually, the cold water main line reaches the location of the hot water heater or boiler.

The cold water enters this appliance cold (unless it has been pre-heated in a solar system whereas it would enter as hot water) creating a need again for branch lines to run to each bath-

room, kitchen, laundry room, and bar sink. Since the entire fresh water system is under pressure, the water pipes may travel up and down the walls, across and under floors, above in the ceilings, or even on the outside of the building. Because this is a pressure system, it pays little heed to gravity. The plumber may install these lines in the particular wall and floors as he sees fit. And very few home dwellers give it any thought until one such pipe bursts and makes itself uncomfortably evident.

Cold and hot water pipes within a private home averaging 2,000 square feet seldom exceed 1 inch in inside diameter, and it is most common to find them in ¾ inch and ½ inch diameter. Common pipe material for fresh water systems are galvanized plated steel, copper and, in some unfortunate states, CPVC plastic. There are very specific guidelines that a plumber relies on when he "sizes" up the piping system for a building. This ensures that the fresh water pipes are large enough in diameter to deliver sufficient amounts of fresh hot and cold water to all room locations calling for it.

1

## Drains, Waste, And Vents

The piping system that takes away the waste water from our sinks, tubs, and toilets is much larger in diameter than the fresh water system because it is a *gravity* system. By this I mean that there is no pump to push the waste water through the pipes. It is the mere weight of the water (produced by gravity) that causes the water to run down the drain lines and out of the building.

There are also very specific guidelines determining the diameters and "inches of fall" (slope) for this drain, waste, and vent system to ensure that all of the waste water and sewerage will flow out of the building without causing blockages.

Since the drain, waste, and vent pipes are much larger in diameter than the fresh water supply pipes and both systems terminate at a water usage location, the plumber first installs the drainage system because this gravity system (not having aid of pressure) needs the most direct route out of the building.

To the layperson, the concept of fresh water piping and the drains and waste system are pretty easily understood. But the vent system usually leaves them a bit stymied. Have you ever climbed up upon a roof and seen those pipes sticking out of the roof, the ones you knew were too small to be chimneys, and you wondered what the hell they were for? They are the vent pipes (stacks) and are an integral part of the drains and waste system. Those pipes are directly connected to the drain lines in your bathroom, kitchen, laundry and bar.

The purpose of those vent stacks is to let atmospheric pressure into the building's drains and sewer. Without them, the waste water and sewerage would not run down the pipes and out of your building. As a matter of fact, it has been known for years by some very unsavory fellows that potatoes and squashes pounded down a neighbor's vent stacks will project water and deposits in toilet bowls out onto the bathroom floor. In San Diego, in the late 1800s, when the first municipal reservoir was completed and a piping system installed to bring the fresh water from miles away into the little town, a grand celebration was planned to witness the first, lucid flow. Dignitaries came from far and wide for the event. The bright engineers of this project forgot about atmospheric pressure and gravity, however. The pipe ran downhill from the reservoir all right but there were no vents installed on the pipe. When the gates of the reservoir were opened, the crowd waited in vain for the real fresh water to show up in their town. In desperation, the city fathers had the line hacked open just outside of town and the usual foul fare was surreptitiously poured into the hole so as not to disappoint the assemblage. Everyone remarked what a great improvement the new arrival was over their old reprehensible swill.

An easy way to demonstrate this phenomenon is by using the old drinking straw in a glass of water trick. Place a straw into a glass of water, then put your thumb over the top of the straw and lift the straw out of the glass. Remaining inside the straw is a column of water about the depth of the water in the glass. Now take your thumb away from the straw and the water immediately runs out, back into the glass. Now in our drain, waste, and vent system, the vent stack is the straw.

Keeping these basic systems in mind should help you to understand what is meant when we speak of a *gravity leak* (i.e., a leak in the waste water system) versus a *pressure leak* (i.e., a leak in the fresh water supply).

*It's eleven o'clock...
do you know where your
main water shut-off valve is?
Do you know how to operate it?*

# Finding The Water Shut-Off

Before beginning any plumbing repair, you first must know the locations of any hand-operated shut-off valves at your building and the location of the water meter, if you are not on a private well system. If you are on a private well, it is common not to have a water meter. See Illus. 1.

If you are not aware of any hand-operated shut-off valves, first locate the meter box. It is usually located in the parking strip or near the street, in front of your building. Now, visually draw a line from the meter to the house, and then go look. The valve will generally be within the first two feet from the ground.

If your home or building has a full basement, many times the shut-off will be down there at the same two-foot height, on the inside of the exterior wall. If it is not there, then look above your head, near the bottom of the floor joists. If your house has only a crawl space underneath it, and you find an access door to the

crawl space when you have followed a straight line to the house from the meter box, open the door and look to either side of the entrance for a gate valve (Illus. 2) installed in a run of water pipe, either galvanized or copper pipe.

If you find a valve, place a rag over the handle and rotate the handle in a clockwise direction as far as you can turn it. Now, on the outside of the building, go to the lowest faucet and open the valve. Next, go to the highest cold water faucet in the building and open it. This will drain the building of the residual cold water (water still inside the pipes).

If you were not able to locate a hand-operated shut-off valve at the building, or there was one but it does not shut the water off, go back to the meter box. Lift the lid with the handle of the water meter key or a large screwdriver. Down in that cobwebby place is the main water valve for the building. Between the round face of the recording mechanism and the

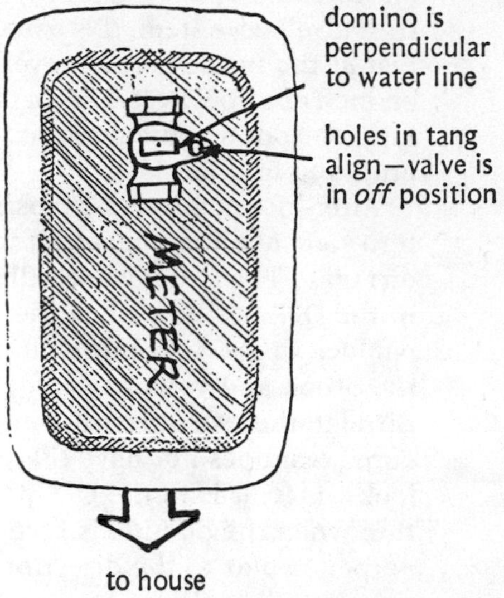

domino is perpendicular to water line

holes in tang align—valve is in *off* position

to house

Illustration **1**
Water Meter, Top View

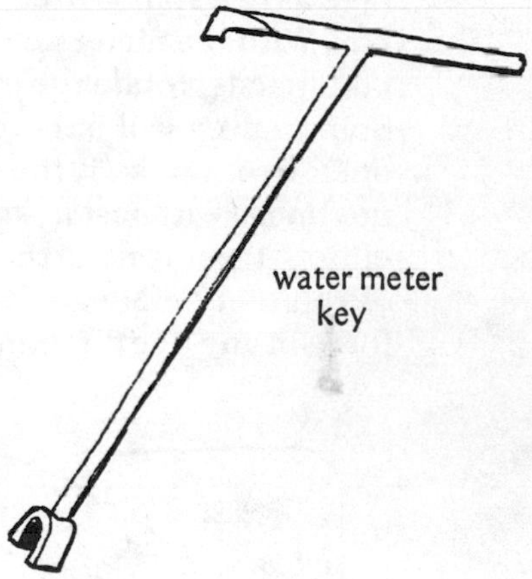

water meter key

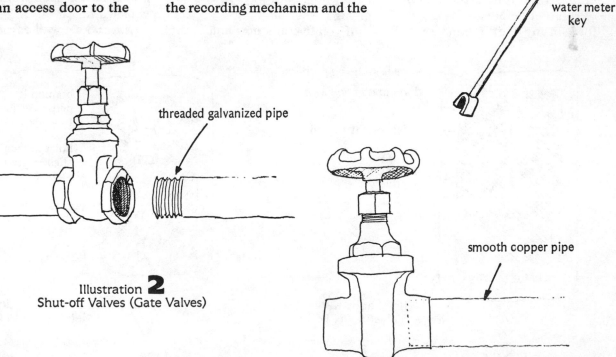

threaded galvanized pipe

Illustration **2**
Shut-off Valves (Gate Valves)

smooth copper pipe

3

street end of the cement box (Illus. 3) look for a small rectangular domino, which is the top of the valve's core stem. It is usually just at the inside ground level or an inch or so below it. Use an old kitchen spoon and dig around until you find it.

After locating it and exposing it to view, use a rag and clean the dirt off it. The meter valve will be in the OFF position when the two padlock wings align, one on top of the other, and you can see through the two holes. If your core stem does not have the padlock wings, it is in the OFF position when the domino is turned perpendicular to the direction of the water line (Illus. 4).

To rotate the core stem and thus. . .shut the water off, place the slot in the end of the water meter key over the domino and take a wide stance over the meter box. With the meter key handle in both hands, rotate the core stem. Some valves will only rotate in one direction, so if the stem does not budge with just a "small grunt effort," try reversing the direction of rotation before applying great force in any one direction, or you

might get an unplanned very powerful sitz bath, standing up.

These meter valves are seldom activated and sometimes it is very hard to get them turning even in the proper direction. A very embarrassing situation arose once when I was trying to turn off a very large water meter in front of a YWCA. I had taken my full stance over the meter, key handle in both hands and I gave it my "gut-busting" best. Well, nothing happened. The stem wouldn't budge. So I took a deep breath, gritted my teeth and this time really put my *all* to the task. My all this time proved a bit too much. The core stem rotated alright. Several old ladies who happened to be walking down the sidewalk and passing behind me, rotated all the way to vermillion when I accidently let loose a very loud 1,000 cubic feet of methane. After they were down the block a ways, they turned around and looked back at me, breaking into belly laughs. I wanted to crawl into the meter box. Maybe you'd better look both ways before giving it your all.

If you live in a new home, the

water meter valve might turn a full 180 degrees before the wings align. In the not so new neighborhoods, the core stem will usually require only a 90 degree rotation. If you are unsuccessful in getting the valve turned off, you call the water company out and request that they turn the valve off for you. It will not cost you anything to have this service performed.

With the meter turned off, see if you can drain all of the building's residual cold water off so that there is no leakage past the meter valve, which shows up as a continued stream out of the lowest hose bib. Give the water a good fifteen minutes to drain.

I have found many times that the hand shut-off valve is defective and turning off the water meter is necessary. It is also not uncommon to find both the hand shut-off valve and the meter valve to be defective in stemming the flow of water. If you should find yourself in this predicament, you will have to leave the building's lowest faucet open while you do your work.

Now take a well earned break!

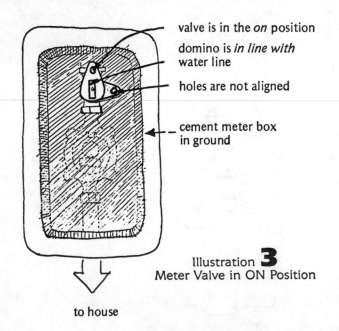

valve is in the *on* position

domino is *in line with* water line

holes are not aligned

cement meter box in ground

Illustration **3**
Meter Valve in ON Position

to house

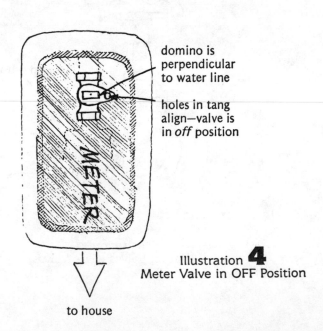

domino is perpendicular to water line

holes in tang align—valve is in *off* position

Illustration **4**
Meter Valve in OFF Position

to house

# The Compleat Do-It-Yourself Plumber's
# Tool Kit

Below is a list of tools that you should have to be totally prepared for repairing or replacing every item covered in this book. There is a tool-to-job cross-reference also. Illustrations of the tools follow.

    All of these tools should be available at your local tool rental agencies, and some possibly through special programs run by many cities, one in ~~Bezerkeley~~ Berkeley.

  A.   adjustable wrenches (6, 8, 12 and 15 inch)
  B.   pipe wrenches (8, 12 and 18 inch)
*C.   basin wrench (RIDGID #1017)
*D.   mini-hacksaw
  E.   standard 12 inch hacksaw with 32 teeth-per-inch blade
  F.   #2 slotted screwdriver, medium length
  G.   #1 Phillips head screwdriver, medium length
  H.   tubing cutter for ⅜ inch to 1½ inch diameter tubing (preferably the PAPCO 500)
  I.   two 10 inch slide-jaw pliers (I prefer the angle of the CRAFTSMAN brand)
  J.   pipe nipple back-out for ½ inch pipe (ACE brand #EX-7)
  K.   cold chisel, ¼ or ⅜ inch
  L.   ballpeen hammer, 10 to 13 ounce
  M.  adjustable safety goggles or glasses
  N.   propane torch and striker
  O.   water meter key
  P.   adjustable beam flashlight (preferably a SPORTSMAN or PASCO)
  Q.   Teflon tape, ½ inch wide (preferably PASCO or DU PONT brands)
  R.   plumber's putty, 1 to 3 pound can (preferably DAP or BLACK SWAN brands)
  S.   pipe joint compound, (preferably RECTORSEAL or SLIC-TITE brands)
  T.   penetrating oil (the smallest can)
  U.   stem grease, 1 to 3 ounce can
  V.   faucet handle puller (I use a PASCO #4658)
  W.  plumber's seat wrench
  X.   plumber's socket wrench set
  Y.   strainer wrench (CHICAGO SPECIALTY)
  Z.   ⁷⁄₁₆ inch open end/box wrench

* The basin wrench and mini-hacksaw may be difficult to find for rent. Your best bet may be to buy these.

## Tools You Will Need
Rent Them or Buy Them

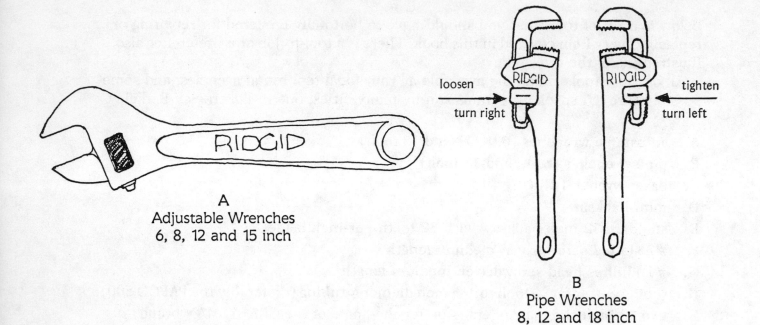

**A**
Adjustable Wrenches
6, 8, 12 and 15 inch

loosen
turn right

tighten
turn left

**B**
Pipe Wrenches
8, 12 and 18 inch

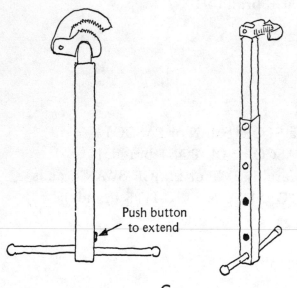

Push button
to extend

**C**
RIDGID #1017 Basin Wrench

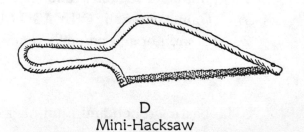

**D**
Mini-Hacksaw

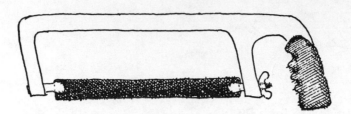

**E**
Standard 12 inch Hacksaw
(32 Teeth per Inch Blade)

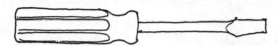

**F**
#2 Slotted Screwdriver

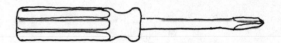

**G**
#1 Phillips Head Screwdriver

**H**
Tubing Cutter
For 3/8 inch to 1½ inch
Diameter Tubing

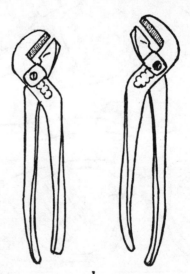

**I**
Two 10 inch Slide-Jaw Pliers

**J**

Pipe Nipple Back-out for ½ inch Pipe
Ace Brand #EX-7

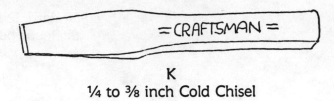

**K**

¼ to ⅜ inch Cold Chisel

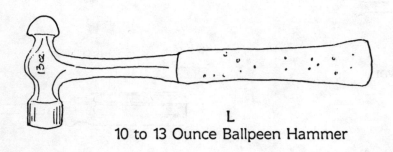

**L**

10 to 13 Ounce Ballpeen Hammer

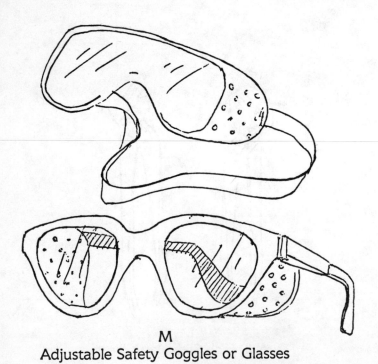

**N**

Propane Torch
and Striker

**M**

Adjustable Safety Goggles or Glasses

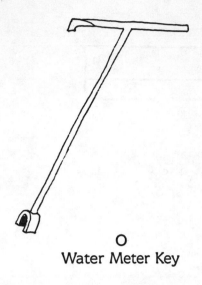

O
Water Meter Key

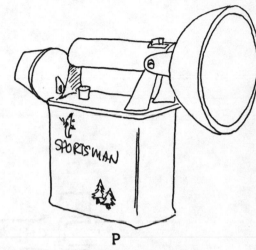

P
Adjustable Beam Flashlight
(Preferably a SPORTSMAN or PASCO)

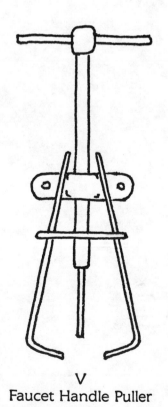

V
Faucet Handle Puller

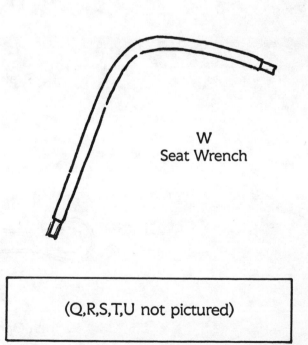

W
Seat Wrench

(Q,R,S,T,U not pictured)

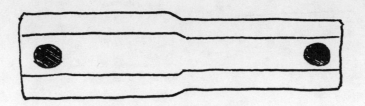

**X**
Plumber's Socket Wrench Set
(One from the Set of 5 or 6)

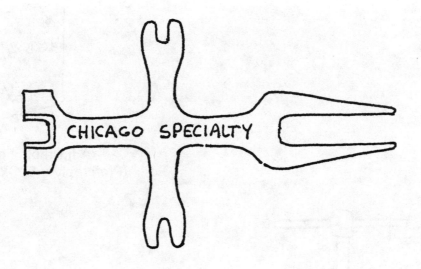

CHICAGO SPECIALTY

**Y**
Strainer Wrench

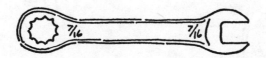

**Z**
7/16 inch Open-end/Box Wrench

# Tool Chart
## The Tools You Need For Each Job

*Note: The letters in parentheses refer to illustrations on pages 5 to 10.*

| TO REPAIR | YOU NEED— |
|---|---|
| ANGLE STOPS AND SUPPLIES | adjustable wrenches 6, 8, 12 & 15 inch (A) • pipe wrenches 8, 12 & 18 inch (B) • basin wrenches (C) • mini-hacksaw (D) • tubing cutter (H) • Ace EX-7 pipe nipple back-out (J) • safety goggles (M) • propane torch and striker (N) • water meter key (O) • ½ inch wide Teflon tape (Q) • pipe joint compound (Rectorseal or Slic-Tite) (S) • faucet handle puller (V) |
| 4 INCH CENTER SETS | adjustable wrenches 6, 8, 12 & 15 inch (A) • basin wrench Ridgid #1017 (C) • standard 12 inch hacksaw (32 t.p.i.) (E) • #2 slotted screwdriver (F) • #1 phillips screwdriver (G) • two 10 inch slide-jaw pliers (I) • safety goggles (M) • water meter key (O) • ½ inch wide Teflon tape (Q) • plumber's putty 1 to 3 pounds (R) • pipe joint compound (Rectorseal or Slic-Tite) (S) • faucet handle puller (V) |
| WIDE-SPREAD FAUCETS | adjustable wrenches 6, 8, 12 & 15 inch (A) • basin wrench Ridgid #1017 (C) • standard 12 inch hacksaw (32 t.p.i.) (E) • #2 slotted screwdriver (F) • #1 phillips screwdriver (G) • two 10 inch slide-jaw pliers (I) • safety goggles (M) • water meter key (O) • ½ inch wide Teflon tape (Q) • plumber's putty 1 to 3 pounds (R) • pipe joint compound (Rectorseal or Slic-Tite) (S) • faucet handle puller (V) |
| SINGLE-POST FAUCETS | adjustable wrenches 6, 8, 12 & 15 inch (A) • basin wrench Ridgid #1017 (C) • #2 slotted screwdriver (F) • #1 phillips screwdriver (G) • two 10 inch slide-jaw pliers (I) • safety goggles (M) • water meter key (O) • ½ inch wide Teflon tape (Q) • faucet handle puller (V) |
| SINGLE-COCKS | adjustable wrenches 6, 8, 12 & 15 inch (A) • basin wrench Ridgid #1017 (C) • #2 slotted screwdriver (F) • #1 phillips screwdriver (G) • safety goggles (M) • water meter key (O) • ½ inch wide Teflon tape (Q) • plumber's putty 1 to 3 pounds (R) • pipe joint compound (Rectorseal or Slic-Tite (S) • penetrating oil (T) |
| WALL-HUNG KITCHEN SINK FAUCETS | adjustable wrenches 6, 8, 12 & 15 inch (A) • #2 slotted screwdriver (F) • #1 phillips screwdriver (G) • Ace EX-7 pipe nipple back-out (J) • safety goggles (M) • propane torch and striker (N) • water meter key (O) • ½ inch wide Teflon tape (Q) • pipe joint compound (Rectorseal or Slic-Tite) (S) • stem grease 1 to 3 ounces (U) • faucet handle puller (V) |
| DECK-MOUNTED KITCHEN FAUCETS | adjustable wrenches 6, 8, 12 & 15 inch (A) • basin wrench Ridgid #1017 (C) • #2 slotted screwdriver (F) • #1 phillips screwdriver (G) • safety goggles (M) • water meter key (O) • ½ inch wide Teflon tape (Q) • plumber's putty 1 to 3 pounds (R) • pipe joint compound (Rectorseal or Slic-Tite) (S) • stem grease 1 to 3 ounces (U) • faucet handle puller (V) |
| WALL-HUNG LAUNDRY FAUCETS | adjustable wrenches 6, 8, 12 & 15 inch (A) • pipe wrenches 8, 12 & 18 inch (B) • #2 slotted screwdriver (F) • #1 phillips screwdriver (G) • Ace EX-7 pipe nipple back-out (J) • 10 to 13 ounce ballpeen hammer (L) • safety goggles (M) • propane torch and striker (N) • water meter key (O) • ½ inch wide Teflon tape (Q) • pipe joint compound (Rectorseal or Slic-Tite) (S) • faucet handle puller (V) |
| DECK-MOUNTED LAUNDRY FAUCETS | adjustable wrenches 6, 8, 12 & 15 inch (A) • basin wrench Ridgid #1017 (C) • #2 slotted screwdriver (F) • #1 phillips screwdriver (G) • safety goggles (M) • water meter key (O) • ½ inch wide Teflon tape (Q) • plumber's putty 1 to 3 pounds (R) • pipe joint compound (Rectorseal or Slic-Tite) (S) • faucet handle puller (V) |
| BAR SINK FAUCETS | adjustable wrenches 6, 8, 12 & 15 inch (A) • basin wrench Ridgid #1017 (C) • #2 slotted screwdriver (F) • #1 phillips screwdriver (G) • safety goggles (M) • water meter key (O) • ½ inch wide Teflon tape (Q) • plumber's putty 1 to 3 pounds (R) • pipe joint compound (Rectorseal or Slic-Tite) (S) • faucet handle puller (V) |
| TRAPS AND CONTINUOUS WASTES | pipe wrenches 8, 12 & 18 inch (B) • mini-hacksaw (D) • standard 12 inch hacksaw (32 t.p.i.) (E) • two 10 inch slide-jaw pliers (I) • safety goggles (M) • water meter key (O) • ½ inch wide Teflon tape (Q) • pipe joint compound (Rectorseal or Slic-Tite) (S) |
| TUB AND SHOWER VALVES | adjustable wrenches 6, 8, 12 & 15 inch (A) • #2 slotted screwdriver (F) • #1 phillips screwdriver (G) • two 10 inch slide-jaw pliers (I) • ¼ or ⅜ inch cold chisel (K) • 10 to 13 ounce ballpeen hammer (L) • safety goggles (M) • ½ inch wide Teflon tape (Q) • stem grease 1 to 3 ounces (U) • faucet handle puller (V) • plumber's socket wrench set (X) |

# THE DIRTY DOZEN

The Dirty Dozen is designed to be a troubleshooting guide for most common plumbing problems. Sometimes all you will need to do is tighten a nut or change a washer. Other problems may require replacement of the fixture, at which point you will be referred to the later section where that is covered and you can decide whether to do it yourself or call a plumber. If you call a plumber, be sure to read the checklist on page 40, on how to save on your plumbing bill.

And now, a baker's dozen of plumbing problems...

## How To Determine If It Is A Gravity Leak

If you find water on the floor, check to see if waste water is escaping from the waste piping (pop-up waste, trap, sink strainer, garbage disposer or continuous waste — see glossary). If so, you have *a gravity leak*, that is, water leaking from the drain system.

Another sign of a gravity leak is splash water lying on the sink shelf or counter, or finding its way to the floor from underneath a loosely mounted faucet.

Gravity leaks can be caused by loosely installed fixtures, poorly grouted tile, or water escaping from under your faucet handles. If you have a leak under a sink with a bathroom widespread faucet on it (Illus. 5), look closely at the spout and valve connections. (1 to 7).

To find the source of a leak, try putting small bowls under each *angle stop* and one under the trap. I put dry colored tissue in each bowl because it's easy to tell if it's wet without having to get down on your hands and knees to check.

The source of the leak will be almost directly above the bowl. On bathroom lavatory sinks, many times the water shows up on the rubber stopper or pop-up waste, just below the friction lock nut. The drip will then run down the waste onto and down the trap until it drops off the bottom of the trap. So look carefully at the waste before condemning the trap.

If you are looking for leaks under a sink which has a garbage disposer in it, make sure to run the disposer as you make your check because the vibration from the disposer often loosens the slip nuts used with tubular brass waste systems. (This is one reason why I stay away from cheap stainless steel and enameled steel sinks. They tend to vibrate a lot when a disposer is hung in them.) Unless you make your inspection while it's running you'll never know the garbage disposer is the culprit.

If you have a sink that is mounted in a rim or "hootie ring," look for gaps between the top surface of the sink and the ring. If there is a gap, and it is 1/16 of an inch or less, a squirt of DAP Tub and Tile Caulk in the crack will cure your problem. If the gap is larger than 1/16 of an inch, then either the mounting screw-brackets under the counter are loose or one or more is missing. Try tightening the screws with a long appropriate (slotted or Phillips) screwdriver or nut driver.

## Dirty Dozen #1
"I find water on the floor under the sink but cannot tell where it is coming from."

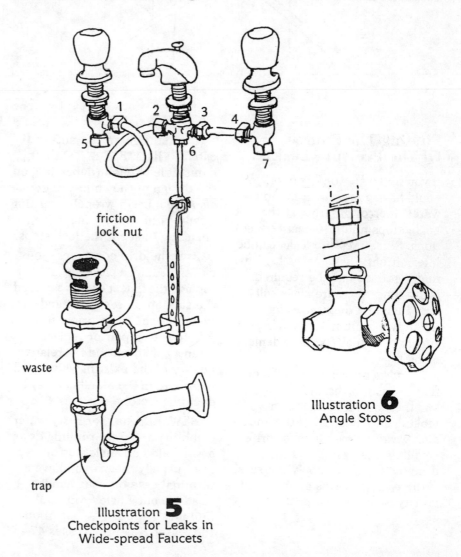

friction lock nut

waste

trap

**Illustration 5**
Checkpoints for Leaks in Wide-spread Faucets

**Illustration 6**
Angle Stops

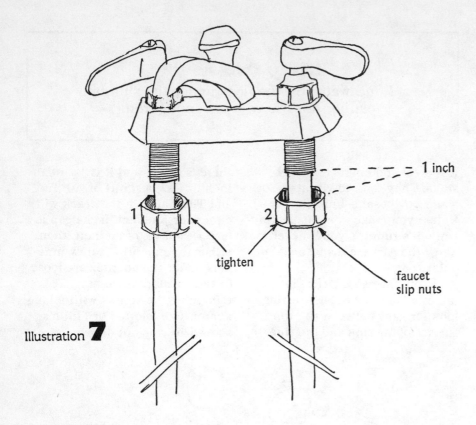

1 inch

1

2

tighten

faucet
slip nuts

Illustration **7**

## Finding The Source Of The Pressure Leak

If you find water on the floor, you could have a *pressure leak* in the water lines originating at the angle stops and/or faucet connections. Since pressure leaks can be intermittent, they can be hard to find. Patience may be required. Many times pressure leaks will only manifest themselves *late at night*, when municipal water pressure is at its peak (because demand is low).

To rule a pressure leak in or out, fill the basin or basins to the brim and then start draining them while looking closely at all of the under-sink waste connections for drips. By filling the basins and then draining them, we apply pressure. If there are no leaks at any point, gravity is not the culprit.

1. First, tighten the nuts indicated in Illus. 5, 7 & 8 with an adjustable wrench (depending on the design of the sink; you could also use a basin wrench), turning slowly ¼ turn at a time, then checking to see if the leak stops.

2. If the drip continues, you can either pay a plumber to fix or replace the faucet or you can read the section on removing and installing the appropriate faucet. Whether to repair or replace it is often a coin toss, and the relative quality of the existing valve (and your faith in the plumber) may be deciding factors.

BEWARE: Rust, or rusty water dribbling or slowly running down a wall below an angle stop or trap arm, usually means you have a terminal case on your hands. Read "About Angle Stops and Supplies" through "What About the Water Heater?" (pages 47–56).

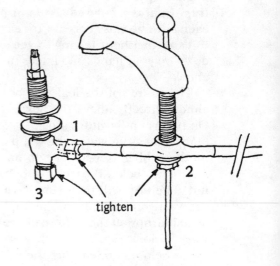

1

3

tighten

2

Illustration
**8**

## How To Determine If It Is A Gravity Leak

If the water is not seeping out from under the toilet bowl when you flush the tank, the source could be one of several other gravity leaks or even a pressure leak at the angle stop and/or fill valve connection.

If indeed the water does seep out from under the bowl when you flush the toilet, you probably have a bad seal between the toilet's horn and the closet flange. See glossary. This could be due merely to a failed bowl wax or wax ring, or worse, it could be due to a corroded and broken closet flange. You might want to read the first eleven titles (don't panic, they're short ones) listed in the TOILET section of the Table of Contents.

The water on the floor could also be due to a poor mating of the tank to the bowl (old dried out tank to bowl gasket and/or tank bolt washers); if you have a tank to bowl gravity leak, read pages 128–153. The water might also be the case of the toilet "sweating," a condition manifested by water droplets forming on the tank and bowl and consequently (due to gravity) dropping off onto the floor. You will find that this happens when the inlet water to the tank is chilly and the room temperature is real warm.

If the toilet does sweat, you can purchase, from your local department store, a tank and lid "sweater" and install it on the toilet. This is a method of insulating the cold tank from the warm room. If this fails to check the sweating, call in a plumber for an estimate on the installation of a metering valve, which will raise the inlet water temperature, and solve the problem.

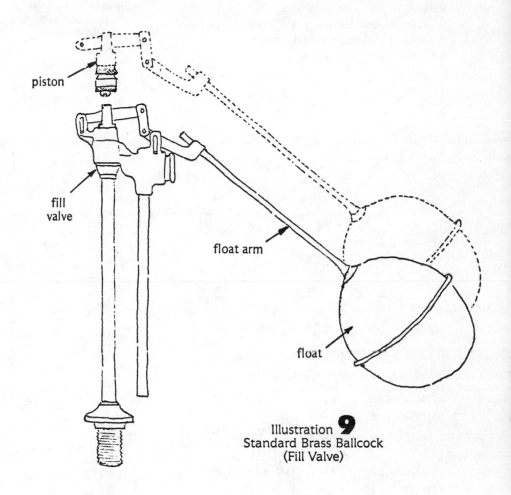

### Dirty Dozen #2
"There's water on the floor around the toilet but I can't tell where it is coming from."

piston

fill valve

float arm

float

Illustration **9**
Standard Brass Ballcock
(Fill Valve)

If you're still groping for a solution, then it's time to LIFT THE TANK LID. Do just that, and then flush the tank, paying careful attention to the fill valve/ballcock (see Illus. 9). Many times, a small stream or "squirt" of water will issue out of the top of the fill valve and hit the top inside of the lid and then run down (you got it!—due to gravity) the outside of the tank and onto the floor. If this is indeed happening, then read pages 37–38 and 138–141 on changing washers and fill valves.

The most dire gravity leak possible is a cracked tank and/or bowl, in which case you're in for the ULTIMATE REPAIR. You poor chaps might want to read the entire toilet section before deciding to do anything. Sure, it could take you several hours, but it could save you megabucks.

## How To Determine If It Is A Pressure Leak

If you cannot find an obvious pressure leak at either the angle stop connections (female threads, packing nut, compression nut) (see Illus. 10 & 11) and/or fill valve connections (see Illus. 12) then it is time for the ole colored tissue in bowl night safari, as first discussed on page 13.

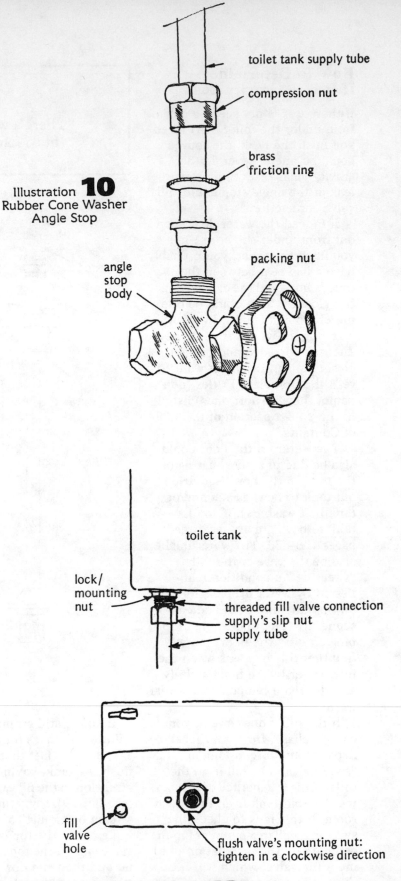

Illustration **10**
Rubber Cone Washer
Angle Stop

toilet tank supply tube

compression nut

brass friction ring

angle stop body

packing nut

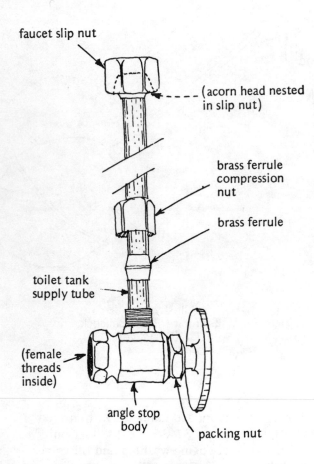

faucet slip nut

(acorn head nested in slip nut)

brass ferrule compression nut

brass ferrule

toilet tank supply tube

(female threads inside)

angle stop body

packing nut

Illustration **11**
Brass Ferrule Compression
Angle Stop

toilet tank

lock/ mounting nut

threaded fill valve connection
supply's slip nut
supply tube

fill valve hole

flush valve's mounting nut:
tighten in a clockwise direction

Illustration **12**
Fill Valve Connections

# Dirty Dozen #3

"Whenever I flush the toilet, water comes out from underneath the bowl."

If all other drains in the house are running freely, you probably have a poor seal of the toilet 'horn' (the hole in the underside of the toilet bowl) over the waste line in the floor. This condition might have been brought on by loose or missing closet bolts in the foot of the toilet (see Illus. 13 & 14).

Very old installations sometimes used plumber's putty and plaster of Paris instead of the superior sealing bowl wax or wax ring in use today.

If you can easily move the toilet bowl by shifting force from one side of the bowl to the other, there is a good chance that the situation calls for the installation of a new wax ring. You might want to read pages 128–153.

I admit it, it is a stab in the dark; but, you might first try just tightening the nuts on the closet bolts. It's maybe a one-out-of-eight to ten shot.

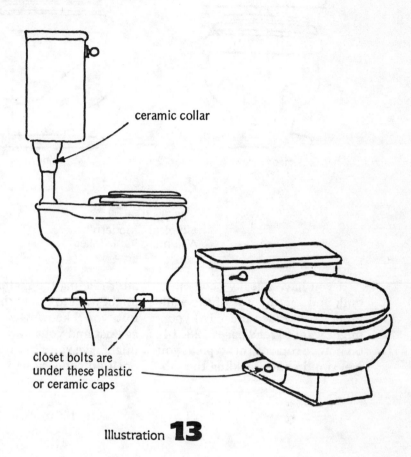

ceramic collar

closet bolts are under these plastic or ceramic caps

Illustration **13**

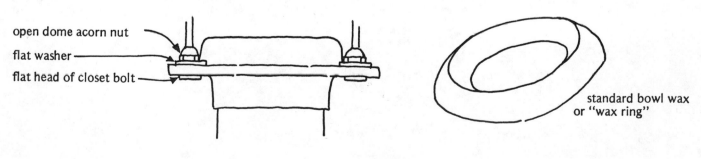

open dome acorn nut

flat washer

flat head of closet bolt

standard bowl wax or "wax ring"

Illustration **14**

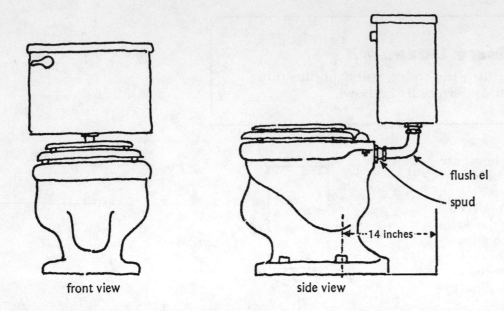

front view        side view

flush el

spud

14 inches

Illustration **15**
Typical "Modern"
Wall-hung Tank Toilet

If you have a leaky bowl or tank and the toilet is of the wall-hung variety (see Illus. 15) you might want to read pages 128–144 on how to replace this type. If you feel timid about tackling the job after reading the material, you might want to call in the plumber. But, you'll know what he's up against and your new insight might give you a better bargaining position concerning his fee.

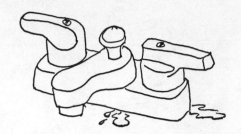

## Dirty Dozen #4

"Every time I turn the faucet on, water
dribbles out underneath the handle
(or around the spout base)."

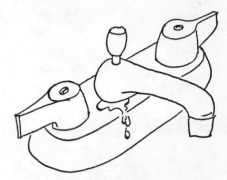

If you have a deck-mounted bathroom lavatory faucet (4 inch center set — see Illus. 16) with a fixed spout, and water is escaping between the spout and the base, then it's Sayonara Pal. Read pages 46–82 and/or call your trusted plumber.

Regardless of what type of deck-mounted faucet you might have (4 inch center set, 6 or 8 inch deck-mounted kitchen sink faucet or deck-mounted laundry faucet) if water is coming out from *under* the base, you probably have a terminal case on your hands. After the faucet is lifted off the counter or sink, you can inspect the underside.

If the water was coming out a corroded hole, throw the faucet away.

However, if the water was escaping a threaded joint at the juncture of the supply connections and the base of the faucet, you first might try reassembling the threaded connection after applying RECTORSEAL/Slic-Tite to the female threads and then testing the faucet for leakage, before tossing it on the trash pile.

Should replacement be necessary, you can save good money by removing the defective faucet before calling in the plumber. Depending upon which faucet you have — kitchen, lavatory, laundry or bar — look up removal and installation in the Table of Contents.

A number of drips *can* be fixed. If water issues from underneath hemispherically shaped handles resembling those in Illus. 17 or any handle that hides the stem underneath, it can usually be repaired, if it has not been a *chronic* problem.

Illustration **16**
Leaks in Deck-mounted Faucets

After the faucet's water supply is turned off, and the handles are removed you can look for the wrench flats on the bonnet or packing nut, underneath (see Illus. 17). Use the adjustable wrench and try to tighten the nut in a clockwise direction. Now test for leaks.

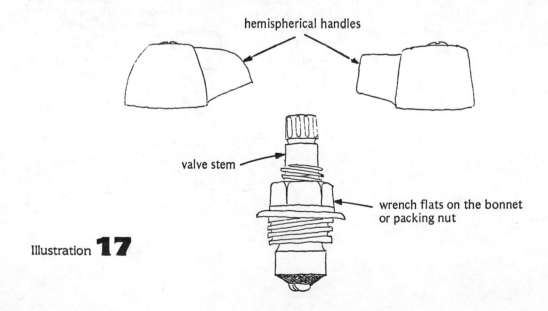

hemispherical handles

valve stem

wrench flats on the bonnet
or packing nut

Illustration **17**

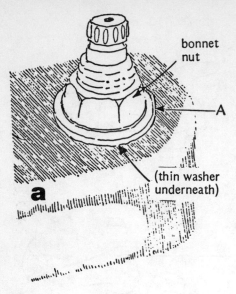

bonnet nut

A

(thin washer underneath)

**a**

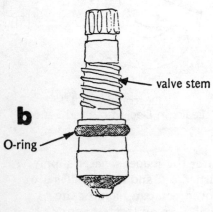

**b**

valve stem

O-ring

Illustration **18**

If the leak is at lip A (Illus. 18a), remove the bonnet nut and stem from the faucet and replace the thin fiber washer underneath. On many faucets, this washer might also be clear, hard plastic. If you cannot get the handles off, you might have to visit a tool rental agency and get a faucet handle puller to do the job.

If water leaks out around the stem, back the stem out of the bonnet and replace the O-ring on the stem (see Illus. 18b).

With the O-ring replaced, grease the female cavity in the bonnet nut and the male threads on the stem and don't forget the O-ring on the stem. An 'acid brush' available at any hardware store makes a good tool for applying the grease in these small, hard-to-get-at areas. Do not be afraid to apply a liberal amount of grease.

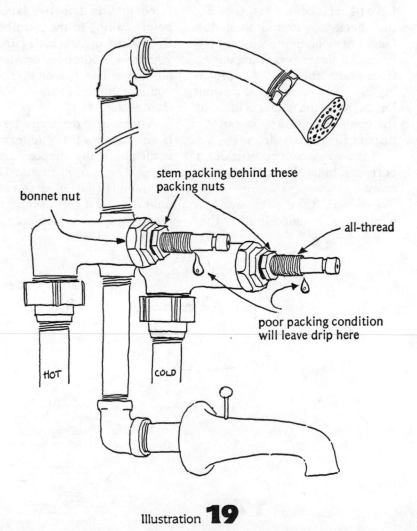

bonnet nut

stem packing behind these packing nuts

all-thread

poor packing condition will leave drip here

HOT

COLD

Illustration **19**

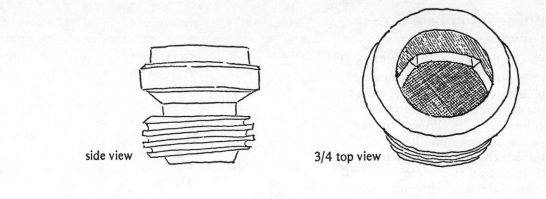

side view

3/4 top view

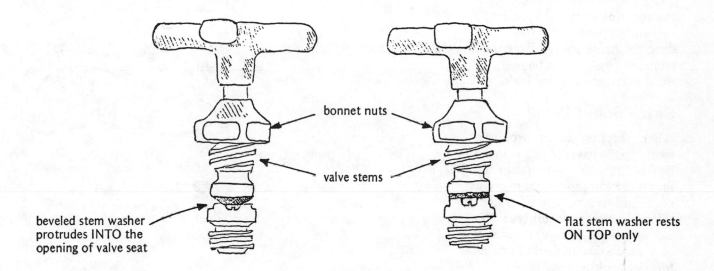

bonnet nuts

valve stems

beveled stem washer
protrudes INTO the
opening of valve seat

flat stem washer rests
ON TOP only

Illustration **20**
Removable Stem Washer Seat

## Tub And Shower Valves

For valves with packing nuts that accept an escutcheon nut or all-thread (Illus. 19), the leak is most commonly found at the stem and packing nut junctures.

If you cannot simply tighten the packing nut further into the valve (clockwise rotation) and cure the drip, then back it all the way out of the valve but not all the way off the stem.

Now, wrap from one to four complete wraps of suitably sized 'impregnated string' type packing around the stem and then re-thread the packing nut back into the valve. Further tightening of the packing nut compresses the new packing against the stem. This will often but not always stop the drip.

Tub and shower valves are often affected by leaks involving out-of-round stems. People apply a good deal of side force on these longest of valve stems. New packing may not fix a leaking bent stem. You might want to take the old bent stems to the plumbing supply or real hardware and purchase new stems, bonnet nuts and packing nuts.

If your tub and/or shower valve has replaceable seats (Illus. 20), you can try removing them and replacing them with new ones. You can buy a seat wrench at a plumbing supply and at most hardware stores. The hole in the center of the seat will be either hexagonal or square. The seat wrench will have a graded diameter hexagonal end and graded width square end.

21

## Kitchen And Laundry Faucets

On single cocks (see Illus. 21) and wall-hung kitchen and laundry faucets, after you have removed the handles and have freed the bonnet nuts all the way off the stems, you can purchase and replace the packings in one piece.

To do this, first remove the flat, brass washer on the underside of the bonnet nut, and then use a sharp pointed object and dig out the remains of the old packing and simply install the new. Now drop the brass washer over the stem, followed by the bonnet nut. Snug it up and test for leaks.

## Swing Spout Base

When water issues out around a swing spout base, it can usually be fixed, if only for a matter of months. Swing spout connections are found in a variety of designs. Whether the spout nut (see Illus. 22) is male or female, there will be a recess for an O-ring or some form of packing.

Some 'Full-Service' suppliers and hardware stores have salespeople who will replace any O-rings or other packings for a modest fee. You might wish to remove your spout and take it with you to such a supplier and have the packings replaced. Read page 106.

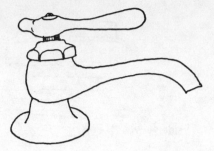

Illustration **21**
Single or Individual Cock

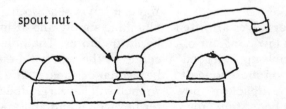

spout nut

spout nut

Illustration **22**
Swing Spouts

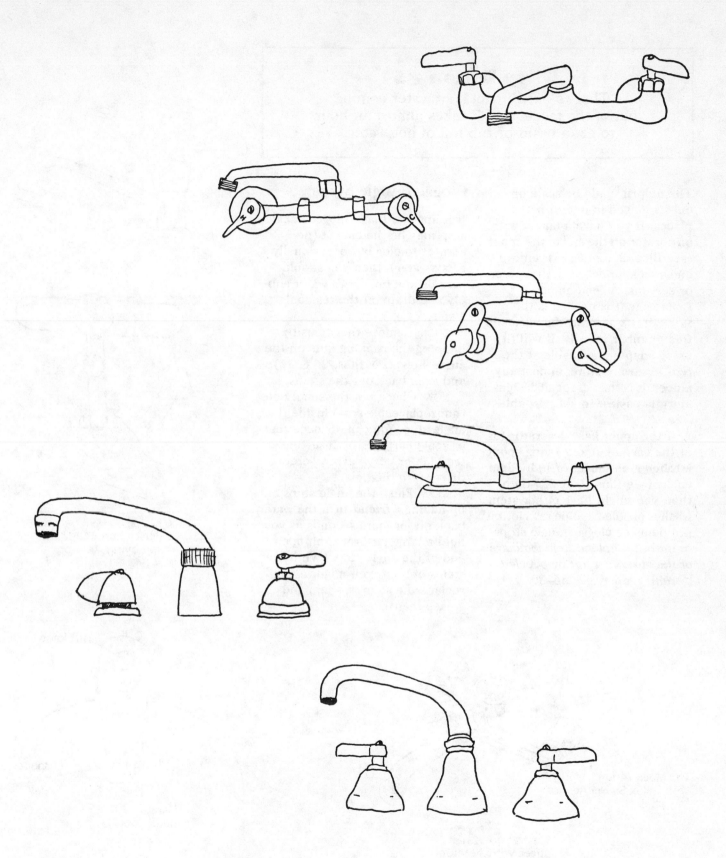

Illustration **22**
Swing Spouts, continued

## Dirty Dozen #5

"There's only a trickle of water coming
out of the faucet and it takes almost an hour
to get a basin or tub full of hot water."

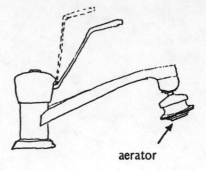

aerator

The culprit could be scale or debris lodged in one or more places. If you have a faucet with an aerator on the end of the spout (see Illus. 23, 24 & 25) remove it and check for debris in the screen or screens. A good choice if replacement is needed is the MOEN DELUX aerator, the *only* one this plumber installs. It will fit, using adapters available at the *real* hardware store, almost any faucet. It is the best of all designs and the easiest to keep trouble free.

If the spout has no aerator (as in the case of an *old* swing spout kitchen sink faucet or individual cocks (see Illus. 21 & 22) then then you might have either stem washer problems, pipe restriction problems or clogged angle stops or both. *To replace stem washers of the standard flat or beveled design, read pages 36–39.*

### Clogged Angle Stops

If it appears that a clogged angle stop may be the culprit (no aerator to clog but occasionally rusty water), then you should turn off the building's water supply and drain off the residual water.

THEN: Remove the stems by undoing the packing nuts on the angle stops (see Illus. 26 & 27) and then back out the stems.

NOW: Check out the small hole (nonreplaceable seat) inside the angle stop. You can dislodge rust or scale particles by inserting an ice pick or *very* narrow screwdriver into the hole.

NEXT: Flush the angle stops out by having a *friend* turn the water back on for mere seconds as *you* hold a large jar over each open end of the angle stop. (While the stems are out, you might as well replace the stem washers and grease them).

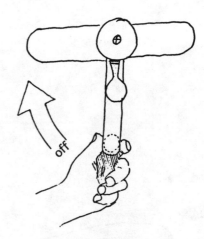

off

Illustration **24**
Removing Aerator

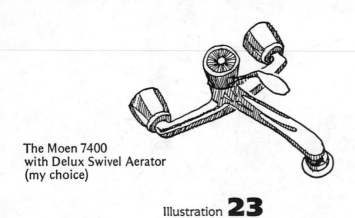

The Moen 7400
with Delux Swivel Aerator
(my choice)

Illustration **23**
Faucet with Aerator

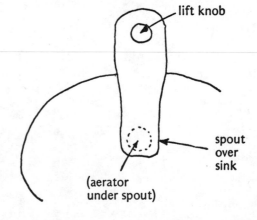

lift knob

spout
over
sink

(aerator
under spout)

Illustration **25**

NOTE: You could have loose bib screws inside the spout and/or pieces of broken stem washer clogging the spout. You might try inserting a piece of wire up the spout to loosen the debris.

## Check The Screens

On automatic clothes washers, as the water enters the machine, it must pass through electrically operated valves which can clog very easily. For this reason, the manufacturer will install fine mesh wire screens at the juncture of the hot and cold rubber supply hoses and the backside of the machine. (If there are no screens here, check at the other end of the hose where it attaches to the washer bib.)

To clear the screens of debris, turn off the hose bibs (washer bibs) or laundry water supply and remove the hoses from the back of the washing machine. Look inside the threaded connections on the back of the machine. If the scale or debris is very heavily built up and will not come off with just a simple scraping, use a sharp pointed object and peel the screen out of the machine. You can purchase a hose washer with fine wire mesh fused in the center to now install in the end of the supply hose after removing the standard rubber hose washer.

If none of these remedies produces more water, it is definitely time to call in the plumber.

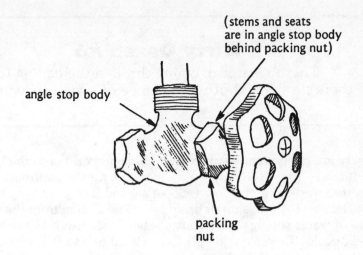

(stems and seats are in angle stop body behind packing nut)

angle stop body

packing nut

Illustration **26**
Rubber Cone Washer Angle Stop

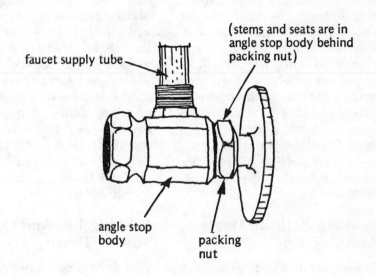

faucet supply tube

(stems and seats are in angle stop body behind packing nut)

angle stop body

packing nut

Illustration **27**
Brass Ferrule Compression Angle Stop

# Dirty Dozen #6

"There's water dripping through the ceiling (or there's a sag and other evidence of a leak above me)."

There are many unpleasant possibilities — toilet seepage, bathtub waste and overflow leakage, leaking bathtub/shower drain line or water supply piping (hot and/or cold). Unless it is simply a loosely mounted toilet bowl, a leaking overflow gasket or poorly grouted tiles, you will probably have to call in a plumber.

One common cause that is not difficult to fix is a leaking wax ring under the toilet. If it is the toilet, read pages 123–126, and then decide whether to call a plumber or jump in yourself. If you have a wall-hung toilet, and it is the ONLY one in the house, unless you have good self-confidence, it would probably be prudent to call the plumber.

Another possible cause is discussed in number SEVEN of the Dirty Dozen.

## Leaking Bathtub Waste And Overflow

The waste and overflow (Illus. 28) is usually out of view unless you have a bathtub that is up on legs, and there are often leaks in several places.

However, there is one case where most laypersons could effect the repair, if the overflow is the true and only cause of the leak (Illus. 28).

This one case is a crudded, dried-out rubber overflow gasket. When the gasket has deteriorated, if the tub is filled to overflowing, the excess water will run down between the tub and overflow hole and drip onto the floor (and ceiling, if the bathroom is on the second floor).

The stream from the shower head will also many times be aimed just so that it shoots into the overflow and also have the same effect.

In either case, you can remove the overflow plate and any linkage (on lever type overflows) and then push the remaining portion of the old gasket out of the way. It will usually fall down in back of the tub, and that's O.K. No? Who is going to ever see it?

Now go buy a new gasket. With the beveled gasket's thin radius on top, carefully position it between the overflow hole and the inside, back of the tub. Reinstall any linkage and then put back the screws holding the overflow plate.

## Leaking Tub And/Or Shower Drain

This devil is best handled by a plumber. In most cases the floor and/or ceiling will require surgery, removing material directly below the trap and affected drain line. To complicate matters, the place where the sag or drip has formed is often NOT directly under the leak.

On shower stalls, the leak is often blamed on the trap and/or drain when the real cause is poorly grouted tile walls, rotten shower pan, or poorly closing door or curtain.

## Leaking Tub And/Or Shower Valve

This can be the toughest valve in the house to repair. That is why, if it needs replacing, I recommend to my customers that we install a new MOEN valve. It rarely needs more than a cartridge change.

The standard valve may leak because: the packing nuts need more packing and/or just tightening; the stems are bent and worn; the bonnet nuts are loose; the valve union is loose (in which case it is "bust a hole" time); or the riser pipe which takes water up to the shower head is corroded out at some point (bust a hole time again). Also, make sure that the shower head arm is tightly threaded into the fitting inside the wall (see Illus. 29).

## Leaking Waterline

If you have galvanized water piping (plated steel pipe) in your home, sometimes a nipple or intersecting pipe run will become corroded and leak where it threads into a fitting. This is because where the threads have been cut on the plated steel pipe, there is no more galvanizing left, and invariably the rust/corrosion process begins at this juncture.

If you have copper water piping, sometimes a leak will occur at a soldered joint where expansion and contraction of the pipe has weakened the joint. This usually happens when the installer of the pipe initially was in too much of a hurry and did not have the pipe FULLY penetrating the female fitting.

Unless the leak was caused by a loose-threaded union (that you can merely re-tighten), you should probably call the plumber. *In any case*, a building with a water pressure regulator or 'reduc-

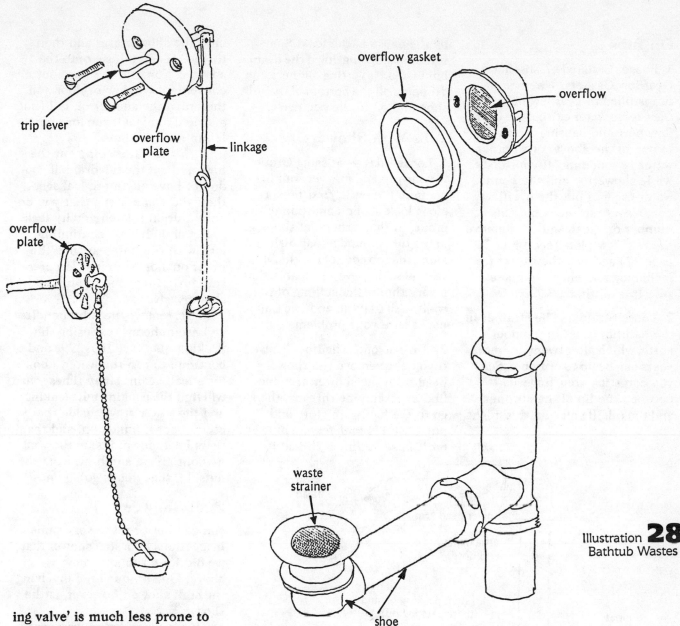

trip lever

overflow plate

linkage

overflow plate

overflow gasket

overflow

Illustration **28**
Bathtub Wastes

waste strainer

shoe

ing valve' is much less prone to piping system ruptures.

You can purchase a water pressure test gauge at a real hardware outlet and test your pressure. The gauge threads onto an outside hose bib. When you turn the water on, the needle indicator on the gauge face tells you your present pressure. Anything above 80 p.s.i., read at twelve midnight, indicates that you should have a regulator installed (see page 119).

## Roof Leak

If the cause is none of the above, might you have a roof leak?

## "Hello!...What Have We Here?... Dr. Watson The Hose Please!"

If your wet sag or drip from the ceiling is below a tub or shower, discovering whether you have a pressure leak or a gravity leak can sometimes be quite exasperating. At least 70 percent of these complaints that I look at end up being a gravity leak.

## On Tubs

**1. Loose, Cracked or Missing Overflow Gaskets.** Whether the tub is filled to overflowing with the excess water exiting the overflow port and causing a leak due to one of the above, or whether water is bouncing off your body while showering and the bounce water escapes out the overflow port also, *first* check out this number one leak source. Remove the overflow plate (see Illus. 28, page 27) and test the gasket for resiliency and check to make sure it is all there.

**2. Loose Strainer.** The strainer in the bathtub is set in plumber's putty, which after twenty or more years can begin to crumble. See if you can stick your fingernail between the lip of the strainer and the tub. If you *can*, this might be the cause of the leak. Some water is not going down the drain but instead is getting out here and dropping off the bottom of the tub shoe and on to the ceiling.

## Tubs With Showers

**1. Loose Tiles — Missing Grout.** If your tub and shower wall has ceramic tile on it, *first* take a *close* look at the condition of the grout. In the corners, at the edge of the tub, around a soap dish and along the top edge of the tile. It is very possible, even probable that a very thorough caulking of the walls with DAP Tub and Tile Caulk could cure your problem.

**2. "Dr. Watson...The Hose Please."** If you can remove the shower head from the shower arm and find exposed pipe threads, then go to the hardware store and purchase a *½ inch female pipe by male hose adapter*. Thread it onto the shower arm and then thread a garden hose onto the adapter. Now run the hose out a convenient window or door and then turn the shower on full (hot and cold) and let it run for a good ten minutes or more.

With the water going out the hose and not the tub drain, if you do not have any more leakage, then you can assume that you do have a drain related gravity leak.

If you do have a continuing leak with the hose carrying the water outside, your leak is a pressure leak, involving the tub and shower valve.

*First*, remove the valve handles and escutcheons, exposing the packing nuts (see Illus. 29) and continue to run the water. Look for a leak again. Many times you will find the packing nuts leaking, and the water stays inside the escutcheons, builds up, and then flows back down, inside the wall without giving any hint, from the outside, that this is going on.

## Stall Shower

You can perform the very same inspections for a stall shower that we did for a tub and shower, above. One unique area involving the stall shower, however, is the shower *pan*.

This is a membrane, composed of sheet metal (lead, copper, galvanized steel), vinyl sheeting or tarred felts. The pan is placed on the subfloor before the concrete setting base for the tile is laid. When this membrane cracks, water from poorly grouted tile and saturated concrete gets below the drain in the floor and runs horizontally until it falls down on the ceiling below.

If this situation proves to exist, you are going to have an expensive repair to make. Get three estimates from your local friendly tile experts.

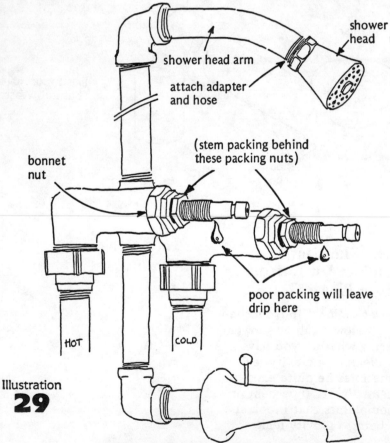

shower head arm

attach adapter and hose

shower head

(stem packing behind these packing nuts)

bonnet nut

poor packing will leave drip here

HOT

COLD

Illustration **29**

28

# Dirty Dozen #7

"There's water on the bathroom floor every time we use the shower."

This happens more often on tubs with shower doors than on shower stalls with doors. However, it does occur with both.

On tubs with shower curtains, the water can bounce off your body and run down the wall to rest on the ends of the tub, and from there to the floor. Putting curtain magnets on the bottom ends of the curtain will keep it pulled in from the edge (on cast iron or enameled steel tubs). On nonmagnetic plastic tubs, small plastic suction cups or velcro tabs (available at the hardware) do the same job.

If the tub is enclosed with sliding glass doors, the culprit is often the bottom track which the door slides in. You should be able to find several small holes in the bottom of the track. They are there to let collecting water drip out and back into the tub. If these holes are clogged with hair and soap film, they will not let the water drain, and the water will build up in the track until it spills out over the top and down onto the floor. Use a nail or narrow knitting needle to clear the holes.

You could also slide the door to one end and drill a few more holes in the bottom of the track.

The bottom track of the tub enclosure is apt to be caulked on the outside, where it contacts the edge of the tub. To leave an exit for collecting water, the inside length of the track should NOT be caulked.

Shower stalls with leaking doors are tougher to cure because most stalls have a hinged door, not a sliding one. The hinged shower door usually leaks when the door becomes warped and out of plumb, leaving a gap between the door edge and bottom splash for water to drip through.

To solve this problem, you don't need a plumber — you need a glass company. OR, you could have your plumber, or better yet yourself, install a shower rod and clear curtain liner *inside* the enclosure.

# Dirty Dozen #8

"The garbage disposer hums or makes no noise and will not run."

This topic is covered in-depth on pages 120 & 121. After you have read them (c'mon, it won't take long) you will have a better idea whether to call a plumber or try to remedy the situation yourself.

One special note: If water runs or drips out of the disposer itself, DO NOT FUSS WITH THE DAMN THING! Water and 110 volt house current are deadly. Call your plumber.

## Dirty Dozen #9

"I smell gas."

Open all available windows; extinguish any and all flames; DO NOT SMOKE; and then call your local gas utility.

If you live in a rural area and use "bottled gas" (propane), call your distributor. If he has no one to send, then call a plumber.

If you have not had this problem before, and there was no new work performed on the gas line, then you probably have an extinguished pilot light, or maybe a dirty one.

But, DO NOT TAKE ANY CHANCES, call in an expert.

## Dirty Dozen #10

"I cannot get the pilot light on my water heater and/or furnace to stay lighted."

As a protective measure, most states require the manufacturer to install a safety control valve on gas-fired appliances. This device is kept open by a tiny amount of electrical current manufactured at the pilot light flame by a little bimetal strip called a *pilot light generator.*

Commercial water heaters can be purchased with an electronic ignition, thus eliminating the need for a pilot light. However, this type of system requires a 110 volt receptacle nearby. I believe it will be a long time before residential water heaters are manufactured in large numbers with this feature.

When the pilot light flame keeps it heated up, the generator produces a tiny, milivolt current. If you follow the metal strip back from the pilot flame, you will find the safety control valve. If the pilot flame goes out, the pilot light generator stops making electricity, and the safety valve closes, shutting off any gas to the burner and pilot.

When the generator fails, it usually means the two metal strips inside the small round tube have burned up, leaving a gap which the small amount of current cannot jump across. Now the gas appliance cannot relight itself, nor will the gas for the main burner continue to pour forth until it snuffs you out or blows you up.

There are many different lengths and shapes of pilot light generators, and a heating and furnace contractor will stock most of them. Give him a call and ask if you can purchase one from him. Have the make and model number of your appliance in front of you when you call. A real hardware will also stock most of the types found in use locally.

## Dirty Dozen #11
"I've got a geyser or a swamp in my backyard."

If you find clean, clear water bubbling up or streaking skyward, then you have a ruptured water line.

First, read pages 3 and 4 to learn how to turn the water off at the meter, if you don't know how already.

If the water smells bad, you probably have a leaking or badly broken sewer line. It might be a good time to break out your Orvis Chest Waders and your L.L. Bean Survival Shovel — or call your plumber.

If you are on a septic tank system, the leach field or leach lines may become oversaturated, causing septic tank effluent to run off near the surface of the ground. Call your local septic tank service company.

## Dirty Dozen #12
"There's an awful rattle and hammering whenever someone uses the water."

In most instances, this is a symptom of a loose stem washer or worn out stem in a faucet, hose bib or toilet ballcock. Pages 36–39 following will tell you how to change common stem washers.

If the problem persists after you have replaced washers and/or stems, call your plumber and let him check out a few of the rarer causes for the noise.

If you have a *very* high water pressure, the plumber can install a pressure reducing valve or "regulator" on the main water line. Also, the Brass Craft Manufacturing Company, Detroit, Michigan 48202, produces a wonderful angle stop with a built-in shock absorption device which will eliminate your problem. The angle stop's patent number is 3343560. You might want to write to them and find out who in your area markets this angle stop. Then *you* could install it at your problem locations with the help of this book.

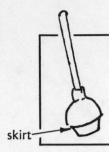

skirt

# Dirty Dozen #13

"STOPPAGES — HELP!
The toilet/sink/tub is plugged up."

This one area, stoppages, accounts for the all-time most common emergency call. Sometimes the blockage happens abruptly; sometimes you may "ride a dying horse" as water goes down ever more slowly, until finally nothing moves.

Try reading pages 56–59 on removing traps. Or use a plumber's helper before you call a plumber. If it's the bathroom lavatory or kitchen that's stopped up, you should check the trap first.

It is harder to get at the trap of a toilet or bathtub, so if one of those fixtures is affected, simply try the plunger (force cup) technique. If this fails, it is time to holler for the plumber.

Try to get the plunger with the extra skirt (see illustration) rather than the flat one because the skirt makes it useful in a tight radius, such as a drain in a bathroom lavatory sink. It also is a better shape for the toilet bowl's exit. But the flat plunger works okay on a kitchen sink, where the drain hole is away from a vertical sink wall.

## "Get Mad And Get Wet"

With the plunger in hand, the important thing is not to be timid. To use it properly, you have to be willing to throw a little water around and get a bit wet yourself. (I know, I know. On a toilet bowl full of paper and bog it isn't very appealing — so wear your raincoat.) So, be prepared to do what you can to minimize the effect on the room of a little water spurting here and there.

Illus. 30 is a diagram of a typical sink and tub trap and drain system. If the stoppage is in the trap, location A, or at any point over to the drain T, then the plunger may be able to clear the blockage. However, if the blockage is located somewhere from location B to the main building sewer, then the majority of force will take the ineffectual path of the dotted line, and go up and out the vent stack.

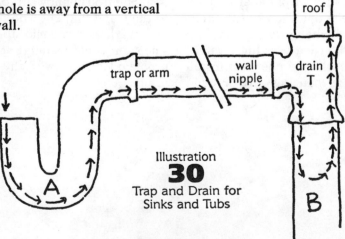

vent to roof

trap or arm

wall nipple

drain T

Illustration
**30**
Trap and Drain for Sinks and Tubs

A

B

When working with force cups to clear a clogged bathroom lavatory sink:

Plug up any overflow holes with a sponge inside a plastic bag. Hold the bag over the overflow with one hand while pumping the cup up and down with the other. If you lack the strength for heavy-duty one-hand pumping, ask a friend to block the overflow. If you don't plug the overflow holes, all the force generated by the plunger (force cup) will go out the overflow holes and do nothing towards unclogging the line.

Place the plumber's helper (plunger/force cup) over the drain hole and shove the handle down fast and very firmly in three or four rapid successions. Don't be too concerned about a little squirting water on the side.

Give it all you've got with back and arms. You might have to repeat this operation a dozen times or so. If things are still not beginning to loosen up after 12 or 13 attempts, you can accept defeat honorably.

A WORD OF CAUTION: When the drain is stopped up, *always* use the plunger *first*. DO NOT introduce drain-cleaning agents into the system first. If you try a chemical attack and then go for the plunger, you could be setting yourself up for a nasty chemical squirt-back that could burn or blind you. See the discussion following on drain cleaners.

If you have two or more sinks connected with continuous wastes (see Illus. 31), you will need someone to help block the additional overflow and drain hole because they are part of the same waste system. Otherwise the applied force from the plunger will merely back up and go out the other sink.

Bathtubs, like lavatories, have an overflow which must be

covered up and held plugged or the majority of the force from the plunger will back up and come out the overflow plate.

It is best to have a tiny bit of water standing in the bottom of the sink or tub. Water shoving up against the obstruction works better than air trying to do the same thing.

On toilets, you do not have overflow holes to plug up, so you can give the plunger your all, using your entire back, legs and arms.

One side effect of using the plunger on clogged toilets is possible seepage of water past the bowl wax seal and out from underneath. Usually, once the stoppage is cleared the seepage disappears, and you do not have to reseat the bowl. (But there is no guarantee.)

## About Chemical Drain Cleaners

I want to say right off the bat that some chemical drain cleaning agents CAN and WILL harm the tailpiece, trap and continuous waste. When you hear the claim that "Our stuff will not harm your pipes," I think that the makers must not consider the tailpiece, trap and continuous waste to be pipes. The trap with its reverse bend in the bottom, "takes it in the neck," so to speak.

As a rule, the drain, waste and vent piping which is inside the walls, under the floors and sometimes in the ceilings can handle the cleaning agents. You can tell when you have found the real "potent" stuff when it has a plastic bag on the outside of a plastic bottle sealed with a bag tie. I hope no one will ever be able to buy this stuff unless they are fully qualified to use it. Most suppliers require the buyer to sign a liability release before they can buy it.

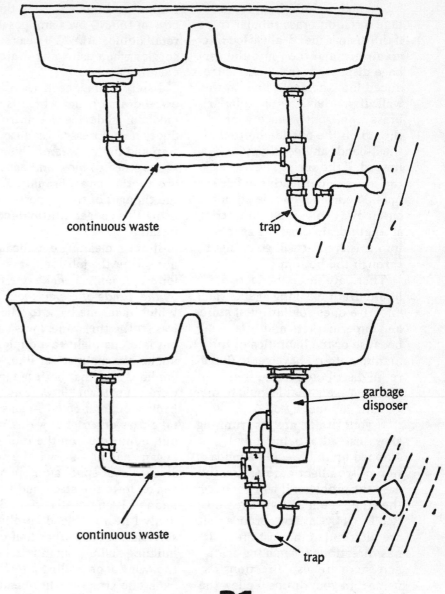

Illustration **31**
Double Compartment Sinks

If *you* were ever to see this stuff being sold retail, I would advise you not to purchase it. It will only cause you more serious problems.

I answered a call once where some college students had gotten hold of some and had dumped it down the bathtub drain to open a clog. The agent ate through the 'shoe' at the underside of the tub, then burnt its way through the subfloor, spilling into a light fix-ture on the ceiling of the apartment below, starting a fire in the light fixture and finally falling onto the tenant below when he came into the room to see what the smoke and odor was all about. He didn't have to shave for a few moons.

Automatic dishwashers use a fairly caustic detergent, and it even helps maintain a clean kitchen sink drain line. It can take a toll on brass tubular traps if the dishwasher drain is fed into an air-gap and then into the garbage disposer before being introduced into the drain line, in the wall. If you have an old tubular brass trap, gently place your thumb on the outside bottom of the J-bend, and *gently* press inward. If the surface flexes easily, the brass underneath the hard, outside chrome, can be all but eaten away. If you put industrial strength drain cleaning agents into this trap, it will go straight through the bottom.

There are more ineffective liquid drain cleaning agents than effective ones sold at retail stores and supermarkets and it is because of the liabilities of the manufacturer. I have yet to find a retail distributed liquid drain cleaning agent that I would bother wasting my money on.

If your drains are just running slow, instead of being fully stopped up, a biweekly application of lye might cure or greatly ease the problem. It will not harm the trap system. Lewis Lye and Red Devil Lye are two brands that are distributed in most areas. It has directions for making soap and there are also directions for using it in your drains. Follow the directions explicitly. The lye in a stubbornly plugged drain forms a cake, on top of the obstruction, further complicating the problem. Also, plumbers and drain cleaning contractors just *love* taking a bath in lye solution when they are called to "snake" your drains. So use it only on *slow* drains.

For a serious stoppage, one that is making the water stand for more than 24 hours after you have tried:
1. Cleaning out the trap, and
2 Using the plunger,

I would recommend using the crystal DRANO over any possible retail liquids. ALWAYS wear safety goggles when using any drain cleaning agents.

Lately we have seen a sophisticated drain opener which is a mechanical device that introduces a compressed gas into the trap and drain system. This unit is supposed to blow and eat the obstruction away. Frankly, I find the thought of the layperson using this gadget a little uncomfortable.

If drain cleaning chemicals are not getting the job done, it is time for a mechanical snake *operated by the hands of experience.* Which takes me back to when I was still getting mine. I was called out late one night to a duplex to unclog the main sewer line. The landlord said that both tenants were out of town but were coming back soon, and could I please take care of it right away. I went out, climbed up on the roof and began snaking — down the vent stack. I sent spool after spool of snake down the stack and still hadn't hit any obstruction. Suddenly I heard a blood curdling scream from the other half of the building and a woman burst out the front door trailing a towel, from one arm, over her head. It turned out she had come back early, unaware that there was any problem with the sewer and she was in the shower. When she came out, all she saw was the entire room *alive* with this icky, gooey thing crawling all over. Well, my snake came up through the toilet bowl instead of heading down the main sewer line.

You too can rent an electric snake, but if you don't know what to do with it or what it's doing when it's in the line, you can waste a lot of time and money and generate a lot of disgust. Leave

that to the golfers. Also, old homes often have lead pipes under the toilets and you can easily drive a powered snake through the bend (pipe) and then have a carpenter, plumber and floor man working for a full day to repair the damage. It is rare when you can get all three to get the job done in one day anyway. You don't have to be very savvy at arithmetic to figure out what that could cost you.

So, if you need a mechanical snake to get yourself out of a predicament, I suggest that you call a plumbing contractor and request his stoppage expert. Most plumbing contractors have a specialist for this job. His knowledge of the entire plumbing system, despite his fee, can actually provide the most economical solution. I tell people (jokingly) that I don't trust any snake man under fifty years old. If he's any younger, he's not been around long enough to know what he's doing.

Whoever you get, I suggest that you do not stand looking over his shoulder; he'll work faster if you don't. A coffee and donut will also go a long way for your cause.

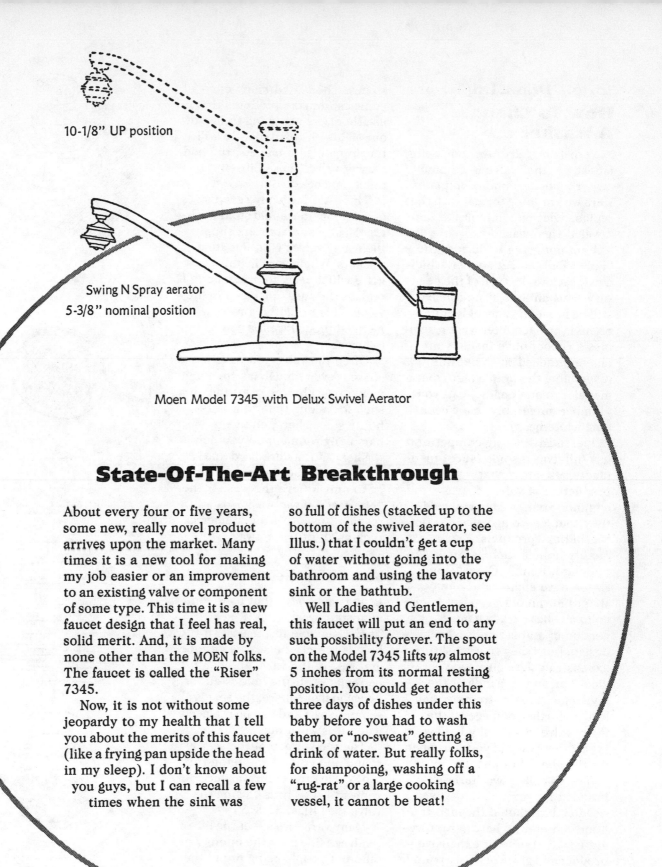

10-1/8" UP position

Swing N Spray aerator
5-3/8" nominal position

Moen Model 7345 with Delux Swivel Aerator

## State-Of-The-Art Breakthrough

About every four or five years, some new, really novel product arrives upon the market. Many times it is a new tool for making my job easier or an improvement to an existing valve or component of some type. This time it is a new faucet design that I feel has real, solid merit. And, it is made by none other than the MOEN folks. The faucet is called the "Riser" 7345.

Now, it is not without some jeopardy to my health that I tell you about the merits of this faucet (like a frying pan upside the head in my sleep). I don't know about you guys, but I can recall a few times when the sink was so full of dishes (stacked up to the bottom of the swivel aerator, see Illus.) that I couldn't get a cup of water without going into the bathroom and using the lavatory sink or the bathtub.

Well Ladies and Gentlemen, this faucet will put an end to any such possibility forever. The spout on the Model 7345 lifts *up* almost 5 inches from its normal resting position. You could get another three days of dishes under this baby before you had to wash them, or "no-sweat" getting a drink of water. But really folks, for shampooing, washing off a "rug-rat" or a large cooking vessel, it cannot be beat!

## "Drip... Drip... Drip..." or
# How To Change A Washer

Next to a plugged drain, a dripping faucet or other valve is a homeowner's most common complaint. Here we are going to deal with the replacement of common flat and beveled stem washers.

I am not going to discuss the "Fuller Ball" faucet washer, which dates back to the turn of the century. This antique system may still be found in some older cities. Should you encounter what resembles a rubber olive inside your faucet attached to something resembling the crankshaft from a model airplane engine, call your plumber, preferably one with a long white beard.

Fierce advertising competition has influenced some faucet manufacturers into deviating from production of valves that use the common stem washer. Instead, they tout 'space age' designs or 'washerless' products. Expensive quality brands such as American Standard, Kohler, Chicago and Crane have engineered new shapes for an old purpose. Each company has a trade name for its version of a nonstem washer design. Until they go wrong, these expensive valves give good service. But, in the hands of the layperson, repair attempts may lead to further damage to the leaky valve. So I really believe it is best that you call your plumber for the above brands.

The so-called 'washerless' brands that you will find advertised and marketed through the homecenters and hardware stores are usually the least expensive product and give you more trouble than the brands that use common stem washers. Since there are still countless faucets and valves in use which employ common stem washers, and many companies still make products that use them, we are going to narrow our sights on this type. We will touch upon sink faucets, tub and shower valves, hose bibs and toilet ballcocks.

There are basically seven sizes of common household stem washers. Most manufacturers supply their new valves with flat stem washers. Whenever I install a new valve which uses stem washers, I replace the ones that came in the valve. This would be a recommended procedure for you to follow also.

Often the valve you have purchased (even though it's spanking new to you) has been sitting on a shelf for a long time in a warehouse somewhere, enduring harsh environments. Even new washers, if they are hard and dried out, will cause a drip.

You might give the washer the "bite test." If the washer is still resilient, use it. If the washer is rock-hard, throw it away.

## Flat Or Beveled?

Inside each valve that uses common stem washers is a "seat." There is a hole in the seat. If the hole is round, the seat is an integral part of the valve and cannot be replaced. If the hole is either hexagonal or square, the seat is a separate part and can be replaced when it is worn out.

The top surface of the seat is round and curved and upon this top surface the stem washer comes to rest, thus closing the valve (see Illus. 32 & 33).

Many variables affect the life of a valve. Aside from the number of different people using it and the care they take of it, the type of water the valve regulates has a great deal to do with how long it performs, trouble free.

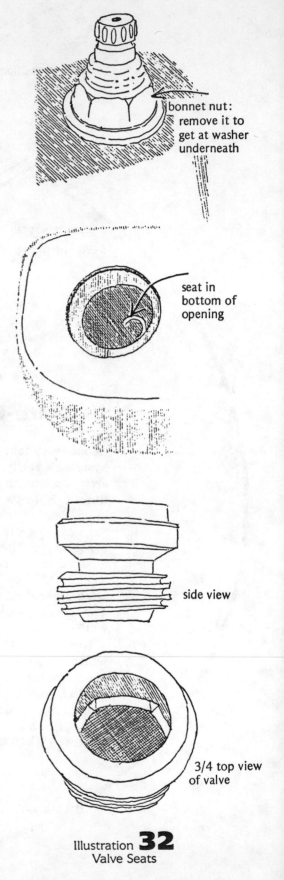

bonnet nut: remove it to get at washer underneath

seat in bottom of opening

side view

3/4 top view of valve

Illustration **32**
Valve Seats

Hard water can leave deposits on the surface of the seat which cause abrasions each time the valve is operated. Other chemical effects of water can be pitting or corrosion of the seat's surface, which can cause the washer to wear unevenly. When you reach the point where you are frequently having to replace the flat stem washer, it is time to try a beveled one (see Illus. 33a).

Why beveled? As a valve wears, the washer is subjected to greater abuse. The beveled surface actually penetrates the *inside* radius of the seat instead of just lying on top, flat. When the stem is turned tightly off, the beveled washer seals both the inside and top surface of the seat.

Most valves (with the exception of ballcocks) will accept either a flat or beveled washer. But, sometimes only a flat washer will permit for sufficient stem travel away from the seat. So, if you replace a flat washer with a beveled one, and not enough water then comes out of the valve spout, you will have to go back to using the flat washer only.

Washers are inexpensive. NEVER cut one down around the edges to make it fit inside the cup on the end of the stem. If you can't get a snug fit, keep looking until you find the washer that fits just right. If you do cut down a washer to fit, you are risking real damage to the stem and seat. The washer, in most cases, will hang up on the inside and the bib screw holding the washer to the stem will back out of the stem and then the bib screw gets jammed in the seat. If your faucet has a nonreplaceable seat, then you have ruined any chances of repairing the valve (see Illus. 33c).

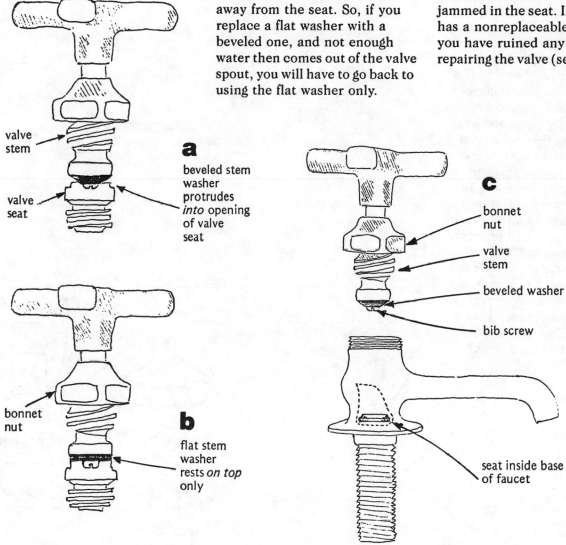

valve stem

valve seat

**a** beveled stem washer protrudes *into* opening of valve seat

bonnet nut

**b** flat stem washer rests *on top* only

**c**

bonnet nut

valve stem

beveled washer

bib screw

seat inside base of faucet

Illustration **33**

As a rule, the beveled washers will not function properly in the toilet ballcock. The piston, which receives the washer (see Illus. 34) travels such a short distance up and down that you need a flat washer to let enough water flow through the valve.

## Bib Screws

Illus. 35a & 35b are of typical stems from single lavatory sink cocks. Illus. 35c is of a typical stem from a wall-hung or deck-mounted kitchen sink faucet. Both types use a machine screw to hold the stem washer in place. If the head of the bib screw is partially or entirely broken off, so you cannot use a new replacement screw, take the stem to the plumbing supply place and ask them to remove the broken screw for you. You might have to pay a very nominal fee for this service.

Bib screws come in many different lengths, diameters, thread pitches, and head shapes. A real hardware will stock all of them. Brass bib screws are likely to corrode more quickly in areas where the water has a high mineral content. A check of real plumbing suppliers may help you locate one selling bib screws made of stainless steel, which will not corrode.

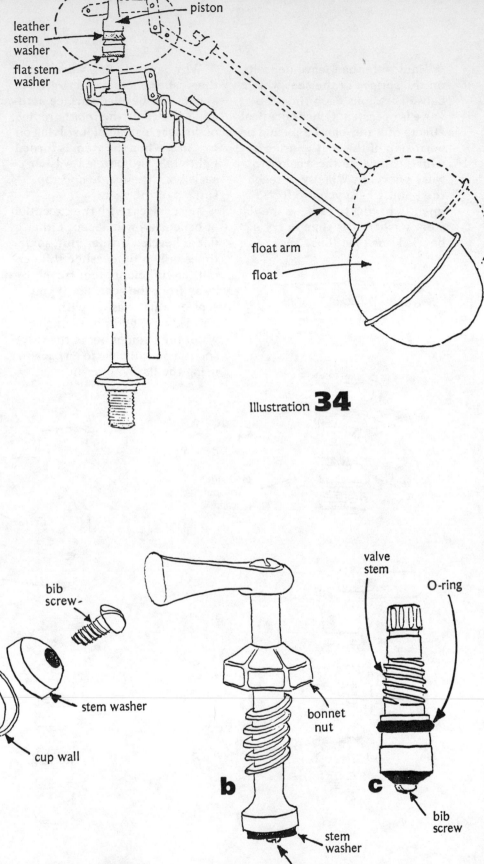

Illustration **34**

Illustration **35**
Stems with Bib Screws

38

## Cup Replacement

In Illus. 35a, you will notice that the end of the stem is cupped, having a rim wall which nests the washer. On old stems, the rim wall starts to break away. Once this begins, replacement washers will not last long. With the rim wall, the new washer is contained and it retains its shape. Without the rim wall, the washer is squashed flat and begins to break apart.

If your cup wall is broken, with a flat metal file remove the remaining standing portion so the end of the stem is filed perfectly flat. Now purchase a new, separate washer cup in either brass or stainless steel if you can find it (see Illus. 36). With a new stem washer inside the cup, screw it to the end of the stem. Really give the screw a good final torque so it will not loosen up.

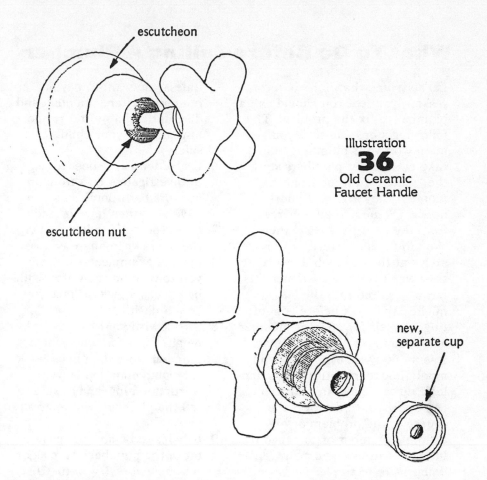

escutcheon

escutcheon nut

Illustration
**36**
Old Ceramic
Faucet Handle

new,
separate cup

## Tub And Shower Valves

In private homes, most tub and shower valves do not have shut-off valves. Before you can start to work on your valve, you will have to turn the water off at the main shut-off valve out at the meter box or at any gate valve in or near the house.

I like to install MOEN single handle tub and shower valves with screwdriver stops. When I rarely have to work on one of these valves, I simply turn the screw to shut the water off *at the valve.*

Removing the stems on conventional kitchen, bathroom, laundry and bar sink faucets is not very difficult. But, sometimes removing the valve stems from a tub or shower valve can be very tricky because it's difficult to get at them.

If you find when you remove the handles and the trim from the valve that there *is* room enough for the bonnet nuts to pass through the holes in the tile, then you might want to invest in a set of plumber's socket wrenches because you will be able to replace the washers yourself.

If the holes in the wall where the valve stems stick out are plugged up with tile cement, cement or the tile dies real close to the stems, you might want to call in a plumber for this one. There is a trick to chipping tile away from the stems without cracking the entire tile and many times it can take an hour or more to just clear the way for the socket to fit into the wall and onto the bonnet nut.

On conventional, two-handle tub and shower valves, after you have removed the handles and the trim and move on to the stems, make sure to put the same stem back into the same side of the valve (hot back into hot, cold back into cold). On some valves you will not have to worry because the threads on the hot and cold stems are reversed and each side will only accept the right valve stem.

I always use a liberal amount of stem grease on the internal female valve threads and on the exposed male threads of the valve stem. An 'acid' brush works well for applying the heat and waterproof valve lubricant. It costs very little and is available at any real hardware store.

If the valve in question is a faucet, and if it has an aerator on the spout, unthread it and remove it before testing for drips because the excess stem grease will clog up the screen(s) in the aerator. You will need alcohol or nail polish remover to clean the grease from the aerator parts.

# What To Do Before Calling A Plumber

Let's assume that, for whatever reason, you feel you should call a plumber to fix the problem. The following steps can save you money on your plumbing bill. Like taxis, most plumbers start the "meter" running from the moment they arrive at your house. (Some actually charge from the time they leave their shop until they return or they arrive at the next job. Usually they won't tell the customer this, but it's figured into the *bill*. It might pay to ask before committing yourself.) Even if the plumber agrees to make a "free estimate," it is unlikely that he will spend much time to investigate a hidden leak without pay. Anything you can do, then, to discover the source of the problem *before* calling a plumber or to expedite his work can save you many repair dollars. For example:

1. Look through the Dirty Dozen and try to find the source of the problem. At least you may be able to rule out several possibilities.
2. If the problem involves an appliance — dishwasher, clothes washer, garbage disposer — read the owner's manual on repairs to rule out common breakdowns. There is nothing so dismaying as paying a repairman the minimum charge to have him press the "restart" button on the garbage disposer.
3. If there is a hand-operated shut-off valve for your building, know where it is (Illus. 37) so you can tell the plumber.
4. Remove bottles and other obstructions from under sinks or wherever the plumber will be working.
5. Keep children away from the plumber while he's working

unless you want to pay $35 an hour and up for a reluctant and disgruntled babysitter (important also for your child's safety).
6. If a ladder will be needed (e.g., to investigate a leak from an upstairs bathroom), and you have one, then have it ready.
7. Make yourself available to help the plumber in any way possible. For example, he may want you to turn on the water while he checks a leak or have you hold a flashlight.
8. Check with your friends and neighbors before choosing a plumber from the phone book. A recommendation is well worth pursuing (and be sure to tell the plumber who referred you).
9. It helps to be able to speak a bit of the plumber's language. If you have reviewed the Dirty Dozen and looked up some terms in the glossary, your plumber should realize at least that you are an informed consumer, and you will feel more secure if you can understand some of the plumber's description of needed repairs.

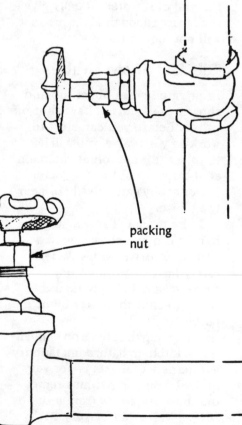

packing nut

Illustration **37**
Shut-off Valves (Gate Valves)

40

# Part II
# Replacing The Offender

## The Ultimate Repair

Not all rescue efforts succeed. Whatever the problem — a leaky faucet or other valve, undersink plumbing, or toilet — a true repair is only made when the problem goes away and *stays* away.

On many of the repair calls I make, it is obvious after a quick inspection that no amount of work will be sufficient to fix the problem. At this point, the only avenue worth pursuing is the *ultimate repair:* replacement with a true quality product. I think you will discover that your mental attitude towards plumbing-related chores will be considerably elevated with the shine of a new fixture, appliance or valve. And a permanent end to a constantly running toilet or dripping faucet can not only save repair bills but also lower your blood pressure, cut down your valium dosage, and . . .well, you get the idea.

Throwing out your old fixture does *not* mean throwing in the towel either. There is no reason why you can't do the installation yourself. This section covers replacement of valves, and toilets, a process that involves three basic steps:

1. Selecting a replacement
2. Removing the old offender
3. Installing new servant

Because Step 1, selecting a new valve or fixture, is crucial to your satisfaction, I will try to provide as many alternatives as possible, with brand name recommendations.

## Brand Name Suggestions

Since you will be performing the labor and saving a lot of money, you can then afford to invest this savings into the purchase of a true quality replacement. I cannot urge you strongly enough to buy *true quality.* One of my foremost goals in this book is to free you from the limitations of those "less than desirable," typically "blister or bubble packaged" products sold at the hardware and "home-improvement" level outlets. One trip by a plumber to attempt repairs to one of these beauties and you have just blown more money than it would have cost to have the very best to start with.

As mentioned earlier, there are new products being developed all the time but the following are *my choices* of quality valves of domestic manufacture:

    1. MOEN    2. CRANE
    3. AMERICAN STANDARD

In this plumber's opinion, MOEN produces the most dependable trouble-free faucet on the market (as of this writing) and it is far from the most expensive. I would especially recommend this brand for you first-timers because all of the MOEN line is very easy to install.

You might write to MOEN, Elyria, Ohio 44305, and ask who in your area sells their product.

## When To Repair Versus Replace

If you know that your present faucet is a true quality product, it is indeed worthy of repairing. When you or a friend are capable of keeping it repaired, it is of little financial consequence. However, if you have to call a plumber to keep it fixed, you will not want to pay his fee twice.

If you've had numerous problems with a fixture and know it is not of especially high quality, maybe it is time for you to replace it.

Bathroom lavatory faucets (4 inch center sets, wide-spreads, and single post designs) may be purchased with or without the pop-up waste.

It becomes very evident when you need to replace a trap . . . water will squirt or pour out a hole in the bottom or side of the J-bend or along the underneath of the trap arm.

Reasons for replacing angle stops are discussed in detail in the angle stop section. Read pages 47–52.

Reasons for replacing or repairing toilets will be discussed in the toilet section. Read pages 123–156.

Some cities, like the city of Berkeley, rent tools on the public library card. You might check with your city hall on the hunch. Most plumbing supply houses sell tools; but most suppliers are wholesale only. However, I have found some suppliers who were both wholesale and retail. If the yellow pages does not tell you if a particular company is or is not wholesale only, give them a call and ask them if you can buy from them. The difference between several retail prices can be substantial. And, those who are both wholesale and retail often have a very good retail price.

It also pays to take your time shopping for your quality faucet. Once you have set your new prize, it will be many years before you will need to do it again (not to mention about wanting to do it again. Just think about all the extra time you'll be spending doing important things like weeding the parking strip, reglazing windows or those wonderfully agonizing rounds of golf).

Also, I suggest that you have *all* of your replacement items before you begin to chase down any rental tools. Which reminds me, have you ever spent blood-boiling hours in a line (Saturday and Sunday especially) in front of the local tool renters? Rent your tools the night or afternoon *before* the big day. You won't want to be wasting precious time in traffic then. If you have any time off coming during the week, your chances of finding all of the tools required at the fewest number of outlets is greatly increased. Also, some of the more complete and economical parts suppliers are closed on the weekends.

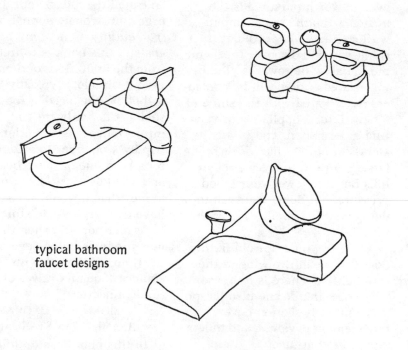

typical bathroom
faucet designs

Illustration **38**
4 Inch Center Set Designs

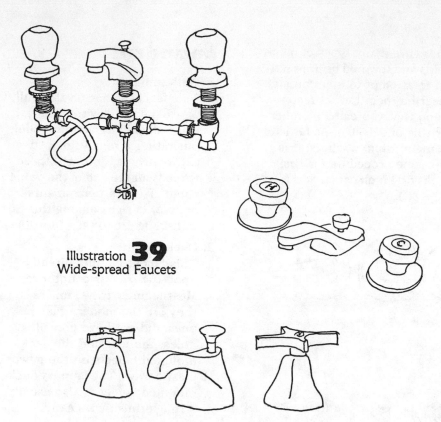

Illustration **39**
Wide-spread Faucets

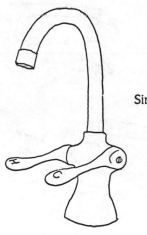

Illustration **40**
Single-Post Mixing Valve

Illustration
**41**
Single or Individual Cock

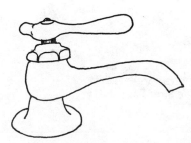

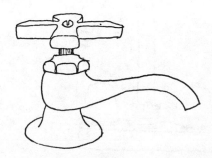

# Faucets

## Bathroom:

1. 4 Inch Center Set:
   These faucets have hot and cold handles and water connections approximately four inches apart, with the spout in the middle. Also, the entire valve rests on *top* of the sink or counter. Single-handle Mixing Valve faucets, such as MOEN, are included in this group (see Illus. 38).

2. Wide-spread Faucets:
   These faucets have individual handles separated anywhere from 6 to 12 inches or more with the spout located in between. The valves themselves hang under the sink or counter top (see Illus. 39).

3. Single-post:
   These faucets are a hot and cold mixing valve mounted in a single hole, either on the sink itself or on the counter top (see Illus. 40).

4. Individual Cocks:
   These separate hot and cold valves are mounted on the sink or counter top (see Illus. 41).

5. Built-in Basin-manifold or Back-shelf Combination: If you have this type of sink and faucet combination, you might have some difficulty in locating replacement parts. Very few manufacturers still produce this design. The porcelain bowl is best removed from the wall to get at the faucet valves and the pop-up linkage.

There are many types of manifolds and it would be unpractical to attempt to mention and describe them here. I recommend that you call a plumber for this one design. As far as changing stem washers, it is the same procedure for single cocks or 4 inch center sets (see page 38).

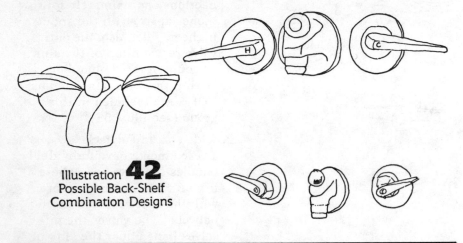

Illustration **42**
Possible Back-Shelf Combination Designs

## Bar Sink:

1. Deck-mount:
   This faucet resembles, very much, the 4 inch center set, except that it has a smaller spread on the threaded connections and handles. It also usually has a high-loop spout with an aerator.

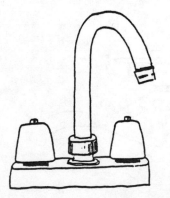

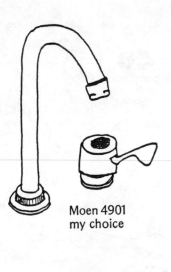

Moen 4901
my choice

Illustration **43**
Bar Sink Faucets

## Laundry:

1. Wall-hung:
   This faucet hangs on the wall above the laundry tray (tub). It is usually not a glamour model, but rather a rough finished satin-chromed job, with hose threads on the end of the swing spout. There are about three popular designs among this wall-hung group (see Illus. 44a).

2. Deck-mount:
   This faucet mounts directly upon the tray or counter top. Most laundry trays, unless they are the modern plastic ones, did not have predrilled holes. You will find the deck-mounted faucets on the newer plastic trays. The laundry deck-mounted faucet is also usually a rough finish with satin chrome plating and hose threads on the end of the swing spout (see Illus. 44b).

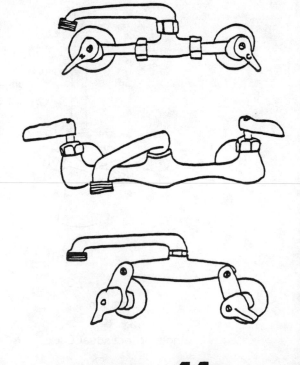

Illustration **44a**
Wall-hung Laundry Faucets

44

## Kitchen:

1. **Top Deck-mount:**
   This faucet is mounted on *top* of the sink or counter, at the back edge of the sink (see Illus. 45a).
2. **Wall-hung:**
   This faucet "hangs" on the wall above the sink (see Illus. 45b).
3. **Under-hung Deck-mount:**
   This faucet mounts on the top of the sink, at the back edge or on the counter top itself (see Illus. 45c).

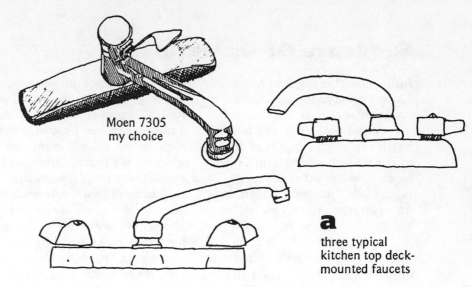

Moen 7305
my choice

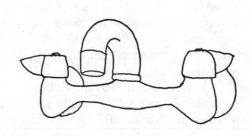

**a**

three typical kitchen top deck-mounted faucets

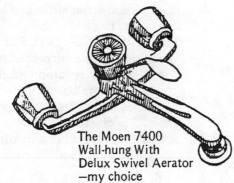

The Moen 7400 Wall-hung With Delux Swivel Aerator —my choice

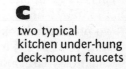

**b**

two typical kitchen wall-hung faucets

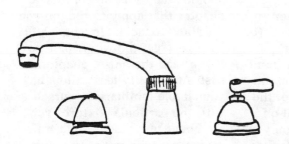

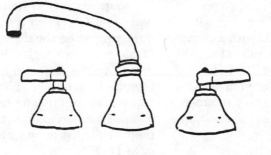

**c**

two typical kitchen under-hung deck-mount faucets

Illustration **45**
Kitchen Faucets

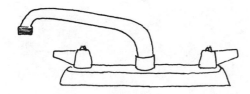

Illustration **44b**
Deck-mounted Laundry Faucets

45

# Sequence Of Operations

After replacing my first hundred faucets (everyone else would probably realize it after ten), I discovered that when the faucet needs replacing the rest of the under-sink plumbing is also ready to go. And, in *many* cases, removal of the waste system is necessary before you can get at the existing faucet to remove it. So, in this book, we are going to make a clean sweep and replace it all with new. That way, on those rare occasions when it is just a rotten trap, supply or angle stop, you can pluck just the information you need to effect that repair, but all the information you need to make a clean sweep is there for the majority of you unfortunate folk.

Getting rid of the old components is *always* more of a problem than installing the new ones. Next time you see some photo advertisement showing some "beautiful people" who are all smiles as they fiddle with a cheap plastic component in a $100,000 kitchen, I hope the "little bells" go off in the back of your head and you have the savvy to steer clear of whatever they are selling.

We will begin by replacing the angle stops if they happen to be rubber cone washer or slip joint types; then we replace the old supplies, the pop-up waste and the trap. The first faucet we will replace is going to be the lavatory 4 inch center set. Following the 4 inch center set will come the wide-spread faucet. After reading about these two faucets, the replacement of a single cock and most kitchen sink faucets will be already evident. The final lavatory faucet we replace will be the single-post mixing valve. As was mentioned before, the built-in basin-manifold or back-shelf combination will not be discussed.

After bathroom lavatory faucets, we move on to kitchen sink faucets, followed by laundry faucets and finish up with bar sink faucets. The manner in which we replace bathroom wide-spread faucets is almost identical to the replacement of under-hung kitchen deck-mounted faucets. Individual cocks are replaced in the same manner as half of a bathroom 4 inch center set.

Having made the decision to tackle your own replacement (or first-time installation on a remodel) start phoning tool and equipment renters and find out which agency rents most of the tools in the list mentioned on page 11. This you can do on your work lunch break. The telephone will also save a great deal of time discovering which plumbing supplier will sell to you and which brand names they carry. For the ease of comparison, I suggest that you visit the outlet that stocks most of the brands, and then see which outlet will sell you your choice for the best price. Ask if you can get a "green money" cash discount.

This next bit of information is EXTREMELY important! While working under lavatory sinks, kitchen sinks, bar sinks and laundry trays, DO NOT USE A 110 VOLT LIGHTING FIXTURE! Water and house current can kill you. I strongly recommend that you buy a stable-based, adjustable beam flashlight. PASCO makes an affordable cheap one and SPORTSMAN brand is a quality one with a very good illumination.

In addition to lining up tools and hardware in advance, you should study sections of this chapter that apply to the job you are about to tackle. In fact, it will help you "get the whole picture" if you read the entire chapter first. At the very least, though, you should familiarize yourself with the particular fixtures you are about to replace. Don't wait 'til you're stuck under the sink surrounded by the unknown.

# About Angle Stops And Supplies

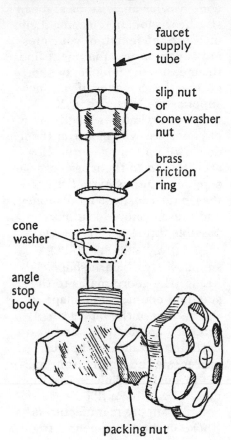

faucet supply tube

slip nut or cone washer nut

brass friction ring

cone washer

angle stop body

packing nut

Illustration **46**
Rubber Cone Washer Angle Stop

Angle stops are the little valves (most of the time they are chromed) under the bathroom lavatory sink, most kitchen sinks with deck-mounted faucets and bar sinks. A round tube, called a *supply*, carries water from out the top of the angle stop up to the faucet above. The angle stops have round, cross or oval handles so that you can turn the water off and work on the faucet.

There are two types of angle stops used with household faucets. They are:

1. Rubber cone washer (slip-joint) angle stops (Illus. 46), and

2. Brass ferrule compression angle stops (Illus. 47).

When I plumb a new home or an addition, I run the water lines in rigid copper pipe. I then solder a special fitting (FIP by copper, winged 90 degree elbow) on the pipe, inside the wall, at the fixture locations. Inside the wall, this fitting is secured in place with pan head sheet metal screws. The fitting has female iron pipe threads into which I thread a ½ inch diameter *brass* nipple. On the outside of the wall (finished wall), this brass nipple protrudes maybe 1½ inches. Onto the end of this brass nipple, I thread a ½ inch female iron pipe by ⅜ inch brass ferrule compression angle stop (see Illus. 47).

I use this type of angle stop *exclusively* and I want to tell you why. The rubber cone washer angle stop, which is still manufactured but of an old design, has an inherent weakness which is two-fold:

1. Excessively high water pressure can blow the faucet supply tube out of the angle stop and cause serious flooding.

2. The rubber cone washer on the hot supply tube usually dries out because of the heated water and then starts to crumble away thus causing a leak, or a real flood if you are not home to check it. This is why it is always a good idea to turn the angle stops off when you will be gone from your home for extended visits.

The ½ inch female iron pipe by ⅜ inch brass ferrule compression angle stop has a little round brass ferrule or "ball" in place of the rubber cone washer. When the brass ferrule squeezes tightly to the supply tubing upon tightening of the ferrule nut, the supply tubing cannot pull out of the angle stop, and cause flooding (see Illus. 47).

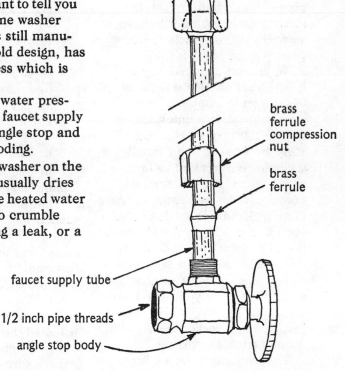

brass ferrule compression nut

brass ferrule

faucet supply tube

1/2 inch pipe threads

angle stop body

Illustration **47**
Brass Ferrule Compression Angle Stop

Some years ago, we began to see another type of angle stop emerge. This one is called a compression by compression angle stop. It allows the plumber to install the angle stop directly to a smooth copper pipe without soldering the special fitting on the end and using a threaded brass nipple. This type of angle stop is held to the copper pipe with a brass ferrule very similar to the one used to grip the supply tubing. This design of angle stop saves a lot of expensive plumber's time, but it has been responsible for a good many floods when used by laypersons. This is because if sufficient torque is not applied to the ½ inch ferrule nut upon installation, the angle stop can also blow off the end of the copper pipe under high water pressure conditions. The copper water pipe is much harder than the softer supply tubing which works so well with the small ⅜ inch compression ferrules.

To determine whether you have a rubber cone washer or brass ferrule compression angle stop, we will do a quick inspection. First, turn off the angle stops by rotating their handles in a clockwise direction as far as they will go. Second, turn the faucet handles or handle (in case of a single handle mixing valve such as a MOEN) to the ON position. No water should issue from the faucet spout. If a stream of water does continue to flow, the stem washers in your angle stops are defective. To perform this inspection, however, we will allow a small trickle or drip.

This is going to be a simple little task that will build your confidence and let you get your feet wet (not literally) gently.

1. With the 8 inch adjustable wrench, or the 12 inch adjustable wrench, adjust the jaws to fit the wrench flats on the angle stop's cone washer nut (see Illus. 46).

2. Turn the nut in a *counter-clockwise* direction as viewed from *above*. Undo the nut all the way off the male threads of the angle stop.

3. Now slide the cone washer nut up the supply tube an inch or so. Where your present supply tube enters the angle stop you will find one of the following:

   a. A rubber cone washer and maybe a thin brass friction ring. The rubber cone washer will probably be gray, black, orange or yellow in color.

   b. Nothing! The cone washer and friction ring are stuck, hiding inside the cone washer nut, and visible only by looking from underneath.

   c. A brass compression ferrule, which resembles a little, round brass ball, with the supply tubing passing up through the center. If you find the latter, and the angle stops DO shut the water off, you are in luck. There is no need to replace them for new ones.

I buy my angle stops and supplies boxed together, with two new chromed escutcheons. Two popular national brands that I recommend are SPEEDWAY, by Brass Craft and SPEED-FLEX, by Eastman.

In the case of bathroom lavatory sinks, it was an accepted practice that plumbers "rough-in" or install the water pipes to be within about 15 inches from the faucet's threaded connections hanging down below the sink or counter. However, many installations that I am called to service were not roughed-in by plumbers and this measurement may not conform to the 15 inch length.

If you do happen to have rubber cone washer angle stops and can see the wisdom in replacing them, measure the length of your present supply tubes. You might find the measurement longer or shorter than the 15 inches. If your new supplies are longer than 15 inches, or whatever length your old ones are, you can trim them down with a tubing cutter. However, to *add* to the length of your supplies requires extra fittings that in turn cost you more money and present more locations for possible future leaks.

SPEEDWAY and SPEED-FLEX supplies have "acorn-shaped" heads. The acorn mates to the standard countersunk shape in the bottom of the faucet's threaded connections, and also nests in the faucet's slip nut, preventing the supply from pulling through the hole in the slip nut and causing a flood.

Some supply manufacturers (those in the home-center trade) produce a "spirally grooved" exterior on their supplies which lends them to easy bending by inexperienced hands. The *only* supply of this type that I would suggest you ever use should have the acorn head on the end instead of the more common rubber cone washer on the end. Also, these supply tubes are thinner than the brands that I mentioned earlier and the grooved supply tubes are subject to cracking in the groove if you end up bending them too much in installing them. The grooves can also get in the way and you cannot trim them down as far as good craftsmanship dictates. For these reasons, I suggest that you stay away from them altogether.

Another warning well worth heeding: Lately, another design of supply tubing has emerged on the home-fix-it market. It is a reinforced plastic hose with metal connections squeezed onto the ends. This type makes a very enticing bid to the layperson because you can bend them around like a piece of wet spaghetti. BUT, stay away from them; they've caused many, many floods when used on respectable water pressures. Whoever is squeezing the metal connections on the end of the plastic is only giving the "dead fish, luke-warm handshake" instead of a required tons-per-inch crusher.

If you find this later, super easy bending design enticing, there is one brand worth buying. It is made by the Fluidmaster Company. Its trade name is "NO-BURST."

This super easy flexible supply differs from the reinforced plastic ones. The "NO-BURST" is stainless steel woven mesh over neoprene with aircraft quality stainless steel connections.

You should be able to find them in good hardware stores.

If the angle stops and/or faucet that you will be replacing is below the level of the water heater, try shutting off the cold water inlet valve to the heater. This valve is rarely activated, so you might want to place an old washrag over the handle to increase your grip. Now, turn the handle in a *clockwise* direction of rotation as far as you can go. If you can shut the valve off (you can tell if no more hot water comes out of the faucets), then turn the burner control (if it is a gas-fired appliance) to the PILOT position. Look on the heater above the control valve; there should be directions for doing this.

If you have an electric water heater, turn off the electricity to the heater at the fuse or breaker panel, unless you know of an on-off switch on the appliance.

By turning off the energy to the heater, you will prevent the burner or electrodes from causing any damage to themselves or to the holding tank, or to any flash tubes if it is a flash-heated appliance. With the cold water inlet valve turned off, you will reduce your chances of siphoning the hot water out of the tank and soaking your tootsies when you replace the angle stops.

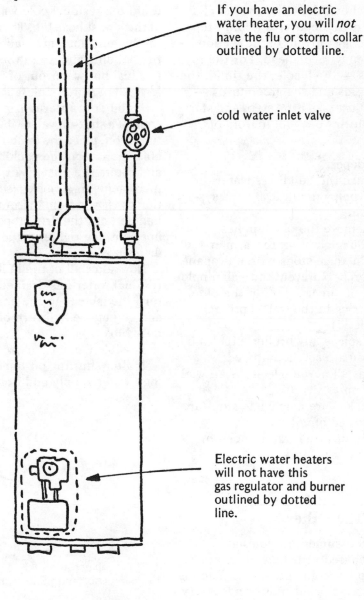

If you have an electric water heater, you will *not* have the flu or storm collar outlined by dotted line.

cold water inlet valve

Electric water heaters will not have this gas regulator and burner outlined by dotted line.

Illustration **48**

# Replacing Angle Stops

This section is the first step in the Clean Sweep for all deck-mounted faucets. And, if you just need to replace some rotten angle stops, you're also in the right place.

All of our movements will be simple and straightforward, so do not panic. Like a challenging hike, we will stop and rest along the way. For you experienced hot-shots, the following list (I'll call it Guidepost) is a long-step-by-long-step tour of the section — you may race ahead. For the rest of us — the feeble, the timid, the cowards and the greenhorns — let's just take little steps and start by putting one foot in front of the other . . .

Guidepost
1. Turn the building's water supply off and drain the system.
2. Remove the old supplies.
3. You might want to warm up the old angle stops with a propane torch to prevent the wall nipple from breaking off in the old fitting in the wall (optional tactic).
4. Replace any broken nipples if you are so encumbered.
5. Install new angle stops on wall nipples.
6. Make sure new angle stops are turned off all the way.
7. Go turn the water back on.
8. Check for leaks.

## One Foot In Front Of The Other

Let's assume that you have purchased your new angle stops, supplies, trap and faucet. The big day has arrived and the necessary tools are accounted for. Some people feel more comfortable with a bathtub full of water and a sink full of water before shutting the building's water supply off. Little Johnnie might get into some mischief and need a quick dunking, and you can make coffee and tea from the water in the sink and flush the toilet by bucketing water out of the tub into the toilet *tank*.

With emergency water accounted for, go turn off the water and drain the residual cold water out of the lowest hose bib. Then open the highest hot water faucet in the building and drain the residual hot water out of the lowest hot water sink faucet.

If you encounter a drip at the stem of a shut-off valve when you turn it off, place the 8 inch adjustable wrench on the packing nut and rotate the nut in ¼ turn increments in a *clockwise* direction as viewed from in front of the handle until the drip stops. *Do not* continue tightening after the drip stops.

Now, after all of the building's residual water has drained off, turn the faucets in the house off and go outside and turn off the hose bibs.

Possible Exception:
If after shutting off the building's water supply and draining the building, you still have water flowing out of the lowest hose bib, leave it open to prevent the water from climbing back up into the building and coming to your work station.

If you have any old bath towels, you might lay them on the floor under the sink or on the floor of the cabinet. Unpackage your new angle stops and supplies. TURN THE HANDLES ON BOTH ANGLE STOPS TO THE *OFF* POSITION RIGHT NOW. Do this by turning the handles in a clockwise direction as viewed from the front. Make sure that the ferrule nut on the angle stop is threaded on far enough to guard against losing the little brass ferrule and the nut.

Pick up the basin wrench. You will notice that the jaws are spring loaded and grasp only when used in a *dragging* direction. The jaws flip from one side of the handle to the other. One side is for tightening and the other side for loosening. I have found the most comfortable position to remove the faucet slip nuts is to lay on my back. Put your safety goggles on and get down in position.

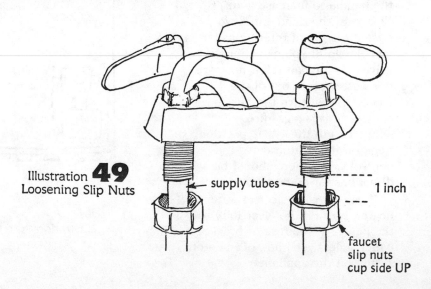

Illustration **49**
Loosening Slip Nuts

supply tubes

1 inch

faucet slip nuts cup side UP

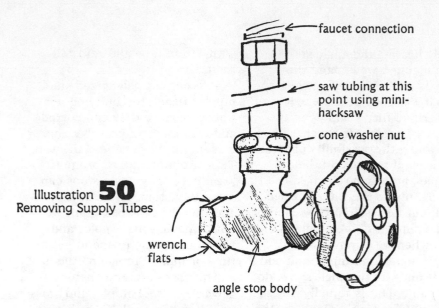

faucet connection

saw tubing at this point using mini-hacksaw

cone washer nut

**Illustration 50**
Removing Supply Tubes

wrench flats

angle stop body

The RIDGID #1017 basin wrench has an extension handle. By pushing in the button on the bottom, you can extend the wrench to the most comfortable length for you. By moving the faucet's slip nut (see Illus. 49) in a *counter-clockwise* direction as viewed from underneath, it will unthread and separate from the faucet connection. Loosen both the hot and the cold slip nuts — when they are backed off all the way, pull them down the supply tubes an inch or so. If you cannot loosen the slip nuts with your basin wrench in hand, adjust the jaws of the 12 inch adjustable wrench to fit the *square* handle and now you can bust them loose with this extra leverage. This is why I like the RIDGID #1017. It has a square handle for this purpose. It's the only basin wrench I've seen that is both height adjustable and square handled.

Now, with the 8 or 12 inch adjustable wrench, loosen the angle stop cone washer nuts by rotating them in a *counter-clockwise* direction as viewed from above. If you have ⅜ inch supply tubing and the angle stop cone washer or brass ferrule compression nuts are loose, try bending the supply tubing in the center and thus drawing one or both ends free of the angle stops and faucet connections. If you already have brass ferrule compression angle stops (in good condition) and you are able to remove the supplies without seriously kinking them, you may try reusing them later when we put them back. If you have the ⁷⁄₁₆ or ½ inch cone washer angle stops, the larger diameter, smooth supply tubing is more difficult to bend. Your best bet is to use the mini-hacksaw and sever the tubing in the center and then pull each piece free (see Illus. 50).

Now, with one hand, wiggle the supplies back and forth or around and around in a circular motion as you pull down on one and up on the other.

Do not be alarmed when a little water dribbles or squirts out the saw cut in the supply tubing when you sever it. It is residual water left standing in the tubing after the building water was drained off. Thus the reason for the old towels on the floor.

If the supply tubes will not part from the faucet connections, just let them dangle there. We'll take care of that problem later (page 67).

Job well done, TAKE A BREAK!

## Using The Propane Torch

Take the 12 inch adjustable wrench and adjust the jaws to fit the wrench flats on the back of the angle stop (see Illus. 50). Then loosen the jaws "just a hair" and set the wrench down close by. This procedure is for the benefit of you first-timers. We employ it in hopes of sparing you any nipple difficulties when removing the old cone washer angle stops. Remember, if you already have brass ferrule compression angle stops and they are functioning properly, then you will not have to replace them and do any of this procedure.

Set the propane torch down on the floor away from the cabinet and any hanging towels, shower curtains, etc. Pick up the flint striker and place the cup end of the striker over the tip of the torch (see Illus. 51 on next page).

Now, open the valve on the propane torch by rotating the round knob in a counterclockwise direction for three complete revolutions. When the valve is opened, start to activate the striker by rapidly squeezing the striker handles together, producing sparks from the flint and igniting the propane. When the torch lights, open the valve another one or two turns and direct the flame *from the side* onto the angle stop and hold it there for a timed 60 seconds.

Then, turn the torch off and without wasting time, set it a safe distance away and place the pre-adjusted jaws of the adjustable wrench on the angle stop's wrench flats. Rotate the wrench in a *counterclockwise* direction as viewed from in front, and back the angle stop up several complete revolutions before stopping to let it cool off. Repeat the process for the other angle stop.

51

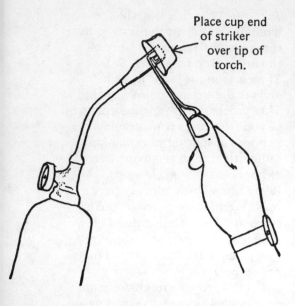

Illustration
**51**
Lighting the
Propane Torch

Place cup end
of striker
over tip of
torch.

By heating the angle stop in this manner, we expand the female threads of the angle stop and it is usually possible to loosen the grip of fifty years upon the nipple. The danger we are trying to avoid is the possibility of breaking several threads off the old nipple and leaving them in the fitting, inside the wall. The second, but far less risky, possibility is the removal of the nipple in the wall when we remove the old angle stop. If the nipples should come out with the angle stops, do not panic. This is actually a blessing. Take the nipple/nipples to the hardware or plumbing supply and ask the counterman to match them up with *brass* ones. If the nipples are brass (very unlikely) grip the wrench flats of the angle stop with the 15 inch adjustable wrench. Then use the 12 inch pipe wrench to grip the nipple. Separate the nipple/nipples from the old angle stops; wrap them

with Teflon tape and reinstall them.

I *do not* use galvanized steel nipples inside the building, for water, because they can corrode and leak long before it becomes evident on the outside of the wall. They are much more prone to breaking. Many angle stops can serve their time on brass nipples and then be replaced again without damaging the nipples and without needing to spend more time or money replacing them.

The cost difference between galvanized steel nipples and brass ones is substantial, but well worth the assurance that brass buys (not to mention higher insurance rates for flood claims). If the old nipples did stay in the wall and the threads are in *good* shape, and the nipples are not nearly clogged with scale and corrosion, you can apply Teflon tape to them and reuse them.

*TAKE A BREAK!*

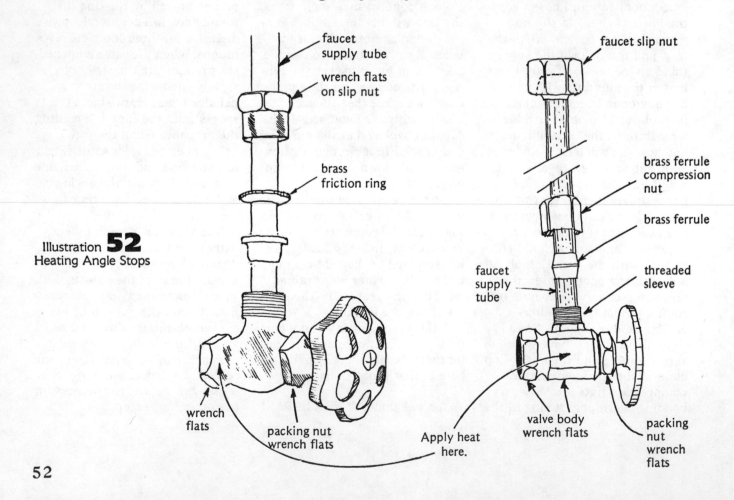

Illustration **52**
Heating Angle Stops

faucet
supply tube

wrench flats
on slip nut

brass
friction ring

wrench
flats

packing nut
wrench flats

Apply heat
here.

faucet slip nut

brass ferrule
compression
nut

brass ferrule

threaded
sleeve

faucet
supply
tube

valve body
wrench flats

packing
nut
wrench
flats

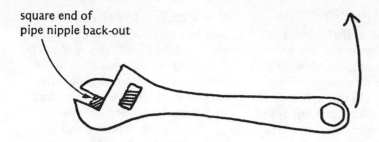

square end of
pipe nipple back-out

15 inch wrench

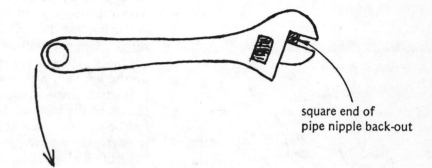

square end of
pipe nipple back-out

Illustration **53**
Removing Broken
Nipples

## What About Broken Nipples—And Using The Nipple Back-out

This very short section is the required procedure if you did break nipples off in the wall or the nipples have damaged outside threads and/or corroded centers.

Paying heed to "Murphy's Law" which in essence translates: When the worst possible thing can happen, it usually does; let's go through the procedure of replacing broken nipples.

We will use the ACE EX-7 pipe nipple back-out for ½ inch diameter iron pipe. If you are not wearing your safety goggles, put them on now. Insert the spiraled, tapered end of the the back-out into the remaining portion of the nipple. If the nipple broke off leaving the majority of itself in the angle stop, the remaining piece left in the wall will not be visible from outside the wall.

Push the back-out through the hole in the wall and into the remaining piece which is hidden from view. You will feel resistance when it is in place. Now, pick up the ballpeen hammer and tap the square end *lightly*, just enough so that the back-out stays in the fitting without falling out. Adjust the jaws of the 15 inch adjustable wrench to fit the wrench flats on the end (see Illus. 53).

I have found it easier to break loose the old broken nipple while *lifting* on the wrench handle instead of pushing down. If room allows, you might pursue this application. In any case, you want to move the back-out in a *counterclockwise* rotation.

It will require a great effort to break loose the old threads, but the 15 inch wrench should provide the leverage to do the job. A piece of scrap iron pipe large enough in diameter to slide down the handle of the wrench can be used to increase your leverage if you are not able to break the joint loose otherwise. After you extract the broken remains, TAKE A BREATHER.

To remove the broken piece of nipple left on the end of the pipe nipple back-out, put the back-out back into the jaws of the adjustable wrench and then place the jaws of the 8 inch pipe wrench on the remaining piece of nipple and rotate the pipe wrench in a *clockwise* direction while looking *down* onto the tapered end of the back-out.

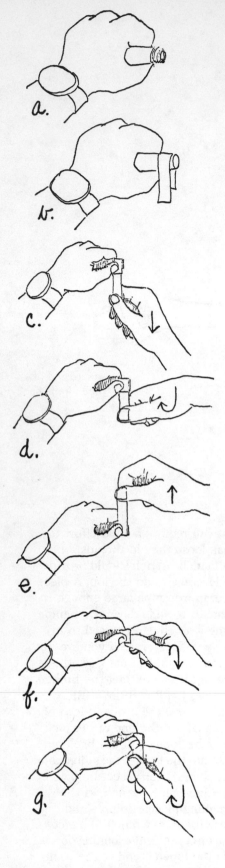

## Wrapping Nipples With Teflon Tape

This little bit of instruction is designed to have you wrap the Teflon tape onto the pipe nipples in the proper direction of wrap. If you wrap it on in the wrong direction, the tape will back out of the threads and not afford you any leak protection.

Pull off about five inches of Teflon tape from the spool and break it off by pulling straight with your thumb and forefinger. While holding the new *brass* nipple. . .in your *left* hand, lay the piece of tape over the threads on the left end, just covering the first thread. Now place your left thumb on the tape lightly and pull on the outside piece of tape until the tape almost disappears under your thumb (see Illus. 54c).

Now, press down firmly with your left thumb and pull down on the outside leg of tape until it begins to stretch. While holding the tape taut, begin wrapping the tape around the nipple in a *clockwise* direction.

Each time you go one full wrap with the tape, move down the threads, closer to your forefinger. When you come to the very end of the tape, rub the end into the threads with your right thumb and forefinger (see Illus. 54h).

I found this procedure one of the most difficult to put into writing. You might find it difficult to follow. What *is* the most important aspect is getting the tape wrapped tightly, in a clockwise direction and covering all of the threads.

So for you "still confused" and you Southpaws, do the best you can.

## Installing New Nipples

If you removed your angle stops and the nipples came with them, or; you had to use the ACE EX-7 pipe nipple back-out to remove broken ones, we will now do a very short exercise in installing new *brass* nipples.

With Teflon tape applied to both threaded ends of your new nipples, we will start the new ones back into the wall fittings inside the wall. Hand tighten the nipples in a *clockwise* direction until you can no longer turn them from lack of strength. Take your time trying to start the nipples threading into the wall fittings — try to keep the nipple as level and straight as you can. Of course if your old nipples protruded out of the wall on angles, then the new ones will only go back in on the same angle.

Now use the 8 inch pipe wrench and snug them up until it becomes an effort to turn them any further with this little wrench. If there is no smooth shoulder portion for you to apply the pipe wrench to, then after reading about chromed sleeves which follows, there is a concise explanation on how to install the nipples without damaging the threads in the section titled Installing New Angle Stops (next page).

Illustration
**54**

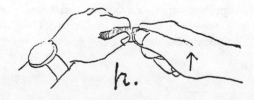

## Chromed Sleeves

Back in the "Good Ole Days" plumbers usually left several inches of nipple sticking out of the wall. The escutcheons, which were flatter then, were slid down the nipple to the wall. Then, a piece of chromed sleeve was cut to length and slid over the outside of the nipple, leaving just about six threads exposed (sticking out the end of the sleeve). When the chromed angle stop was then threaded onto the nipple, everything was shiny chrome. This was also done for good reason. In the Good Ole Days, most bathroom sinks were either of the pedestal or wall-hung variety. The longer nipple positioned the angle stop on the end to an equal distance from the wall as the faucet connection above it. The chromed sleeve hid what would have been an unsightly galvanized pipe.

The faucet supplies back then were *very* heavy gauge brass tubing which was no easy task to bend by hand. So having the angle stop out from the wall meant that the plumber only had to bend the supplies to one dimension: sideways. Today's supplies are three to five times thinner (not to mention cheaper) and made of copper for easier bending.

If you find this outer chromed sleeve on your nipples and you do not wish to fuss with them due to rust or corrosion or paint, subtract the length of the sleeve from the overall length of the nipple. Then pick new nipples closest to this measurement. *BUT, always* go to the next longer nipple length (½ inch increments) if the sleeve leaves you between standard nipple lengths.

## Installing New Angle Stops

Sometimes it is necessary to *gently* place the jaws of a pipe wrench or slide-jaw pliers on the threaded end of a nipple. Whenever possible, use only the smooth portion of the nipple on which to apply tools. Sometimes rather than risking damage to the threads, I hand-tighten the nipples as far into the wall fitting as possible and then place the escutcheons over the nipples followed by new angle stops. After starting the angle stop onto the nipple by hand, I use the 8 inch adjustable wrench to tighten the nipple into the wall fitting and tighten the angle stop onto the nipple *simultaneously.*

If you choose this technique, make sure that the jaws of the adjustable wrench do not loosen up and *strip* or round off the wrench flats on the new angle stop. (Like candy bars, angle stops have shrunk in mass tremendously and they have very thin female thread walls compared to wonderfully meaty ones of years gone by.) It is also very important that you do not overtighten the angle stop onto the nipple. The angle stop is brass, so it is soft to begin with. The thinner female thread walls of today's angle stops will crack and split if you overtighten them.

I would go three or four complete revolutions in a *clockwise* direction of rotation using the 8 inch adjustable wrench, *slowly,* after tightening the angle stops onto the nipples by hand as far as possible. Come to a stop with the threaded sleeve and ferrule nut pointing up.

Here is another good reason for buying *brass* nipples. If you have a good handle on biology, the reasoning will be very clear. Both mating parts being made of soft brass (angle stop and nipple), it

requires less torque and fewer revolutions to make a watertight seal. A *harder* steel nipple would make the angle stop's female threads do all of the accommodating (stretching) for a tight fit on the male nipple. Whereas, if *both* mating parts are made of pliable brass, *both* parts do the adjusting.

If your angle stops did come free from the existing nipples, leaving the male threads in good shape, then wrap the male threads with Teflon tape in a *clockwise* direction. Applying the Teflon tape to nipples in the dark, confined "pullman" or vanity cabinet will be more difficult than wrapping nipples laying in your hand. It can be a drudge using your arms while lying down, so take your time even if you have to sit up and rest several times.

After threading your new angle stops on the existing nipples, leaving the threaded sleeve and compression nut pointing up, make *sure* that you turn the angle stops all the way off, *now* (lest you forget). This is also important: make sure that no one else in the house turned on a faucet that you don't know about. If you turn the water back on, an open faucet could overfill a basin and cause a flood.

Now, go back and turn the water on to the building. Go to the lowest hose bib and turn it off slowly (if you had to leave it open during the angle stop replacement). Without wasting any time, go back to your work station and check the new nipples and angle stops for drips. If you have a drip, go shut the water off again but don't bother draining the building. Further tighten the angle stops onto the nipples one or more complete revolutions and resume the water service and check for drips again.

## What About The Water Heater?

If you did manage to shut the cold water inlet valve to the water heater off, you cannot test the hot side for drips until you resume water service to the water heater. Leave the burner control in the PILOT setting if it is a gas-fired appliance, until the angle stops pass the leak test. Then, turn the burner back to ON. If you have an electric water heater, you would leave the switch or circuit breaker in the OFF setting likewise until passing the leak test before flipping the switches back to ON.

Many times on new angle stops, the packing nut behind the handle will have a drip around the stem, where it enters the valve (see page 52). With your 8 inch adjustable wrench, tighten this nut in ¼ turn increments, until the drip stops.

Okay — the new angle stops are installed and we have no leaks . . . right? *TAKE A BREAK!*

# About Sink Traps
## Plastic Versus Brass

There are two plastics used in the manufacture of traps used in the residential plumbing trade. They are ABS and PVC. It is not important to know what the ingredients the initials stand for are. The trade names are ABS and PVC. ABS is usually black in color and PVC will be white or cream color. (Electricians use a gray PVC pipe, but to my knowledge that specification remains in their trade only.)

Most ABS trap systems consist of a trap arm (which is a cut-to-length piece of Schedule 40 pipe) glued to a Schedule 40, individual P-trap. Under accessible fixtures (sinks) the P-trap should have a union nut. By undoing the union

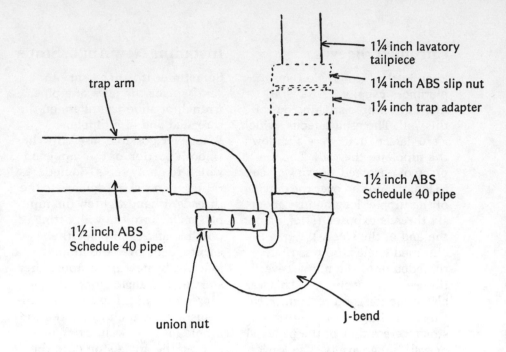

1¼ inch lavatory tailpiece
1¼ inch ABS slip nut
1¼ inch trap adapter
1½ inch ABS Schedule 40 pipe
trap arm
1½ inch ABS Schedule 40 pipe
union nut
J-bend

Illustration **55**
ABS P-Trap with Union Nut

nut, you can separate the J-bend portion of the P-trap from the trap arm (see Illus. 55).

In recent years, however, ABS sink traps have become available in the same (smaller) outside diameter as tubular brass traps. This new plastic trap comes with a trap arm included. This way, you can use the standard wall nipples used with tubular brass traps (also brass waste adapters) and the standard 1½ inch slip nut washers and nuts also used with tubular brass systems.

One thing I do *not* like about these new traps is the *thinness* of the material. The new traps are a flimsy cousin compared to the much thicker, larger diameter Schedule 40 ABS pipe and P-trap. If you have the Schedule 40 trap system, you will not have to repair or replace it anywhere near as often as the flimsy plastic version *or* the tubular brass trap arm and P-trap.

## Removal Of Tubular Brass Traps

This section deals with a game familiar to all of you . . .TUG-OF-WAR, but this time with a different partner. If you only have to replace or repair a leaking brass trap, you are in the right place. It is also among the Clean Sweep topics, under the umbrella of HOW TO REPLACE A FAUCET. Compared to replacing angle stops, it is a CINCH!

Guidepost

1. Loosen upper slip nut (on top of J-Bend (see Illus. 56).
2. Loosen lower slip nut (see Illus. 56).
3. Pull J-bend down.
4. Loosen trap arm slip nut at the wall (see Illus. 57 & 58).
5. Pull trap arm out of the wall nipple or waste adapter.

If you have a leak in your trap system at locations 1, 2 and/or 3

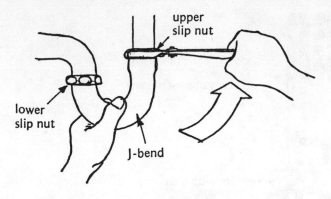

upper
slip nut

lower
slip nut

J-bend

Illustration **56**

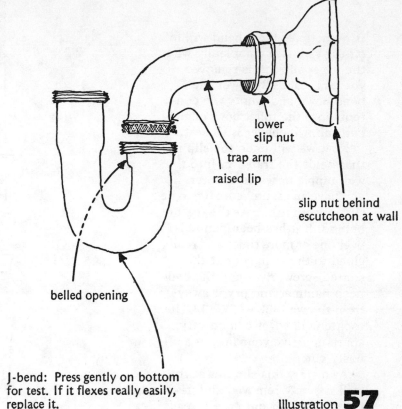

lower
slip nut

trap arm

raised lip

slip nut behind
escutcheon at wall

belled opening

J-bend: Press gently on bottom
for test. If it flexes really easily,
replace it.

Illustration **57**
Tubular Brass Trap

in Illus. 58, the slip joint washers are no longer effecting a good seal, and they need to be replaced. Read the following section and then go to Installing A New Trap, page 90.

You will simply install new slip joint washers using your old trap and trap arm.

We will now remove the existing trap. If you are working under a sink, inside a cabinet, you had better get a pillow for your back. With the 10 inch slide-jaw pliers, adjust the jaws to the *upper* slip nut of the trap's J-bend, the one grasping the tailpiece (pipe carrying waste water out of the sink). *If you have a pedestal sink,* read on — what we do here will apply in that situation (see paragraph 2, page 73).

If the handles on the slide-jaw pliers are too far apart to grip comfortably, slide the lower jaw down to the next notch. The front of the jaws should point to the right, with the handles swinging in a *counterclockwise* direction. With the pliers in place, loosen the upper slip nut by using a *counterclockwise* direction as viewed from above. If you cannot break loose the slip nut, try using the 12 or 18 inch pipe wrench.

Next, loosen the lower slip nut on the *low* side of the trap's J-bend, giving the J-bend support from the bottom, using your other hand (see Illus. 56).

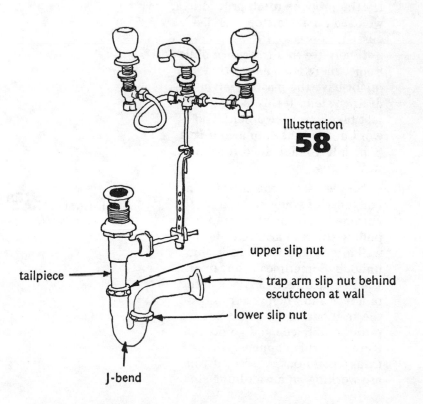

Illustration
**58**

tailpiece

upper slip nut

trap arm slip nut behind
escutcheon at wall

lower slip nut

J-bend

Sometimes the J-bend will fall off the tailpiece completely when the lower slip nut is removed. If you can, carefully lower the J-bend down and empty the contents into the toilet bowl or the bathtub, whichever is closest.

Now, we will undo the slip nut that holds the trap arm into the wall nipple or waste adapter. If you have an escutcheon, it can be slid forward to expose the slip nut behind. If it has been painted over one or more times and really glued to the wall, get out the slotted screwdriver and the ball-peen hammer and pry it away from the wall. BE CAREFUL! The escutcheon edges can be very sharp and give your fingers a nasty cut.

As a rule, this slip nut at the wall is rarely removed and it takes a real set onto the threads of the drain nipple or adapter. You may have to use the 18 inch pipe wrench on this slip nut. Turn the nut in a *counterclockwise* direction. If you cannot break it loose, try the propane torch procedure we used on angle stops, as discussed on pages 51 & 52.

If you live in a tract or mobile home, there is a chance that you might have the plastic trap and drain system. If this is the case, just take down the J-bend and work around the trap arm if it is Schedule 40 and glued into the wall fitting.

Now we get to the tug-of-war. For those of you who do have the chromed, tubular brass trap, try pulling the trap arm out of the wall after you have the slip nut undone. Sometimes the trap arm will line up directly in back of the tailpiece and when you try to pull the trap out, it will run smack into the tailpiece and go no further. If this happens, something's gotta budge. Also, if you are working on a wall-hung sink

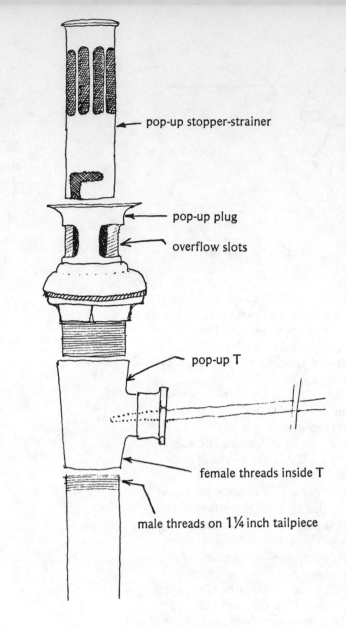

pop-up stopper-strainer

pop-up plug

overflow slots

pop-up T

female threads inside T

male threads on 1¼ inch tailpiece

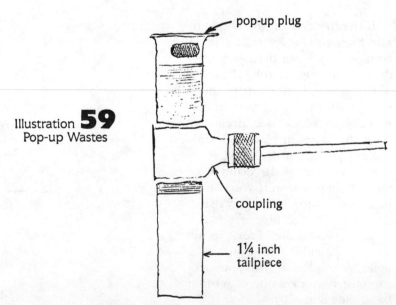

pop-up plug

Illustration **59**
Pop-up Wastes

coupling

1¼ inch tailpiece

58

that has a pop-up waste in it, you might have an easy way out. You can remove the sink from the wall by backing out any screws holding it in place (they will be underneath each side, at the wall) and then lift it up and off the wall.

Or, if you can, unthread the tailpiece from the waste T and then pull the trap arm all the way out. The tailpiece on 99 percent of all pop-up wastes, threads into the T or coupling (see Illus. 59). Grip the tailpiece with the slide-jaw pliers (jaws pointing to the right) and back the tailpiece out using a *counterclockwise* direction of rotation as viewed from underneath.

However, if you have a rubber stopper waste or a pop-up waste resembling the ones in Illustrations 68 & 75, you are not so fortunate. In these two cases, the tailpiece does not unthread. Your only course of attack is to remove the entire waste from the sink — pull out the trap arm, then install a new trap arm, and then put the old waste back into the bowl (using new beveled waste gasket). See pages 65 & 66 for instructions.

If you were only going to replace the rubber slipjoint washers on the J-bend because of a leak at the slip nuts, you won't have to mess with the waste or slip nut at the wall.

## Removal Of A Stubborn Trap Arm

If your trap arm did not pull out of the wall after you removed the J-bend portion and the slip nut at the wall connection (behind the escutcheon), we will now tackle the task of removing it.

Place the 12 inch pipe wrench on the trap arm about one inch away from the wall. We want the handle on the *left* side, with the jaws on *top,* so when we rotate the wrench in a *counterclockwise* direction, it will grip the trap arm. Now, swing the wrench handle in the *counterclockwise* direction while simultaneously pulling straight out on the trap arm. If the trap arm collapses under the twisting strain, do not panic.

With safety glasses on, pick up the 12 inch standard hacksaw or the mini-hacksaw and sever the trap arm in two, about one inch from the wall. Next, place the ¼ inch wide cold chisel between the outside of the remaining piece of trap arm and the inside of the wall nipple. With the ballpeen hammer, drive the cold chisel between the two parts at about six equally spaced points around the circumference of the broken trap arm. Tap the cold chisel in far enough to leave an impression in the wall of the trap arm. By doing this, you actually reduce the outside diameter at this point. It is a good idea to squirt some penetrating oil into the grooves and let it set for several minutes. It might take several applications of the chisel at each location and repeated applications of the penetrating oil before you shock the tubing loose. Take it slow and you should have few problems.

Make sure that you wear your safety glasses/goggles while doing this!

If there is *no* slip nut behind the escutcheon at the wall, your trap arm is probably soldered into a brass bushing which is then threaded into the fitting in the wall. If the trap arm is corroded and leaking and must be replaced, you will have to peel the brass solder-ring bushing out of the wall fitting.

After severing the trap arm outside the wall, about one inch from the wall surface, use the mini-hacksaw and make about six cuts, equally spaced around the inside of the bushing. Then use the ¼ inch cold chisel and drive the pieces out of the fitting.

Before installing your new trap arm, you'll have to purchase a 1¼ or 1½ inch by close galvanized nipple (depending upon which size fitting is in the wall) and rethread it into the wall fitting. Liberally apply RECTOR-SEAL/ Slic-Tite to the threads of the wall fitting and wrap both ends of the new nipple with Teflon tape before installing.

Take a well-earned break!

# Removal Of The Lavatory Pop-Up Waste

This is the last obstacle in our way before removing the faucet itself and making The Clean Sweep. It is one of the longer sections because we will be discussing all of the most common designs of pop-up wastes found in use today. First, take a good look at your pop-up waste. Then study Illus. 60-64. If yours resembles one of these, you can go directly to the appropriate sections. There are many designs though, and you might find yourself with one not illustrated here. However, by reading the section, you will gain insight into the possible *other* ways such a system might be joined together. Even the various, popular designs differ only in slight ways.

Guidepost

1. On very old ones, sever lift rod with mini-hacksaw (see Illus. 65).
2. On newer designs (see Illus. 66) undo set-screw on lift strap.
3. Pinch spring clip and slide off adjustment strap from pop-up adjustment arm.
4. Study Illus. 60-64.
5. If yours resembles Illus. 60 (Female T Type) then:
   a. Remove T portion with adjustment arm from plug in sink.
   b. Remove plug in sink.
6. If your pop-up waste resembles Illus. 61 (Male T Type) then:
   a. Remove pop-up stopper (see Illus. 67).
   b. Backdown friction/lock nut.
   c. Remove as much of beveled rubber waste gasket as possible.
   d. Lift waste *up*, into sink.
   e. Use slide-jaw pliers and remove pop-up seat flange from T (see Illus. 68).
7. If your pop-up waste resembles Illus. 62, then:
   a. Remove pop-up adjustment arm and gland nut.
   b. Remove friction/lock nut, washer and waste gasket from waste.
   c. Lift waste up and out of sink.

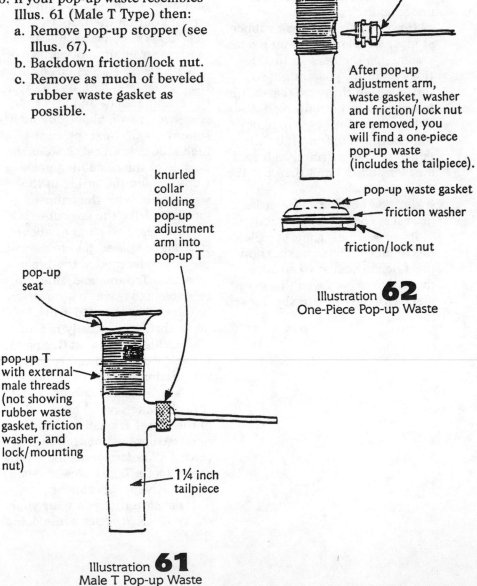

pop-up adjustment arm assembly

After pop-up adjustment arm, waste gasket, washer and friction/lock nut are removed, you will find a one-piece pop-up waste (includes the tailpiece).

pop-up waste gasket
friction washer
friction/lock nut

Illustration **62**
One-Piece Pop-up Waste

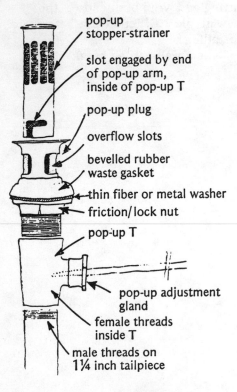

pop-up stopper-strainer

slot engaged by end of pop-up arm, inside of pop-up T

pop-up plug

overflow slots

bevelled rubber waste gasket

thin fiber or metal washer

friction/lock nut

pop-up T

pop-up adjustment gland

female threads inside T

male threads on 1¼ inch tailpiece

Illustration **60**
Female T Pop-up Waste

knurled collar holding pop-up adjustment arm into pop-up T

pop-up seat

pop-up T with external male threads (not showing rubber waste gasket, friction washer, and lock/mounting nut)

1¼ inch tailpiece

Illustration **61**
Male T Pop-up Waste

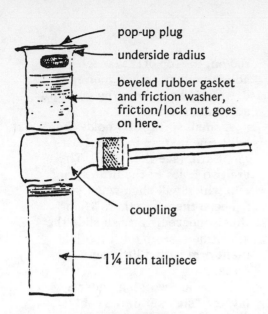

pop-up plug

underside radius

beveled rubber gasket and friction washer, friction/lock nut goes on here.

coupling

1¼ inch tailpiece

Illustration **63**
Coupling Type Pop-up Waste

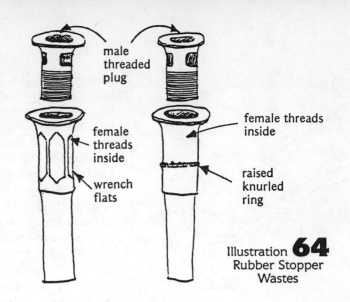

male threaded plug

female threads inside

wrench flats

female threads inside

raised knurled ring

Illustration **64**
Rubber Stopper Wastes

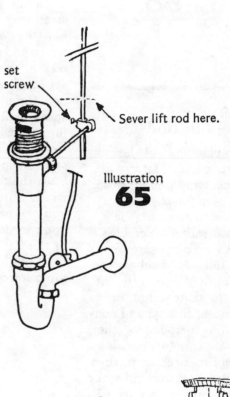

set screw

Sever lift rod here.

Illustration
**65**

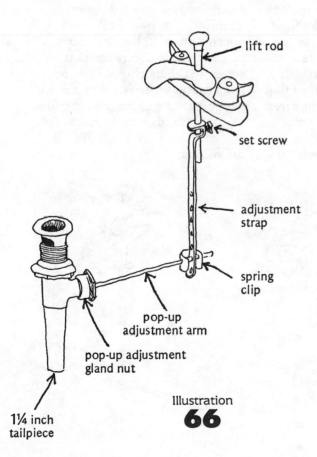

lift rod

set screw

adjustment strap

spring clip

pop-up adjustment arm

pop-up adjustment gland nut

1¼ inch tailpiece

Illustration
**66**

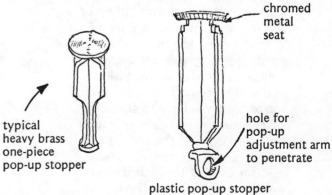

typical heavy brass one-piece pop-up stopper

chromed metal seat

hole for pop-up adjustment arm to penetrate

plastic pop-up stopper

Illustration **67**
Pop-up Stoppers

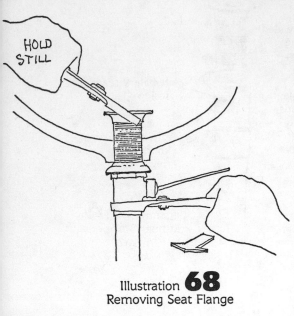

HOLD STILL

Illustration **68**
Removing Seat Flange

## Removing Lift Rods

If you are replacing an old fashion 4 inch center set (and later, wide-spread faucet) and pop-up waste, and the pop-up waste does not use an adjustment strap (see Illus. 69) but rather resembles the lift rod with a set-screw connection in Illus. 65, back up the set-screw and try to pull the lift rod out of the connection. In most instances, this type of connection will be corroded together, and if you are going to *install* a new one, *not just repair it,* then take the mini-hacksaw and sever the rod as discussed in Illus. 65.

If you need to remove the existing pop-up waste to replace a leaking, corroded waste gasket and wish to reuse your old pop-up waste, you will have to squirt penetrating oil on this connection until you *can* lift the rod up and out of it.

After cutting through the lift rod, try pulling it out the top of the faucet from above. Some old designs had a two-piece lift rod. A short length hung down under the

sink which had a hole in the lower end. Another length with a hook in its top end hung in the hole of the section, above. The bottom of the lower section attached to the lift rod with the set-screw type connection (see Illus. 70). If you have this type, after cutting the lower rod free, swing it up and remove the hook from the eye and then lift the upper length out the top of the faucet.

If your faucet is of a newer manufacture, you will probably see a flat, pop-up adjustment strap with a series of holes in it, hanging down in back of the waste and tailpiece (see Illus. 69). At the top of this strap is a set-screw with a hexagonal head or a thumb-screw head. This screw binds the strap to the round lift rod (which protrudes out the top of the faucet with a knob of some shape attached to the top). With the 6 inch adjustable wrench, undo the set-screw. If you can position yourself so that you can view the face of the screw or the flat of the screw, it will back out in a *counterclockwise* direction of rotation. Now, lift the

rod out the top of the faucet. The adjustment strap will then fall down and hang from the pop-up adjustment arm.

A small spring clip holds the adjustment strap to the adjustment arm (see Illus. 69b). There are two holes in the little spring clip which will align when you squeeze them together. When thus squeezed, you can slide the adjustment strap off the adjustment arm with a little outward force.

If you are working under a lavatory sink set into a cabinet, one with double doors and a dividing stop or stick dividing the entrance, you can now appreciate my great hatred for designers of such cabinets. Just try to squeeze your body into one of those horrible little boxes and then have room for your arms to move about. The owner of the cabinet doesn't know it, but they have just spent the difference that separated their choice from a good cabinet when they first went shopping. The extra time it takes my 225 pounds to go in and out of one of these makes just such a difference.

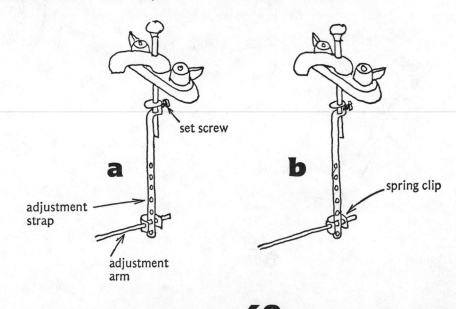

Illustration **69**

62

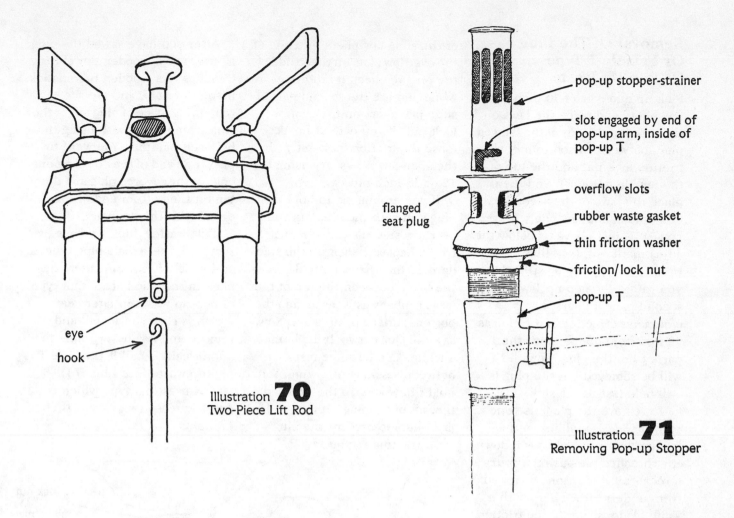

eye

hook

Illustration **70**
Two-Piece Lift Rod

pop-up stopper-strainer

slot engaged by end of
pop-up arm, inside of
pop-up T

overflow slots

flanged
seat plug

rubber waste gasket

thin friction washer

friction/lock nut

pop-up T

Illustration **71**
Removing Pop-up Stopper

## The Pop-Up Stopper

The pop-up stopper is, in essence, a "mechanically actuated" cork and it tells us a lot about the particular type of pop-up waste in which it operates. On the pedestal sinks, many times the pop-up stopper was tubular with a flattened dome on top. Near the top, but under the dome, were vertical slots which acted as a strainer (see Illus. 71).

If you have this type, you can remove it by pushing down on the lift rod and raising the stopper off the flanged seat plug in the bottom of the bowl. Now, grasp the top of the stopper and rotate it in a *counterclockwise* direction until you can turn it no further.

You might have to grasp the stopper with the slide-jaw pliers to turn it due to corrosion. Then lift *up* on the stopper while still grasping it, maybe wiggling it a bit in a circular motion.

With the stopper out of the flanged seat plug, you will be able to see two slots in the wall of the plug. These two openings allow water that enters the overflow high up on the bowl to drain into the waste without the bowl overflowing and causing a flood (see Illus. 71).

The flanged seat plug has threads running down its outside circumference. This plug was inserted into the hole in the sink bottom and it protruded out the

bottom side of the sink by maybe 1½ to 2 inches. The large, black rubber waste gasket, the thin friction washer and the lock nut were then threaded up the plug from underneath, to make a tight, waterproof seal against the underside of the sink.

Pop-up stoppers of newer designs ceased to be hollow, and were produced of cast, solid brass and later plastic. . .of course. We will discuss these later types further on.

On the next page and next section, we will begin the process of dismantling the flanged plug or Female T Type pop-up waste which we mentioned in the first paragraph.

63

## Removal Of The Plug Or Female T Type Of Pop-Up Waste

Pick up one pair of 10 inch slide-jaw pliers and place the jaws on the exposed threads of the flanged plug, between the bottom of the friction/lock nut and the top of the female pop-up T, and then place the jaws of the second pair of 10 inch slide-jaw pliers on the pop-up T, just above or below the adjustment arm (see Illus. 72). Hold the stopper plug still while you rotate the pop-up T with the second pair of pliers. Use a *clockwise* direction of rotation as viewed from *above*, until the T parts from the plug. Now the T will be removed but the plug is still held fast to the sink.

To remove the plug, use one pair of slide-jaw pliers on the friction/lock nut and back it down the threaded plug using a *counterclockwise* rotation as viewed from underneath. Then, with a knife blade, separate the friction washer (a thin brass or plastic one) from the bottom of the rubber waste gasket. With a sharp knife (a utility knife is best), make a series of deep cuts in the rubber waste gasket, from the center to the outside. BE SURE to keep your face to one side. Then, with the slide-jaw pliers, try to remove as much of the gasket as possible by gripping sections between the knife cuts and then tugging. With a piece of scrap wood placed up against the bottom of the plug, use the ballpeen hammer to lightly tap on the wood — lifting the plug out of the hole in the bottom of the sink.

If the plug rotates in the sink when you try to back down the friction/lock nut, put one handle of the slide-jaw pliers into one of the overflow slots on the inside of the plug to check its rotation, while you use the second pair of slide-jaw pliers on the friction/lock nut. If you cannot break loose the friction/lock nut with the slide-jaw pliers, try using the 12 or 18 inch pipe wrench.

If you are unable to hold the plug still with the pliers in the overflow slot, it's time for the trusty hacksaw. Pick up the standard 12 inch hacksaw and place the blade between the top of the large rubber waste gasket and the bottom surface of the sink. Now, saw the plug in two. It might take a while, so take some rests between sessions of sawing. You might have to grip the exposed threads of the plug with the slide-jaw pliers to prevent the plug from rotating as you saw it.

After you have sawed the plug in two, use a wooden dowel (saw 8 inches of a wooden broomstick if you have to), and tap the remaining piece of plug out of the sink from underneath using the ballpeen hammer. You want to place one end of the dowel on one edge of the severed plug and then tap on the bottom end of the dowel with the ballpeen.

This waste which we have just removed, the female plug type, is still widely used. But, there has been the addition of another type of pop-up waste in later years which is easier to install and remove and has fewer joints to afford leaks. I call it the Male T pop-up waste (see Illus. 73). MOEN uses this type which is another reason why I use their products.

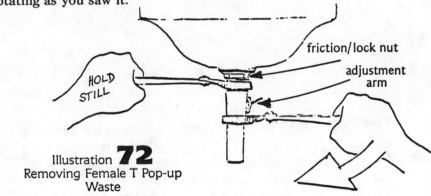

Illustration **72**
Removing Female T Pop-up Waste

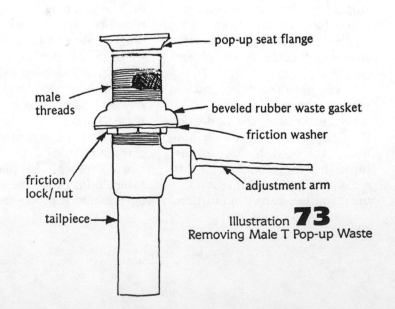

Illustration **73**
Removing Male T Pop-up Waste

## Removal Of The Male T Type Of Pop-Up Waste

On this type of design, the pop-up T is one piece, with male threads on the top portion (see Illus. 73). The male T, with friction/lock nut, friction washer and pop-up waste gasket already installed, is inserted up through the sink hole from underneath. When the male threads of the pop-up waste T protrude out of the hole in the sink bowl bottom a small pop-up *seat flange* is threaded onto the male threads (see Illus. 64).

You will notice that the male threads of the pop-up T are the same diameter as the smooth lower portion of the pop-up T. This fact is the giveaway: you can see that the T is one piece, not a threaded plug with a larger diameter coupling threaded to it (see Illus. 63).

The pop-up stopper for this type of waste will be one of two kinds mentioned on page 63.

The first possibility is a stopper of heavy brass. (This ain't much of a possibility these days. Even the Mercedes-Benz of all faucets, the Grohe of West Germany, now has a plastic one.) It used to be that the mere weight of this stopper (an all *brass* one) made a good, watertight seal when the adjustment arm lowered it onto the seat flange. Our other possibility, actually a probability, is a plastic stopper with a hole in the bottom leg. No, it's not James Watt. The top of the plastic stopper is covered with a chrome or stainless steel disk—convex on top with beveled edges to seal in the seat flange. The end of the adjustment arm passes through the hole in the bottom leg of the stopper (see Illus. 67).

The adjustment arm pulls the lighter weight plastic stopper down onto the seat flange to create a watertight seal. Some-times you might find a very thin O-ring on the beveled edge of the stopper. There is one benefit to this plastic design, however, but it is not due to the choice of materials but rather to the shape of the stopper itself. With the adjustment arm passing through the bottom of the stopper, it never fails to lift off the seat and return to the seat with accuracy. On the solid brass variety, it was sometimes possible to have the adjustment arm swing to one side of the stopper bottom and miss its mark when you wanted to lift the stopper up.

To remove the male T pop-up stopper waste, use one pair of slide-jaw pliers to back down the friction/lock nut *all the way down* to the last thread using a *counterclockwise* direction of rotation as viewed from underneath. Then, again, with a knife blade separate the friction washer from the large rubber waste gasket. After doing this, use a sharp knife (utility knife) and make a series of cuts in the gasket, from the inside to the outside edge. Keep your face to one side of your working hands.

Now, with the slide-jaw pliers, pull away as much of the gasket as possible. Then, place a scrap piece of wood on the bottom of the tailpiece and use the ballpeen hammer to lightly tap on the wood, thus lifting the pop-up waste slightly out of the hole in the sink bottom. The waste is prevented from coming all the way out by the adjustment arm. Now, with one pair of slide-jaw pliers grasp the outside edge of the seat flange and with the other slide-jaw pliers, grasp the outside of the pop-up T, just above the adjustment arm. Holding the stopper seat flange *stationary*, rotate the pop-up waste T in a *clockwise* direction as viewed from *above*, using the second pair of pliers. The pop-up T will un-thread from the seat flange and fall free from the underside of the sink (see Illus. 68).

## Removal Of The One-Piece Type Of Pop-Up Waste

This third and rare possibility of pop-up waste design is less common than the first two mentioned and the fourth to follow, but I felt I should give it some attention. Who knows, if I ever sell one copy of this book and it doesn't have this type in it, it would be my luck that the reader *would* have it.

The one-piece pop-up T is also a male T, but this design has the 1¼ inch tailpiece as a homogenous part. (It doesn't unthread from the waste.) The only mating parts other than the rubber waste gasket, friction washer and friction/lock nut, are the pop-up stopper and the adjustment arm (see Illus. 62).

To remove this type, first unthread the adjustment arm gland nut free from the waste. This arm gland nut with the adjustment arm sticking out will unthread in a *clockwise* direction of rotation as viewed from in *front* of the waste. If you **are** actually looking directly at the gland nut from behind the waste, it will unthread in a *counter-clockwise* direction of rotation. Now, unthread the friction/lock nut down in a *counterclockwise* direction of rotation as viewed from underneath; back it down *all the way* until it falls free of the waste completely. Next, separate the friction washer from the rubber waste gasket as we did on the two previous designs. With a block of wood held to the bottom of the tailpiece, tap on the wood with the ballpeen hammer and the *entire* one-piece waste T will lift out of the hole in the sink.

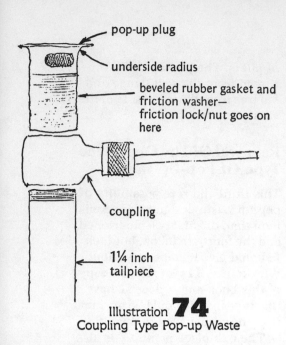

pop-up plug

underside radius

beveled rubber gasket and
friction washer—
friction lock/nut goes on
here

coupling

1¼ inch
tailpiece

Illustration **74**
Coupling Type Pop-up Waste

## Removal Of The Coupling Type Of Pop-Up Waste

Removal of the coupling type pop-up waste is identical to the removal of the female T or plug-type waste, *except* that the coupling is smaller than the female T and it is more difficult to grasp with the slide-jaw pliers (see Illus. 74).

## Removal Of The Rubber Stopper Waste

If you have the old, rubber cork waste, the one which uses a rubber stopper, or one using a Lift-And-Twist metal stopper, you will find either wrench flats or a raised, knurled ring several inches below the bottom of the basin (see Illus. 75).

If your waste has wrench flats, use the 15 inch adjustment wrench on the flats and rotate the outside casing in a *clockwise* direction of rotation as viewed from *above*.

If your waste has the knurled ring, place the jaws of the 12 inch pipe wrench on the ring and rotate the outside casing in a *clockwise* direction as viewed from above. When using the pipe wrench, place the jaws on from

*behind* so the handle points to the *right*. This way, you have more control and it is easier to *draw* the handle towards you to loosen the waste.

Regardless of which casing you have, once it is broken loose, you may use the lighter weight slide-jaw pliers to back the casing all the way off the plug-type seat flange.

I have poor luck trying to remove this type of waste in one piece. What usually happens to me is:

1. The casing collapses and can not be unthreaded
2. The casing breaks all the way off, flush with the bottom of the sink (so much the better).
3. The damn thing rotates in the sink because the two halves are married together with years of corrosion.

I usually end up taking the 12 inch hacksaw and sawing the waste in two as we did previously for another waste. Place the blade of the hacksaw between the top portion of the rubber gasket and the bottom of the sink and then sever it.

Anyway, look down into the waste from above. It might have a metal cross in the center. You might place a screwdriver (on an angle) into one of the pie-shaped holes of the cross in an attempt to prevent the seat flange from rotating as you try to back down the casing. If the stopper seat rotates in spite of the screwdriver, you might as well right now do the hacksaw trip mentioned above.

Once the bottom half of the waste is sawn away, use that dowel or broomstick section and the ballpeen to tap the remaining seat flange out of the sink. Once the waste is totally removed, it would be a nice idea to use some cleanser and steel wool and clean away the old scum line which is witness to the outline of the old waste.

The Chicago Specialty Strainer Wrench illustrated on page 10 has a forked end which might help prevent the waste from rotating in the sink if the forks were introduced between the cross in the waste.

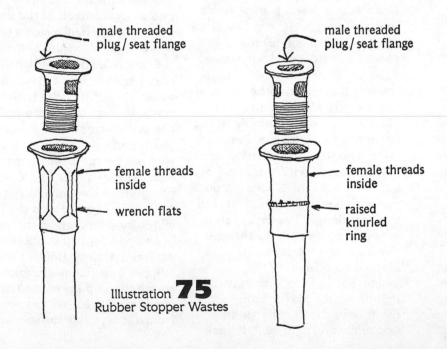

male threaded
plug / seat flange

female threads
inside

wrench flats

male threaded
plug / seat flange

female threads
inside

raised
knurled
ring

Illustration **75**
Rubber Stopper Wastes

It has been my experience that the fork merely busts out the cross when attempting to hold it still from above and use the wrench or slide-jaw pliers on the casing below.

## Alternative To The Rubber Stopper Waste

If you are going to replace a rubber stopper waste, I would suggest that you purchase another rubber stopper waste *only* if you find one made of 17 gauge material (*brass*). Most all of the rubber stopper wastes that I have seen lately are of such poor, flimsy workmanship and materials, that I do not even choose to install such *junk*.

I would suggest that you purchase a Lift-And-Twist waste as mention on the previous page. It is made from 17-gauge brass, and is well worth your investment and installation efforts. It is about four times as expensive as the rubber stopper designs, but it is a hundred times better. Chicago Faucet Company, among others, used to make this type years ago, and due to popular demand, they are back in production. There are two companies in my locale that have these superior designs, and they both do international exporting. They are:

Ohmega Salvage
2407 San Pablo Ave.
Berkeley, CA 94702
415-843-7368

Plumbers Supply Co.
P.O. Box 3088
415 40th Street
Oakland, CA 94609

Now, with the waste, *and* the trap out of the way, we have a clean shot at the mounting/lock nuts of the faucet and have almost completed the Clean Sweep.

Take A Break! Go have a short one, even!

## Removal Of The Faucet Slip Nuts And Supplies

These brief instructions are for the benefit of those who sawed through the supplies in order to replace the old angle stops and who still have portions of supply tubes dangling down from the faucet (page 51).

We are getting very close to completing the Clean Sweep. The old angle stops are gone and new ones installed. The trap system has been taken down and the waste has been removed from the sink. It's now just those two pesky supply tubes and the faucet before we have a naked sink.

It is time to remove the faucet slip nuts and pull down the old supplies. If the supplies have been in place for many years, the rubber cone washers can be rock hard, and like a cement holding the supply tubes in the faucet connections.

I have found the easiest way to tackle this operation is to lay down on my back with my *safety glasses on*. With the RIDGID basin wrench in hand, flip the jaws to the side of the shank for *loosening* and then place the jaws on the faucet slip nuts (see Illus. 76). As viewed from underneath, you should turn the faucet slip nuts in a *counterclockwise* direction of rotation. If the nuts are badly corroded or just very stubborn and will not budge, then apply the jaws of the 12 or 15 inch adjustable wrench to the square handle of the basin wrench to gain the additional torque necessary to turn the nuts.

Once you have pulled the old supplies free of the faucet, once again apply the jaws of the basin wrench to the faucet's thinner, lock/mounting nuts (see Illus. 77). Again, it might be necessary to use the adjustable wrench in

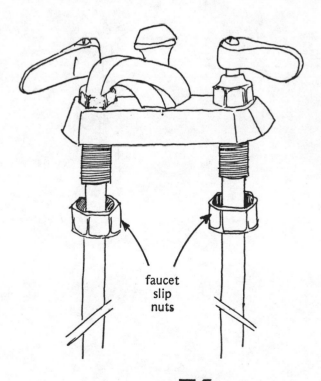

faucet slip nuts

Illustration **76**
Removing Faucet Slip Nuts (4 Inch Center Set)

connection with the basin wrench to loosen these nuts. If you have any difficulty with these nuts, it is almost unanimously because the nuts are not brass, but rather pot metal.

If you do have pot metal nuts (usually gray in color) and they will not come free regardless of how much force you apply to them, you might have to use the ¼ inch cold chisel to crack the nuts off the faucet connections. It is times like these that I wish I had the man or men responsible (for the implementation of such trash quality parts) in the room with me. It would be an unforgettable education for them.

With the lock/mounting nuts all the way off the faucet connections, try lifting the old faucet off the sink by gripping the spout and applying force in a circular motion while at the same time lifting upward. If this does not separate the two, use the wooden dowel/broomstick method of "shock separation" as we discussed in the removal of pop-up wastes.

Take a Well Earned Break... and rest your aching back and creaking knees.

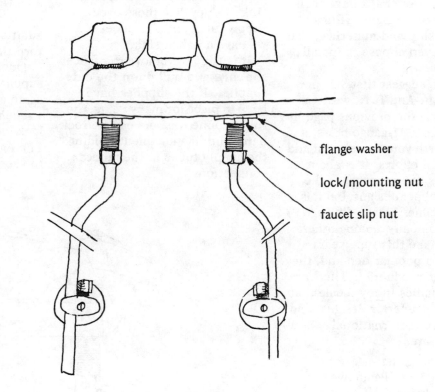

flange washer

lock/mounting nut

faucet slip nut

Illustration **77**

# Removing Old Faucets

## Removal of Single Handle Faucets (4 Inch Center Set)

If you are replacing a newer, single handle bathroom lavatory faucet, it may have the threaded connections like other 4 inch center sets. However, the chances are good that it will have the "drop-leg" leads of ⅜ inch diameter soft copper, with *brass* ½ inch male pipe thread adapters soldered to the ends (see Illus. 78).

These ½ inch male adapters will have thin wrench flats on the top, where they are soldered to the copper drop-leg leads. If your faucet does indeed have these drop leads, it will not have the large, thin lock/mounting nuts; but, *instead* it will use small ¼ inch threaded studs and small machine nuts to secure it to the sink or counter.

You may use the 6 inch adjustable wrench (given there's room) to loosen these machine nuts and remove them. The RIDGID basin wrench will also work (with a little patience). The nuts unthread in a *counterclockwise* direction of rotation as viewed from underneath.

To undo the faucet slip nuts, you will have to first put the 8 inch adjustable wrench on the wrench flats of the male adapters *before* using the RIDGID basin wrench on the slip nuts. If you do not, you will only twist (wind-up) the drop-leg leads without loosening the slip nuts.

After the faucet is lifted off the sink or counter, it is a good idea to thoroughly clean the surface with cleanser and a steel wool pad to remove the old scum line left by the old faucet. Rarely does the outside perimeter of the new faucet match that of the old one.

If you wait until the new faucet is set before doing the clean-up, it is very difficult to accomplish without scratching the finish on the new faucet.

## Removal Of Lavatory Wide-Spread Faucets

With the removal of the 4 inch center set, we accomplished the Clean Sweep (riddance of all funky plumbing). For those with wide-spread faucets, the removal process for angle stops, supplies, trap and waste is identical, only the faucet itself differs. In this section we are going to dismantle the few, more popular designs still found in existence.

Guidepost:

1. Remove the pop-up lift rod if you haven't already done so.
2. Remove faucet handles.
3. Remove escutcheon nuts.
4. Remove escutcheons.
5. Undo flat mounting nuts at base of valve (on *top* of sink).
6. Undo the manifold nut at spout base.
7. Lower valves down away from sink.
8. Remove spout base nut.
9. Clean up sink.

If you are removing a wide-spread faucet from a bathroom sink, the removal process will take a little bit longer than the average 4 inch center set; not because it is more difficult, but because there are more connections to undo. As far as total swear word count, the wide-spread might be less.

Okay, let's get started. First, remove the hot and cold monograms on the top of the wide-spread's handles. I have found the blade of a pocket knife or steak knife works well if the monograms are plastic and rest flush on top of the handles. Some of the older faucets had monograms that

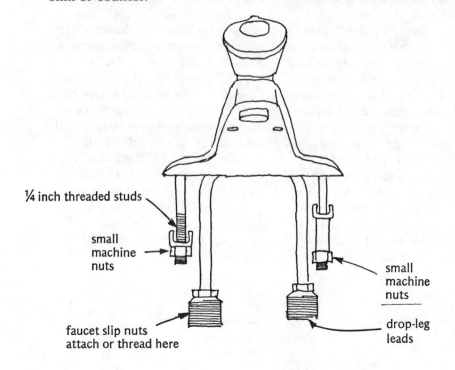

¼ inch threaded studs

small machine nuts

faucet slip nuts attach or thread here

small machine nuts

drop-leg leads

Illustration **78**

69

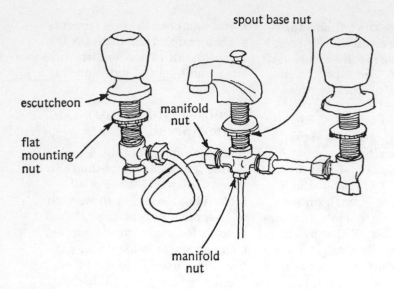

spout base nut

escutcheon

manifold nut

flat mounting nut

manifold nut

Illustration **79**
Widespread Valve Depicting Both
Flexible Manifold Tubing, and Smooth
Rigid Manifold Tubing

threaded into the handles and these monograms will have ridged edges, like coins, that give them away. They will unthread in a *counterclockwise* direction.

You may use the slide-jaw pliers, horizontally, to grasp the edges of the threaded type of monograms. At the bottom of the holes in the faucet handles, you will discover a machine screw, which holds the handles to the stems. The screw will be either a slotted or Phillips head screw. Now, with the appropriate screwdriver, remove the screws in a *counterclockwise* direction. You can lift the handles off the stems. If the old faucet is going into the garbage and the handles won't come off after the screws are removed, then open the jaws of the slide-jaw pliers all the way so you can grasp the handles in them. Now wiggle them while lifting up. It won't matter if you scar the handles if the faucet is to be junked.

There is a special tool for removing handles without causing them any damage. It is called simply a "handle puller." I think my dentist's got one hid away in his pile of tooth tools. My tool is a PASCO#4658. It's going on seven years old and still works as well as it did brand new. I don't know if most tool rental agencies will have one for rent; but, since you are removing your faucet for good, go ahead and squash the old handles.

Once the old handles are off, you will see the valve stems protruding from the center of a flanged escutcheon. Look around

the top, outside edge of this escutcheon for two wrench flats (see Illus. 80). If your faucet *does* have these flats, use the 12 or 15 inch adjustable wrench, or slide-jaw pliers and rotate the escutcheons in a *counterclockwise* direction as viewed from above, until the escutcheons part from the threaded exterior of the valves.

If your faucet does not have these wrench flats, use the slide-jaw pliers and place them on the elevated diameter of the flanged escutcheons and move them in a *counterclockwise* direction.

On old wall-hung and pedestal sinks, the handles might not have removable monograms. Instead, you might have a "jam nut" underneath the handles (see Illus. 81). Undo this nut *down* the stem by rotating it in a *clockwise* direction as viewed from *above*. Then grip the handles with a slide-jaw pliers and rotate the handles in a *counterclockwise* direction until they unthread completely free of the stems. When the handles are off, then use the 6 inch adjustable wrench and unthread the jam nuts off the stems using a *counterclockwise* direction of rotation.

If there are no monograms and no jam nuts, then you might find a set screw in the side of the handle base or on the end of the cross-shaped handles. In this case (if you're junking the faucet), just . . . mini-hacksaw the stems in two, just above the escutcheon nuts, on top of the escutcheons (see Illus. 82).

Illustration
**80**

valve stem
packing nut removed
threaded exterior of valve
wrench flat—(another one on opposite side of escutcheon)

70

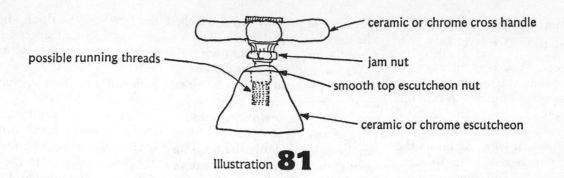

ceramic or chrome cross handle

possible running threads

jam nut

smooth top escutcheon nut

ceramic or chrome escutcheon

Illustration **81**

Once the handles are off, undo the escutcheon nuts with the slide-jaw pliers used horizontally. Undo them in a *counterclockwise* direction of rotation as viewed from *above*. In many instances, these escutcheon nuts will have smooth, beveled edges which present a challenge to grip with the pliers. When you get them off, then lift off the escutcheons themselves (see Illus. 83).

If your domed escutcheons are chromed metal, you might not have escutcheon nuts. Instead, underneath the top of the escutcheon, there are female threads. These female threads receive a section of hollow, male running thread, which holds the escutcheons to the valve bodies. For this type of escutcheon rotate them while gripped in the slide-jaw pliers, held horizontally. Grab them near the top. They will unthread in a *counterclockwise* direction of rotation. This design

of escutcheon is found most prevalently on tub and shower valves, but now and then you run into one on a sink.

Hang in there, just three paragraphs to go. After you lift the escutcheons off, you will see a large flat mounting nut at the bottom of the threaded exterior of the valve. Underneath it will be a large, flat washer. Using the 12 or 15 inch adjustable wrench, unthread this mounting nut up and off the valve by rotating it in a *counterclockwise* direction of rotation as viewed from above.

On the bottom of the widespread faucet spout, underneath the sink or counter, you will see a small *brass* nut. This nut holds the manifold T that carries water from the valves over to the spout. When lying on your back, try using the RIDGID basin wrench to undo this nut in a *counterclockwise* direction as viewed from underneath. Remember, have

your safety glasses/goggles on. This little nut is the only thing holding the faucet valves and manifold tubing from coming down on your head. When you remove the nut all the way off the spout connection, the valves could fall. It is a very good idea to hold onto one of the valves with one hand while backing off the nut with the other. The 6 inch adjustable wrench is a good tool to use on this little nut.

After the valves and manifold tubing are removed, use the RIDGID basin wrench to undo the mounting nut for the spout. It is a junior sized version of the mounting nuts used to hold the valves to the sink or counter. It also unthreads in a *counterclockwise* direction as viewed from underneath. When this nut is removed, you can lift the spout off, from above. Now clean up the sink or counter.

Congratulations! Take a break.

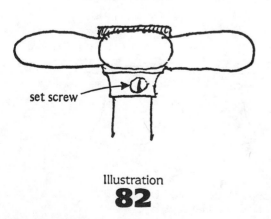

set screw

Illustration
**82**

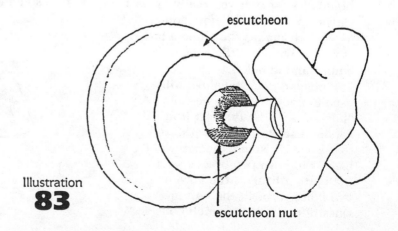

escutcheon

Illustration
**83**

escutcheon nut

## Removal Of Pedestal Sink Wide-Spread Faucets

This section is a tiny bit more involved than the previous section for wide-spread faucets in general. The physical shape of the pedestal sink is a more time consuming object to work with. As far as the faucet is concerned, the process is the same. We will, however, give you some tips on working with the sink itself which will save you a good bit of agony.

Guidepost:

1. Turn off water and drain building.
2. Remove supplies.
3. Remove old angle stops and install new ones.
4. Remove J-bend portion of trap.
5. Provide clean, uncluttered work space on floor near sink.
6. Remove bowl from pedestal and move to work space.
7. Remove old waste.
8. Remove old valves.
9. Remove old spout.
10. Clean up old scum lines on sink.

Pedestal sinks are made today in vitreous china. In years gone by, they were made in both vitreous china and cast iron. If you are working on one of the china sinks, you should afford a greater amount of care in handling. I would suggest that you really *warm up* the room before going to work. It makes the china a bit more forgiving of little accidental bumps and knocks.

Porcelain pedestal sinks will usually not have what we call a "horseshoe" that the cast iron version uses to hold the pedestal to the bowl. Instead, the porcelain basin will have two brackets on the bottom back of the bowl or two holes through the bottom sides of the bowl in which bolts

then secure the bowl to the wall. The base of the pedestal will have a bolt securing it to the floor.

We want to remove the bowl from the pedestal so we can work on it without breaking our necks and backs or the sink. So let's remove any screws you find in any brackets holding the bowl up against the wall. Leave any screws you find holding the brackets to the bowl alone.

With the brackets or through-bolts in the sink removed, you will be able to lift the bowl off the pedestal *once* the J-bend portion of the trap and the supply tubes are removed. Removal of the faucet itself is performed exactly as we did for the cast iron bowl, discussed on pages 69–71.

If your wide-spread faucet is a *real* old one, and it is of the old fashion handle design as depicted in Illus. 84, I suggest that you squirt some penetrating oil onto all the connections and mounting nuts (several times) before attempting its removal. In most cases, the pedestal on which the bowl rests does not have enough room on the back opening to use many tools for loosening the upper slip nut on the trap's J-bend and the friction/lock nut for the pop-up waste, or rubber stopper waste.

The easiest procedure that I have found is to remove the bowl from the pedestal and work on

the bowl on the floor where you can easily get at everything. Cast iron pedestal sinks use a "draw bolt" to secure the bowl to the pedestal and the pedestal to the floor.

The sink does not just balance there. Some pedestal sink bowls of the cast iron construction have "horseshoes" cast in the bottom outside of the bowl and the head of a carriage bolt slides into the horseshoe, preventing it from falling and turning as you tighten up the nut. The shank of this carriage bolt passes through a cross-webbing or holes in the top of the pedestal. A nut (usually square) threads up the bolt from the bottom, tightly securing the bowl to the top of the pedestal. You might find a bowl with one horseshoe in the front, middle underside and sometimes one with two horseshoes, one on each side of the middle underside of the bowl.

At the base of the pedestal, there is another cross-webbing and a bolt (coming up from the floor) passes through the hole in the webbing, with a square nut threaded down the shank of the bolt, from above, securing the pedestal to the floor (see Illus. 85).

The nuts of the carriage bolts will *invariably* be rusted together. No one has ever had the presence to use brass nuts and bolts;

Illustration **84**
Old-fashioned Wide-spread Design
with Cross Handles

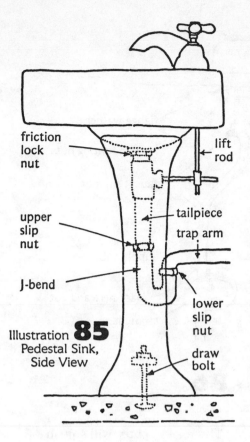

friction lock nut

lift rod

upper slip nut

tailpiece

trap arm

J-bend

lower slip nut

draw bolt

**Illustration 85**
Pedestal Sink, Side View

they're always iron. You should squirt these nuts with penetrating oil to loosen them prior to putting a wrench on them. The square carriage bolts nuts will loosen with a *counterclockwise* direction of rotation as viewed from underneath. I have an 8 inch adjustable wrench and a slide-jaw pliers with the handles cut down so they will fit inside the pedestal base and still have enough room to swing.

IMPORTANT: If I am only going to replace the trap on a pedestal sink, I remove the supplies — pull the J-bend down an inch or so — then loosen the slip nut on the trap arm at the wall, and pull the trap arm out of the wall — then loosen the nut in the base of the pedestal far enough so I can rotate the sink (in one piece) until the back side faces as far out into the room as possible. Usually one corner of the sink will be stopped at the wall. This is usually far

enough to get at the trap with ease.

I then install a new trap, rotate the sink back, install new trap arm and supplies and tighten up the slip nuts on the trap. Don't forget to retighten the nut on the bolt in the foot of the pedestal.

To remove the old faucet at the same time, leave the bolt alone in the pedestal base and remove the upper carriage bolt/bolts and remove the supplies. After loosening the slip nut on the lower side of the J-bend, swing the J-bend to one side as far as it will go and then try to lift the sink free. If the J-bend hangs up on the trap arm, then you will have to pull the J-bend all the way out of the tailpiece before lifting the sink off the pedestal.

You will notice that the slip nuts of the trap on some pedestal sinks are very inaccessible, and on some others, maybe a half or more of the slip nut is visible outside of the pedestal. With the slide-jaw pliers, try to undo the slip nut on the low side of the J-bend. If you can get a purchase on it, it will unthread in a *counterclockwise* direction as viewed from below. If you can loosen it, see if you can pull down the J-bend without loosening the the upper slip nut at the tailpiece, which is invariably inside of the pedestal. Try wiggling the J-bend from side to side while you pull downward on it. We need (in most cases) only to move it down an inch or so. Now, try moving the J-bend out from under the 90 degree bend of the trap arm. If you can, you can now lift the bowl free. If you cannot budge the J-bend, use either the mini-hacksaw or the 12 inch hacksaw and saw the trap arm in two. Then lift the bowl from the pedestal.

If your pedestal sink has indi-

vidual cocks, and they happen to be close to antique, they will also have square, iron nuts. And they are invariably rusted. Pedestal sinks with individual cocks sometimes also had a rubber stopper waste, opposed to the pop-up design. Some pedestal sinks with individual cocks did have a pop-up stopper. Removal of the sink from the pedestal would still be the same process as discussed above.

## Removal Of Individual Cocks

If you have individual cocks on a pedestal sink and only need to change the cocks themselves, not the trap and/or trap arm or the waste, then squirt some penetrating oil on the faucet mounting nuts and slip nuts. The mounting nuts on old cocks were usually square, and invariably rusty. They will unthread in a *counterclockwise* direction as viewed from underneath. Have your safety glasses/goggles on for sure. *Nothing* is worse for damaged sight than rusty flakes of iron inside your eyeball.

Aside from individual cocks, if your pedestal sink has a pop-up waste you should *not* take the easy way out on disassembly as we did in the 4 inch center set section and saw through the pop-up lift rod. The lift rod and linkage for the pop-up waste in your case may be the only one left in the whole state and a little difficult to replace regardless of price. It would behoove you to check around with the plumbing suppliers and see if they can get a replacement pop-up waste and linkage *before* you attempt its removal. The diameters and lengths of old adjustment arms and those of newer ones differ considerably, along with the lift rods themselves.

# Replacing Bathroom Faucets

## Installing (Setting) A New 4 Inch Center Set

We are now going to put back what we took off and out of the sink. We'll start with the 4 inch center set, then do the various wastes, the wide-spread faucet and then the trap. First, let's do the 4 inch center set.

Guidepost:

1. Pack underside of faucet full of plumber's putty.
2. Set faucet on sink or counter and install lock/mounting nuts.
3. Double-check for parallel.
4. Measure, mark and cut supplies to length.
5. Install supplies.
6. Open angle stops and check for drips.
7. Install pop-up or rubber stopper waste.

If you are not able to obtain DAP, BLACK SWAN or HERCULES brand plumber's putty, plunk the can of putty that you did buy into a pot or pan of hot water for five or ten minutes or so. This will help provide for a good plastic consistency. Open the box containing your new faucet. If you purchased a brand other than the ones that I recommend, you might find a separate, plastic base shipped along with the faucet. This base will usually be of clear, black or aqua color. It will be about ⅛ inch thick. If you find one, *throw it away*. It only causes (in the future) splash leaks and it collects slime.

Turn the new faucet upside down and pack the bottom cavity full of plumber's putty. Depending upon which faucet you purchased, it might take a full one-pound container of putty. You want to fill

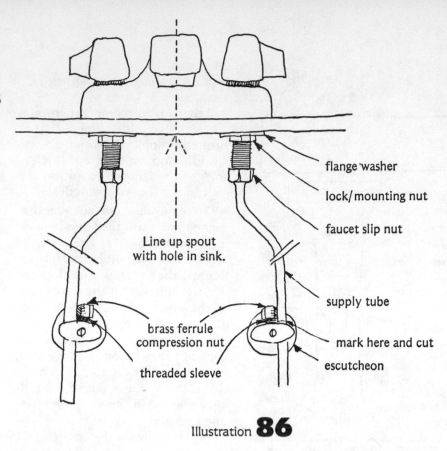

Line up spout with hole in sink.

flange washer

lock/mounting nut

faucet slip nut

supply tube

mark here and cut

escutcheon

brass ferrule compression nut

threaded sleeve

Illustration **86**

the cavity up until you have about ⅛ inch excess of putty sticking up higher than the bottom of the faucet.

Now, set the faucet into the holes on the sink or counter, and press down on the faucet. Open the little bag with the large flange washers and the new brass lock/mounting nuts inside. On some brands, the flange washers might look like wavy clown's collars or maybe shallow cups. If you have the cup variety, the dome should hang down as you slide them up the faucet's threaded connections. This will provide for the spreading of force when you tighten up the lock/mounting nuts and keeps them from loosening up in the future.

Start the large flange washers up the threaded connections with your fingers, turning the nuts up in a *clockwise* direction as viewed from underneath. If you lay down on your back to do this, WEAR YOUR SAFETY GLASSES.

The excess putty will squish out from under the faucet as you tighten the lock/mounting nuts with the RIDGID basin wrench. Make sure that the faucet is setting *parallel* with the back of the sink and wall before *really* tightening the mounting nuts. When the faucet has been checked for parallel twice, really snug up the mounting nuts with the basin wrench. I always try to set the faucet so that the spout is directly over and in line with the hole in the sink bottom (see Illus. 86).

If all is well, really apply all the torque you can with your hands, using the basin wrench. More excess putty will continue to squish out from under the faucet for some time. Use a kitchen knife to trace the outline of the faucet in the same manner that you would trim a pie or cookie dough. The excess strip along the base of the faucet will pull up very easily.

IMPORTANT NOTE: Some of the MOEN faucets, the Chateau line, will have drop-leg supplies and the faucet will use a threaded stud and small machine nut to secure it to the sink or counter *instead* of the usual threaded faucet connection (see Illus. 87).

## Using The Tubing Cutter — Installing New Supplies

With the new 4 inch center set secured to the sink or counter, you are ready to install the new supply tubes.

Slide the faucet slip nuts, cup end up, along the new supply tube until the acorn head of the BRASS CRAFT/EASTMAN supply nests in the slip nut. Using your fingers, start the slip nut onto the threaded connection of the faucet, in a *clockwise* direction of rotation. Tighten up the nut as hard as you can using only your fingers, for now.

Next, *slowly* bend the supply tubing by pulling it over to the *outside* of the angle stop and then bend it down so that it passes parallel to the outside of the angle stop (see Illus. 86).

If you have a pointed felt tip pen, like the SHARPIE, mark a cutting point on the supply tubing, at the distance equal to the bottom of the threaded ferrule compression nut sleeve, *plus* an additional ¼ inch. Then loosen the faucet slip nut and check to make sure that your mark has not been rubbed off.

When you wish to use the tubing cutter, open the jaws of the cutter by turning the handle in a *counterclockwise* direction. Open the jaws far enough to slide the supply tubing between the two lower rollers and the cutting wheel on the stationary, upper jaw. Now, close the jaws by turning the handle in a *clockwise* direction, bringing the wheel down on

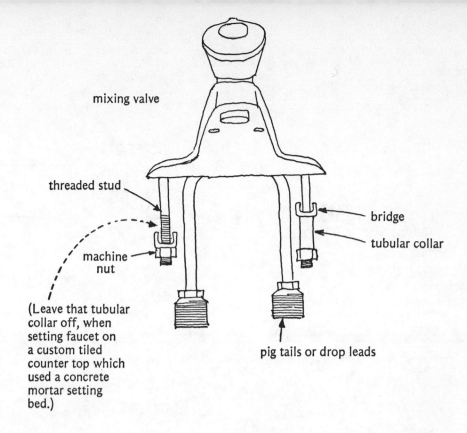

mixing valve

threaded stud

machine nut

(Leave that tubular collar off, when setting faucet on a custom tiled counter top which used a concrete mortar setting bed.)

bridge

tubular collar

pig tails or drop leads

Illustration **87**
Faucet with Drop-Legs

the marking pen mark. After contact, turn the handle on the cutter one additional ¼ turn. Hold the supply in one hand and pull the cutter around the tubing for *one* complete turn, WITH THE CUTTING WHEEL *FOLLOWING* THE HANDLE. Then, reverse the direction for one complete turn. Now, tighten the handle another ½ turn and repeat the process, following this process until the supply tubing separates in two (see Illus. 88).

The cutter is reversed in direction each full revolution so that the cutting wheel will track in the groove made on the very first revolution. Cutting wheels, when dull or getting there, will not track in the first groove when turned only in one direction. They will continue making new grooves or "threading." You can expect rented tools to be operable but well "broken-in." In my esti-

mation, the PAPCO 500 tubing cutter is tops for trimming supplies. Now, unthread the ferrule compression nut from the angle stop. Do not lose the little brass ferrule, underneath the nut. Slide the faucet slip nut up the supply tube (if it came off when you did the trimming). Make sure that it goes back on cup side up. Next, slide the angle stop ferrule compression nut up the supply, cup side down, followed by the brass ferrule which can be started on from either side.

Insert the bottom of the supply tubing into the threaded sleeve of the angle stop, taking care not to let the brass ferrule and ferrule nut slip off. With great care, start the angle stop compression nut onto the threaded sleeve in a *clockwise* direction of rotation as viewed from *above*. You might apply some oil or Crisco to the threaded sleeve of the angle stop.

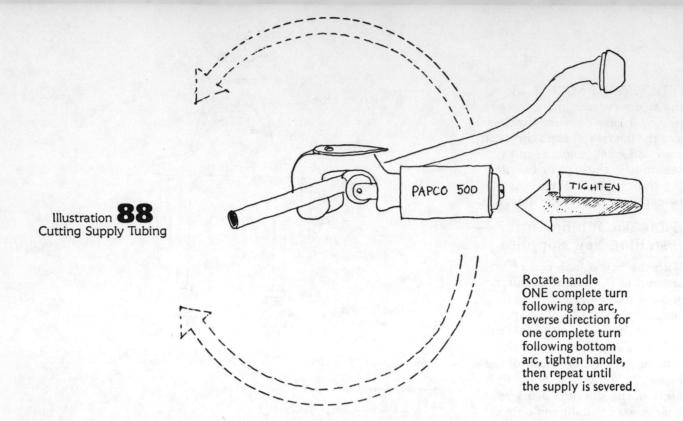

Illustration **88**
Cutting Supply Tubing

PAPCO 500

TIGHTEN

Rotate handle
ONE complete turn
following top arc,
reverse direction for
one complete turn
following bottom
arc, tighten handle,
then repeat until
the supply is severed.

Using only your fingers to start, thread the compression nut onto the sleeve. These threads are very fine and cross-thread too easily. If they should cross-thread, you will have a leak and have to replace the angle stop. I have found the compression nut to be threaded on easily if I wiggle, very slightly, the supply tube from side to side as I turn the compression nut. TAKE YOUR TIME! Turn the nut as far down as you can using only your fingers. Then, rotate the supply in any direction necessary to bring it close in line with the faucet connection.

Next, bend the supply in the middle, very slowly and just enough to get the acorn head of the supply under the faucet connection. Then rebend the supply tube back so that the acorn head nests in the countersunk hole in the bottom of the faucet connection (see Illus. 89).

Now, you want to make sure that the supply tube's acorn head comes into contact with the faucet's threaded connection as perfectly vertical as possible. A slight angle will be okay; but, if the acorn head is too far on its

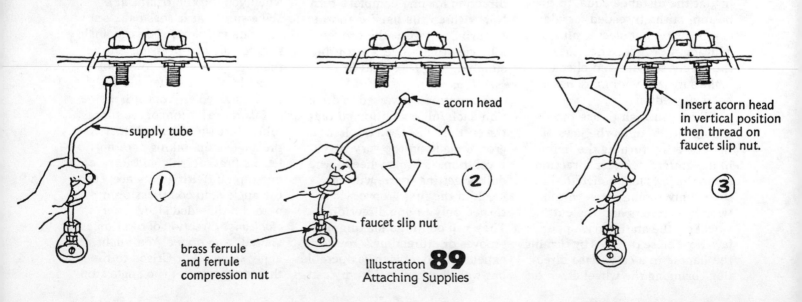

supply tube

brass ferrule
and ferrule
compression nut

① 

acorn head

faucet slip nut

Illustration **89**
Attaching Supplies

② 

Insert acorn head
in vertical position
then thread on
faucet slip nut.

③

side, you will have a leak. Then, put some RECTORSEAL/Slic-Tite in the threads of the faucet slip nut and some on the threaded connection. Start the faucet slip nut onto the threaded connection with your fingers, turning the nut in a *clockwise* direction as viewed from underneath.

IMPORTANT NOTE: Once both nuts (the brass ferrule compression nut and the faucet slip nut) are threaded to their respective mates, as tightly as you can with fingers only, *then* tighten the brass ferrule nut onto the angle stop *first*, using the 6 inch adjustable wrench. Turn the faucet slip nut with the basin wrench. Some manufacturers ship rubber cone washers and brass friction rings with the faucet. You won't need them so you can throw them away.

Okay, we have the new supplies installed and the faucet handles are in the *off* position. If you have a single handle faucet, make sure *the* handle is in the off position.

Now, *slowly* open the angle stops and check for leaks. Turn the handles in a *counterclockwise* direction. If you have a drip at the faucet slip nuts, angle stop ferrule nuts or angle stop packing nuts, then further tighten the nut in question in ¼ turn increments until the drip stops. All nuts will be turned in a *clockwise* direction.

With no drips, we can move on to the installation of the new pop-up waste, AFTER A WELL EARNED BREAK!

## Reshaping An Out-Of-Round Supply Tube

If your supply tubing is out-of-round after trimming it with a hacksaw instead of a tubing cutter, or you accidently stepped on it, etc., you will discover that the ferrule will not slide over the end of the tube. We are now going to do a real quickie and reshape the supply so we may use it.

Pick up the 8 inch adjustable wrench and adjust the jaws to fit the tubing where it is still in a good round condition. Adjust the jaws until they gently contact the outside of the tubing. Now, pull the wrench free of the tubing *without* touching the adjustment of the jaws. Then reposition the adjustable wrench onto the tubing about one inch from the out-of-round end. Holding the tubing tightly in one hand, swing the wrench around and around the tubing, while moving the wrench down towards the end, little by little as you rotate the wrench (see Illus. 90).

You'll feel resistance once you begin to go around the out-of-round portion. The wrench handle will become harder to turn as you begin to reform the bent section back to a round shape. Keep turning the wrench until you encounter the very edge of the tubing. DO NOT turn the wrench until it falls off the end of the tubing —rather, stop when the end of the tubing is *flush* with the outside of the wrench jaws. Now, loosen the thumb adjuster and remove the jaws from the supply tubing.

Now, try once again to slide the angle stop ferrule nut onto the improved end of the tubing, cup end last, followed by the brass ferrule. If you can get the tubing started into the hole in the ferrule nut, then place the ferrule nut on the floor and push down, holding the supply in hand. The supply tube will slide through the hole in the nut. You can do the same for the brass ferrule also.

Congratulations. That wasn't so bad was it?

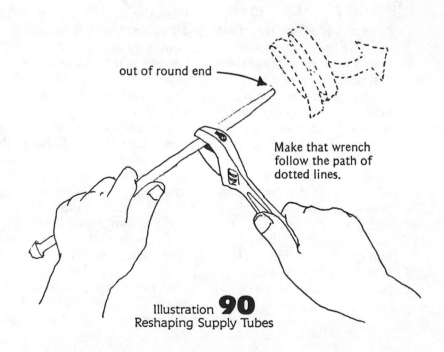

out of round end →

Make that wrench follow the path of dotted lines.

Illustration **90**
Reshaping Supply Tubes

## Installing New Pop-Up Waste

In this section, we put back the pop-up waste. On the very tail end of the section, we do the rubber stopper waste. The section is a fairly meaty one; but believe me, a far cry easier than removing the old pop-up waste — and a lot more enjoyable.

Guidepost:

### MALE T TYPE

1. Putty the seat flange.
2. Install friction/lock nut, friction washer and beveled waste gasket onto the male T waste body.
3. Lift waste up through the hole in the sink and thread the seat flange onto the male T waste.
4. Bring up friction nut, friction washer and waste gasket. Wrap putty snake on top of waste gasket and secure waste *tightly* to basin.
5. Install pop-up adjustment arm, if loose.
6. Install pop-up stopper.
7. Install 1¼ inch tailpiece.

### PLUG OR FEMALE T TYPE

1. Putty the plug and insert into the hole in sink bottom.
2. Install beveled waste gasket (with putty snake on top), friction washer and friction/lock nut securely onto plug.
3. Wrap Teflon tape on bottom threads of plug in sink; apply RECTORSEAL/Slic-Tite in recess of female waste body. Put any fiber or plastic gasket into female recess and then marry the two components.
4. Install pop-up adjustment arm and gland nut if they are loose.
5. Install pop-up stopper.
6. Install 1¼ inch tailpiece.

### COUPLING TYPE

This one is so short that no Guidepost will be given here. Just read the 2 sentence paragraph on page 81.

### ONE-PIECE TYPE

This one is also so short that no Guidepost will be given here. Just read the 5 sentence paragraph on page 81.

### RUBBER STOPPER WASTE

This waste is installed exactly like the one-piece type with the exception that there is no pop-up arm to install. Read the text on one-piece waste.

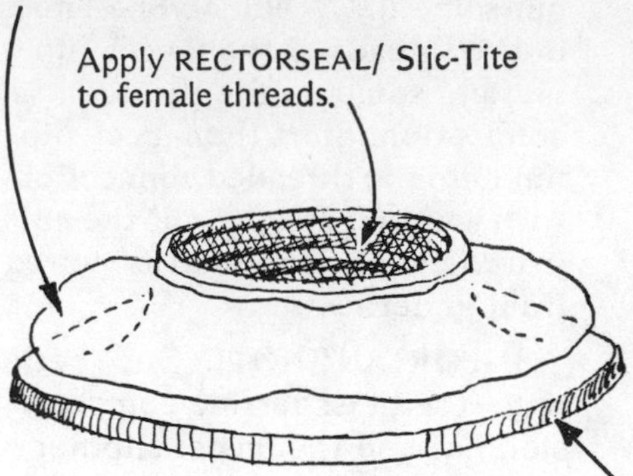

## The Male T Type

Unpackage your pop-up waste. You will find the pop-up seat, the waste T and the adjustment arm and the pop-up adjustment strap. Open the can of plumber's putty and get out a walnut-sized ball's worth and roll it into a little "snake" like you did with modeling clay as a child. Even your therapist might agree this is good for you. Use a clean, smooth surface to roll the snake out on, using the palm of your hand. Make the snake about ⅜ inch in diameter. Wrap it around the underside radius of the pop-up stopper seat flange, making one complete wrap and then part the excess and save it for later (see Illus. 91).

Now press the snake down a bit lightly onto the seat flange so that it will not fall off when the flange is turned over. Also, apply some RECTORSEAL/Slic-Tite to the female threads on the *inside* of the seat flange (see Illus. 91).

In another little bag, you might find a large zinc-plated steel or brass washer; a large black, beveled rubber gasket and maybe a large, flat, clear plastic or black fiber friction washer (see Illus.

plumber's putty

Apply RECTORSEAL/ Slic-Tite to female threads.

seat flange

Illustration **91**
Preparing Seat Flange

92). You should also find a large diameter, thin brass friction/lock nut.

Now, with the pop-up T in one hand, thread the large lock nut all the way down the T until you reach the last thread above the adjustment arm. Next, drop the metal or fiber friction washer down over the male threads of the waste T so that it comes to rest upon the friction/lock nut you have already threaded down. If you have both a metal and a fiber washer, drop the metal one down first, followed by the fiber or plastic one.

Now, start pushing the rubber waste gasket down the outside of the T's male threads, until you reach the washers. This beveled rubber gasket is a little difficult to push down over the threads and it is sometimes easier to get it to the bottom by holding the gasket stationary in one hand and rotating the pop-up T in a *clockwise* direction as viewed from below the gasket. With the rubber gasket all the way down, beveled side up, make two or three wraps of Teflon tape around the top of the male pop-up T (see Illus. 92).

Next, lift the pop-up waste up through the hole in the basin, from below. Push it up until the rubber waste gasket contacts the bottom of the sink. While holding onto it here with one hand, thread the stopper seat flange onto the male threads which are protruding up into the sink, using a *clockwise* direction of rotation as viewed from above (see Illus. 93).

If you wish to hold the stopper seat flange still and rotate the pop-up T, to mate the two parts (which is sometimes easier), then turn the pop-up T in a *counterclockwise* direction as viewed from above the sink. When the stopper seat flange is threaded all the way onto the pop-up T, as tightly as you can do it by hand, then pull the T down into the hole in the sink.

Now, thread the friction/lock nut back *up* the T with your fingers to begin with, if you can. Use the slide-jaw pliers if you cannot thread the nut by hand.

This will carry the thin friction washer or washers and the beveled rubber waste gasket with it. Hold the pop-up T stationary in one hand and use the slide-jaw pliers in the other to rotate the brass friction/lock nut in a *clockwise* direction as viewed from underneath. Now, turn the nut up until the beveled rubber gasket is within ½ inch of the underside of the sink.

Now, take the left over piece of putty snake (or roll another) and wrap it around on the top of the beveled rubber waste gasket. After doing this, then continue to tighten the friction/lock nut with the slide-jaw pliers, really squashing the rubber gasket to the underside of the sink. The excess putty will squish out from under the seat flange and above the rubber gasket as you finish tightening the friction/lock nut.

Except for the pop-up linkage and the tailpiece, this type of waste is done. We will go on to do

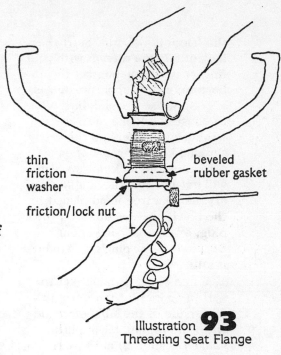

thin friction washer

beveled rubber gasket

friction/lock nut

Illustration **93**
Threading Seat Flange

the Female Plug type *before* installing the linkage and tailpiece.

Take a break!

## The Plug Or Female T Pop-Up Waste

We will now put back the female (plug) pop-up waste (see Illus. 94 on next page). Apply the plumber's putty snake to the underside lip of the pop-up plug. (See instruction for making putty snake on page 78.) Now, insert the plug into the hole in the sink, dropping it in from the top. Push the plug down into the hole until a little putty oozes out from under the plug's lip. Next, push or thread the beveled waste gasket up the stopper plug from the bottom, with the beveled side up. You might just try to get the gasket up far enough so that about ½ inch of the plug's male threads stick out of the bottom of the gasket. Then, slip the friction washer or washers (See Illus. 94) over the plug's male threads followed by

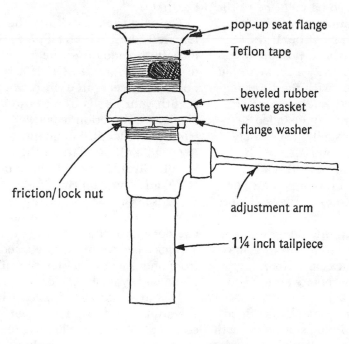

pop-up seat flange

Teflon tape

beveled rubber waste gasket

flange washer

friction/lock nut

adjustment arm

1¼ inch tailpiece

Illustration **92**
Male T Pop-up Waste

the friction/lock nut. Start the lock nut up the threads with your fingers until you contact the bottom of the rubber waste gasket. Now, use the slide-jaw pliers to chase the lock nut, friction washer or washers up the threaded plug. Again, when threading the lock nut up, you will have to hold the plug stationary, using a free hand placed in the bowl, pushing down on the plug; or, by inserting enough fingers into the plug's hole to hold it still.

When you get the gasket to within ½ inch or more from the underside of the sink, stop and wrap the remainder of putty snake (or another one) around on the top of the beveled gasket. Now, continue with the slide-jaw pliers to really crush the gasket to the underside of the sink. Once the gasket contacts the sink bottom, you can usually take your hands free of the plug (for it will remain stationary as you continue to tighten up on the lock nut).

Now, apply some RECTORSEAL/Slic-Tite to the female threads of the larger recess in the female pop-up T waste (see Illus. 94). Next, if you have a thin, clear plastic or fiber friction ring with a wall about 1/16 inch thick, insert the ring into the bottom of the larger recess of the female T. Some wastes do not use the thin washer, so if you do not have one, don't worry about it.

At this point, wrap the last ½ inch of the pop-up plug's male threads with Teflon tape, and then lift the female T up and start threading the T onto the plug, turning it slowly in a *clockwise* direction as viewed from underneath. These threads are pretty fine, so take it easy and do not force them. Thread the female T onto the plug as far as you can go by hand, until you can no longer

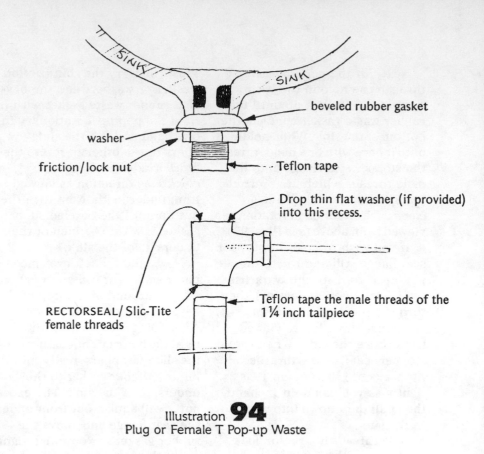

Illustration **94**
Plug or Female T Pop-up Waste

turn it, or until the plug begins to rotate in the sink.

If the adjustment arm should just happen to be pointing to the wall, straight out of the back of the waste, leave it be. If the adjustment arm is *not* already installed into the waste, we would be concerned with the threaded opening for the adjustment arm. The arm is *rarely* installed securely, but usually just loosely threaded into the T. Also, the adjustment arm, or threaded opening, will rarely point a perfect 180 degrees to the wall after snugging up the female T to the plug. So, with the slide-jaw pliers, rotate the T around in the sink hole in a *clockwise* direction until the arm points straight to the wall.

With this accomplished, hold the threaded plug stationary with one pair of slide-jaw pliers, and tighten further the friction/lock nut on the plug with the other

pair of slide-jaw pliers. Tighten the nut further in a *clockwise* direction as viewed from underneath.

On both the male T and the female T, the 1¼ inch tailpiece is loosely threaded into the bottom of the T. Remove it now (if it is not already separated) by turning it with your hands in a *counterclockwise* direction as viewed from underneath. Put some RECTORSEAL/Slic-Tite in the female threads in the bottom of the T and some on the fine threads at the top of the tailpiece. Now, rethread the tailpiece into the bottom of the T, turning it in a *clockwise* direction as viewed from underneath. Tighten the tailpiece with your hands only.

If your waste was shipped with the adjustment arm loose, put some RECTORSEAL/Slic-Tite in the female opening on the back of the waste. Put some RECTORSEAL/Slic-Tite on the male threads of the pop-up adjustment arm gland nut.

If your pop-up waste has a threaded male sleeve on the T and a female gland nut carrying the adjustment arm, also RECTOR-SEAL/Slic-Tite both threads.

HANG IN THERE, WE'RE ALMOST THERE! Now look at the pop-up stopper itself. If it is made of plastic and has a hole in the bottom, this means that the end of the adjustment arm mates to the hole, once the stopper is inside the T.

Regardless of whether you have a threaded sleeve for the adjustment arm or a female thread hole, there will be a small, friction ring to seal the joint. Do not lose the ring when handling the parts.

Now, drop the pop-up stopper into the seat, in the bottom of the bowl. Turn the stopper around in the seat until the hole in the bottom of the stopper comes closest to the threaded opening for the adjustment arm (see Illus. 67, page 61). Slip the plastic male spike of the adjustment arm into the hole in the stopper bottom and thread the adjustment arm gland to the waste T, using a *clockwise* direction as viewed from behind the waste or a *counterclockwise* direction as viewed from in *front* of the waste T.

## THE COUPLING POP-UP WASTE

The coupling type waste is assembled exactly like the female T. The major physical difference is that the coupling (carrying the adjustment) is shorter than the female T and more difficult to grip with the slide-jaw pliers (see Illus. 95).

## THE ONE-PIECE POP-UP WASTE

Another type of pop-up waste you might discover is the one-piece type (see Illus. 96). The pop-up adjustment arm gland unthreads and it is the *only* major part other than the gasket, washers and the lock nut. On this waste, the flanged stopper seat is *not* separate. Apply the putty as outlined on page 78 and drop the waste into the sink hole. Install the gasket and washers and lock nut as done on page 79. And, install the adjustment arm as we did for the female T (see last paragraph on page 80 and first four on this page).

## THE RUBBER STOPPER WASTE

The rubber stopper waste would be installed exactly as we did on the one-piece waste above, except that you would not have an adjustment arm to fool with.

The waste is installed and in the section following, we will install the pop-up adjustment linkage.

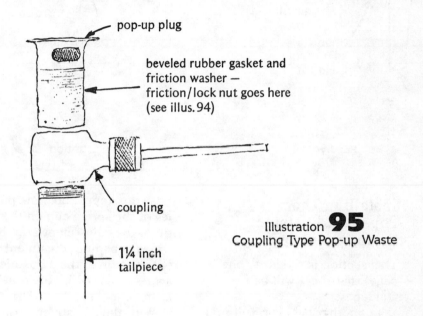

pop-up plug

beveled rubber gasket and friction washer — friction/lock nut goes here (see illus. 94)

coupling

1¼ inch tailpiece

Illustration **95**
Coupling Type Pop-up Waste

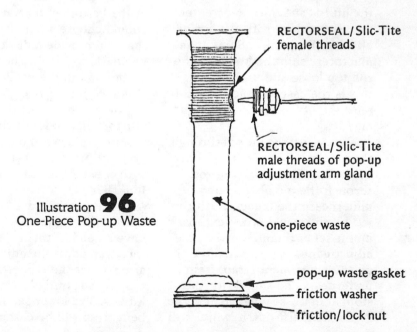

RECTORSEAL/Slic-Tite female threads

RECTORSEAL/Slic-Tite male threads of pop-up adjustment arm gland

one-piece waste

pop-up waste gasket

friction washer

friction/lock nut

Illustration **96**
One-Piece Pop-up Waste

81

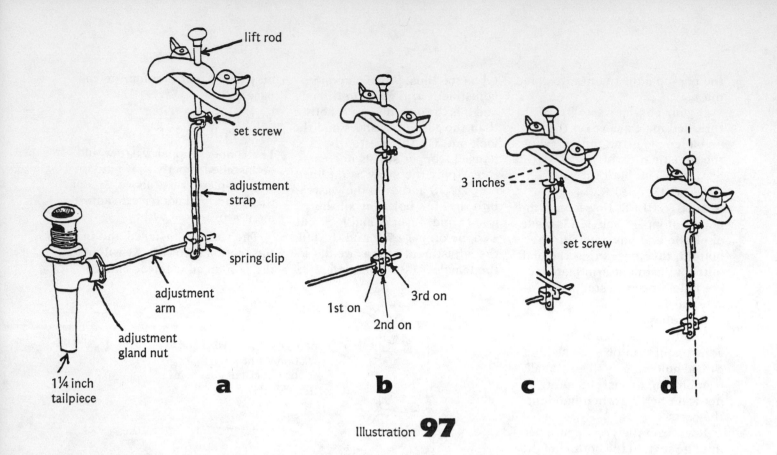

Illustration **97**

## Installing The Pop-Up Adjustment Strap & Linkage

This section is so short (one page) that there will be no Guidepost.

In another bag, you will find the lift rod and the pop-up extension strap along with the spring clip (see Illus. 97a). Some manufacturers ship the knob for the rod top loose and unthreaded. If this is the case, thread the knob onto the lift rod real tight, right now.

Now, insert the lift rod through the hole in the back of the faucet. You will have to push the rod through the plumber's putty underneath the faucet. Push the rod all the way down. Next, back up the set or thumb screw on the adjustment strap so it can be slid up the adjustment strap, from underneath the sink. With the stopper in the seat flange, pull the adjustment arm *down*, which will

raise the stopper up. Now, put one leg of the spring clip on the very tip of the adjustment arm. Next slide the pop-up adjustment strap onto the tip of the adjustment arm — followed by the other leg of the clip (see Illus. 97b).

With the adjustment arm still at the bottom of its travel, you should choose a hole in the strap that will provide a distance of about 2½ to 3 inches between the set screw and the bottom of the sink (see Illus. 97c).

Now pinch the legs of the spring clip together and slide the adjustment strap down the adjustment arm until it forms a straight line with the dangling lift rod (see Illus. 97d).

If you purchased a Kohler faucet, their adjustment straps have a bend in them. Just slide the strap down the adjustment arm so that the top, straight section of the strap is parallel to the lift rod. The lower section of the bent strap will be closer to the

base of the adjustment arm. Personally, I don't care for this design — you cannot use the straight strap like MOEN and others use to repair Kohler ones. Kohler's adjustment arm is short and will not reach the straight strap.

Now, lift the lift rod up from underneath until you can drop the lift rod down through the hole in the top of the adjustment strap. When the rod's knob is resting on the faucet, use the 6 inch adjustable wrench and set the screw, tightly, securing the rod's position. If you wish to readjust the height of the lift rod, back off the set screw and slide the lift rod up.

The 4 inch center set is now ready for the trap. Take a well earned break!

Before doing the trap, we are going to install the wide-spread faucet. For those with 4 inch sets, skip ahead to the installation of the trap (page 90).

See Important Notice
on page 88.

## Installing The Wide-Spread Lavatory Faucet

This section is the meatiest one in this book. We have several designs to discuss, each with its own idiosyncrasies. *The work is not difficult,* just a little tedious. Because of this factor, I recommend a specific brand of wide-spread faucet which is a *real* snap to install. After reading this section, you can weigh for yourself which type you might like to work with.

Wide-spread faucets are made up of a number of components, unlike the 4 inch center set. Therefore, there are more steps in the installation process. The following section will be cross-referenced to some sections in the 4 inch center set installation instruction. These areas will be steps which the two faucet types share in common. Also, we will be taking short breaks at completing the major tasks in the process of setting the wide-spread faucet.

Guidepost:

1. Apply plumber's putty to bottom of spout base.
2. Set (install) spout.
3. Install manifold T tubing (loosely).
4. Set valves into sink or counter (loosely).
5. Mark manifold tubing for proper valve penetration; then, take it down and cut it to length.
6. Take valves back down.
7. Pack underside of escutcheons with plumber's putty.

8. Lift valves back up with manifold tubing attached and secure to counter or sink (for good).
9. Install handles and hot and cold monograms and turn handles to the OFF position.
10. Open angle stops and check for leaks.

Okay, we again want to start with a clean sink deck or counter top. Let's unpackage the faucet, being careful not to accidently throw anything away or lose anything. It is sometimes easy to discard the small, plastic hot and cold monograms among the paper.

First, unwrap the spout and then look for a large flange washer and a brass lock/mounting nut that will thread onto the spout's threaded connection. Some faucets had an extra little hole in the spout's flange washer for the lift rod to protrude. It formed a small arc, in back of the hole for the threaded connection. Today, most all the manufacturers make a special seal so that the lift rod can travel directly through the very threaded connection that carries water up and out the spout.

Now, put a thin layer (⅛ inch) of plumber's putty on the bottom of the spout base. Use your thumb to spread the putty into a thin blanket. Then set the spout in the center hole of the sink or counter. Place the large flange washer over the spout's threaded connection, hanging below. Start the lock/mounting nut up the threaded connection, using your fingers, turning the nut in a *clockwise* direction as viewed from underneath. If you are lying on your back, make certain that you have your safety eyewear on. Now, turn the lock nut up as far as you can by hand, before applying the RIDGID basin wrench to the task. Snug up the nut, but before put-

ting a final, strong torque on the lock/mounting nut, make sure that the spout is pointing as directly as possible over the drain hole in the bottom of the sink. If you have difficulty keeping the spout pointing over the drain hole while snugging up the nut, maybe you could flag down a neighbor long enough for them to hold the spout stationary while you apply the last, setting crush on the nut.

At the bottom of the spout's threaded connection, there attaches a T connection, that we shall call the manifold T. This connection allows the water from the hot and cold valves to enter the spout and be mixed on the way up the spout, before entering the basin. Usually, this connection is shipped in its own little bag. On old installations, mostly American Standard and others, the T was comprised of two, overlapping parts, of rigid brass. On some later faucets, made by such people as Kohler, this T is one piece with ⅜ inch soft copper tubing soldered into a brass T (see Illus. 98).

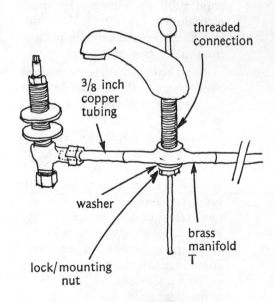

Illustration **98**
Solder d Manifold Tube

threaded connection

³/₈ inch copper tubing

washer

lock/mounting nut

brass manifold T

Some late American Standard models had a manifold T connection with threaded male sleeves on each side, which receive brass ferrules and compression nuts to hold the spirally grooved, flexible connections in place (see Illus. 99). This nut and ferrule are the same ones we used in the section on angle stops (see Illus. 47 on page 47). An even newer design is now available (see Important Notice on page 88).

The top and bottom of the manifold T have recesses, one is usually larger than the other. In the shipping bag for the manifold T, you should find a flat, fiber friction washer, a little rubber washer, a small brass washer and a small brass friction/lock nut. The flat fiber washer fits into the larger recess of the manifold T, *on top*, and it should lie flat in the bottom of the recess. Now, with the fiber washer in place, lift the T up and nest the bottom of the male, threaded spout connection in the larger, top recess. Out of the bottom of the manifold T, a smaller diameter male running thread will protrude. Push the small rubber washer up this smaller male thread, until it is inside the recess on the bottom of the manifold T (see Illus. 99).

Next, put the thin brass washer over the small threaded tube protruding out the bottom of the manifold T, followed by the small brass lock/mounting nut. With your fingers, turn this nut up the threads in a *clockwise* direction as viewed from underneath. This holds the assembly in place. Leave the nut only finger tight for now, because we will be taking down the manifold T after taking some measurements.

Take a short break — not too many beers now.

We will now start fitting up the valves. First, unwrap the valves,

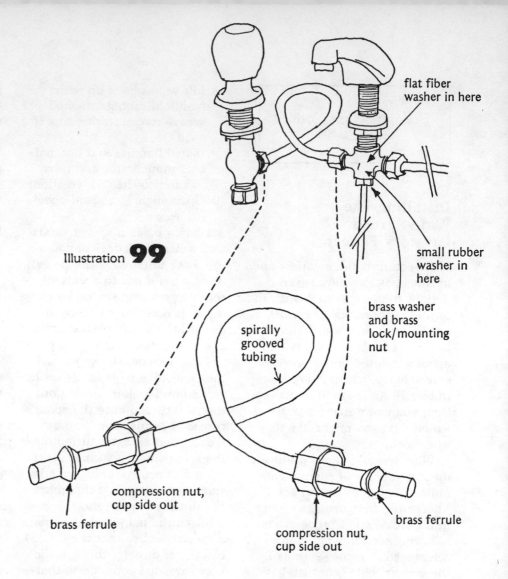

Illustration **99**

flat fiber washer in here

small rubber washer in here

brass washer and brass lock/mounting nut

spirally grooved tubing

compression nut, cup side out

brass ferrule

compression nut, cup side out

brass ferrule

handles and the cone escutcheons. Set the handles on the end of each valve stem and turn the handles in a *clockwise* direction as far as they will go. (They might not both turn in this direction.) If both valves have the stem travel moving downward while using the clockwise rotation, it will not make any difference which valve is used for hot and which for cold unless otherwise stamped or marked on the valve. If the valves have a different direction of rotation for turning on and off, you will have to decide which valve you want for hot and cold, depending upon your personal taste.

Chicago brand faucets, among a few others, do not use a down-

ward travel of the valve stem in the conventional way most other faucets do to shut the flow of water off. Chicago faucets have a unique design which uses the water pressure to shut the valve off; these faucets have to fight water pressure to keep the valve *open*. When the valve closes, the water pressure helps keep the valve closed. This is a good feature, one that you will see makes a price difference, when shopping for your new faucet.

Regardless of the manufacturer of your new faucet, pick up the large cone escutcheons and inspect them for two possible wrench flats on the vertical sides of the upper diameter (see Illus. 100). Not many manufacturers still provide these wrench flats . . . just one more step which is labor-price related. They were a real nice feature for the plumber when installing them. If your escutcheons do not have the wrench flats, do not be concerned. Now, thread the large lock/mounting nuts down the threaded exterior of the valves. Turn the nuts in a *clockwise* direction as viewed from above, until the nuts almost reach the bottom of the thread. If you have the two large flange washers (metal ones) drop one over each valve so that they rest upon the lock/mounting nut already threaded down the valve. If you have two different size diameter lock/mounting nuts, the larger one goes down the valve first.

From underneath the sink or cabinet, lift the valves, one at a time up through the holes above. While holding them there, pick up the large coned escutcheons and thread the escutcheons down the valves from above. Thread the escutcheons on in a *counter-clockwise* direction as viewed from underneath. Thread them on until you have about ½ inch of threads sticking out the top of the escutcheons. With both valves just hanging in their respective holes, thread the lock nuts and flange washers *up* the valve bodies from underneath, until the washers contact the bottom of the sink or counter top. *Do not snug up the nuts for now; for they too will be coming back down.*

Take a break!

If you have a manifold T with the soft ⅜ inch copper tubing soldered into the manifold T, you might find that you need to trim the tubing down to length to fit into the threaded sleeves on the bottom sides of the valves (see Illus. 101). *The spirally grooved manifold tubing is discussed further on, but continue reading.*

We left the manifold T lock/mounting nut loose so we could now swing the ⅜ inch tubing to the side of the valves. We want to mark the tubing where it would be in full penetration of the threaded sleeve on each valve body (see Illus. 101). We do not want to cut this manifold tubing too short, so if you have any doubts in guessing the length of the tubing, make your mark a little on the long side. We can always trim off a little more, but adding to the length after cutting off too much requires extra compression fittings.

Now, mark the manifold for left/right or hot/cold, etc., with a marking pen or crayon, etc., so that you will be inserting the same side of the tubing back into the same valve it was measured for. Wide-spread faucets, if they are mounted in a custom counter top, will be installed in holes which were drilled by hand. Many times the distance from the spout connection hole to each valve hole will not be the same distance.

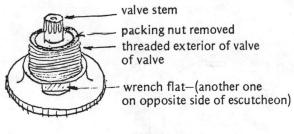

valve stem
packing nut removed
threaded exterior of valve of valve
wrench flat—(another one on opposite side of escutcheon)

Illustration **100**
Cone Escutcheon

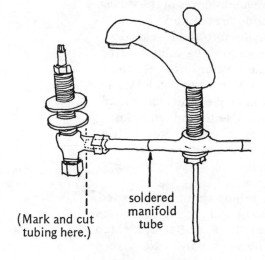

(Mark and cut tubing here.)

soldered manifold tube

Illustration **101**
Measuring ⅜ Inch Tubing

85

With both sides of the manifold T connection marked, undo the brass nut holding the manifold T to the spout connection and take the manifold T down. Be careful not to lose the little brass washer and the little rubber washer on the bottom. The same goes for the fiber washer in the top of the T, in the recess.

Next, use the tubing cutter to cut the tubing at your marks. Count the number of valve threads sticking out of the top of the escutcheons because they should both be equal. Then, unthread the coned escutcheons from the valve bodies and lay them down, out of the way on a clean surface.

Take a break!

Now, find the rubber ⅜ inch cone washers, brass friction rings and the cone washer slip nuts for the manifold tubing. They might have been shipped in their own little bag. Slide each cone washer slip nut onto the ends of the manifold tubing, cup end out (see Illus. 102). Then, slide each brass friction ring onto the tubing followed by the cone washer, cone shape pointing out. Now put some RECTORSEAL/Slic-Tite on the threaded sleeves of the valves. Then slide the manifold T connection tubing into the threaded sleeves on each valve and start the cone washer nuts onto the threaded sleeves in a *clockwise* direction as viewed from behind the nuts. Use the 6 inch adjustable wrench and put just a little torque on the nuts, maybe one complete turn past the "finger tight" limits.

The tubing should be inserted as far as it will go into the valves and stay there, while you tighten the cone washer nuts. Now, we will lift the entire assembly back up into position on the end of the spout connection. Make sure that the valves will protrude up through the holes in the sink or counter and then put the little rubber washer over the smaller threaded tube of the spout connection, followed by the brass friction washer and lock nut. The assembly will hang in position after you thread the lock nut up as far as you can with the use of your fingers (see Illus. 103).

Now, pack the bottom of the cone escutcheons with plumber's putty. After lifting each valve up through the holes in the sink, start the coned escutcheons down the threaded exterior of the valves until they contact the surface of the sink or counter top. Remember, when we looked for the wrench flats on the coned escutcheons in the beginning? If you have them, you can now take the 12 or 15 inch adjustable wrench and *gently* snug up the coned escutcheons until they lay flat on the sink or counter top. The excess plumber's putty will ooze out from under the escutcheons.

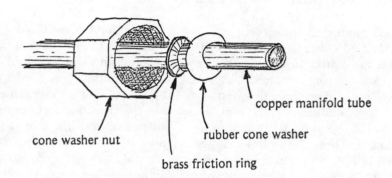

cone washer nut

rubber cone washer

brass friction ring

copper manifold tube

Illustration **102**

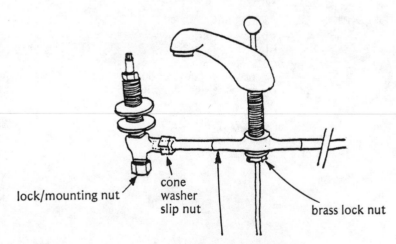

lock/mounting nut

cone washer slip nut

brass lock nut

soldered manifold tube

Illustration **103**
Installing Soldered Manifold T

If your escutcheons do not have the wrench flats, and most of today's faucets do not have them, we have to get the basin wrench and tighten the lock/mounting nuts from underneath the sink or cabinet, using a *clockwise* direction of rotation as viewed from underneath. I know, your poor knees and back! Now you know why the plumber wants so damn much to do the job.

When you finish snugging up these lock/mounting nuts, get the 8 inch adjustable wrench and tighten the cone washer nuts on the manifold tubing, making sure that the manifold T connection tubing is bottomed out in the valve's threaded sleeves.

It is okay to have a slight bend in the center area of the manifold tubing, to accommodate an offset for the spout, but it should be as straight as possible where it enters the valves. This is so the cone washers will make a good seal. After tightening the cone washer nuts, use the 6 inch adjustable wrench or maybe the RIDGID basin wrench and tighten the brass nut on the bottom of the manifold T, once again, snugging it up to the spout connection.

Take another breather.

●

I would like to mention here that all these breaks that I'm giving you folks are for your benefit only and it does not reflect any extra time spent — ending up in your bill when done by none other than yours truly.

●

Now, set the handles back on the valve stems and make sure that the handles can turn the stems to the full OFF position *without* rubbing the slope of the coned escutcheon. If the handles do rub the escutcheons, you will have to back off the lock nuts underneath the sink and then

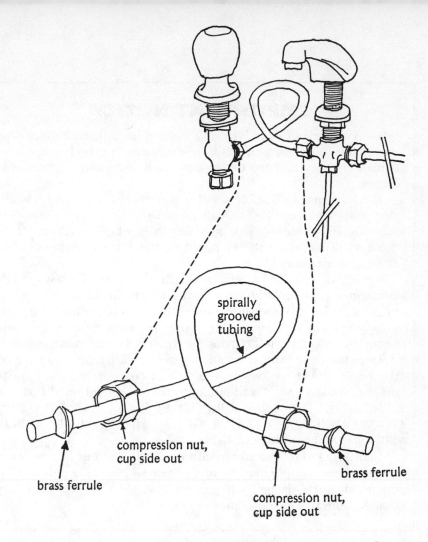

spirally grooved tubing

compression nut, cup side out

brass ferrule

brass ferrule

compression nut, cup side out

Illustration **104**
Installing Manifold T with Flexible Tubing

thread the coned escutcheons further down the valve bodies until the handles do not make contact with the escutcheons. After making this adjustment if you have to, retighten the lock/mounting nuts.

●

If your wide-spread faucet has the spirally grooved flexible manifold tubing that connects the manifold T to the valve bodies, as in the case of some American Standard designs along with some other manufacturers, your task will be somewhat different (see Illus. 104).

Many manufacturers using the flexible, spirally grooved manifold tubing use the brass ferrule and

ferrule compression nuts in place of the rubber cone washers (see Illus. 104).

For this type of manifold design, the adjustment of the lock/mounting nuts on the valve bodies will be identical to the previous instruction for the 3/8 inch copper tubing which is soldered to the manifold T as mentioned above. Checking for proper handle travel is also the same. Set your spout on the sink or counter as we did before. To attach the flexible leads to the manifold T connections and the valve bodies, use the brass ferrules and compression nuts. The nuts go onto the tubing first, cup end out, then the ferrules.

With the ferrule compression nuts and the brass ferrules in place, slip the end of the leads into the manifold T connections and the valve bodies. You might want to do this work with the valves lying on a flat, clean surface. Tighten the four nuts to finger tight limits and then use the 6 inch adjustable wrench and tighten each ferrule nut only ½ turn further, in a *clockwise* direction as viewed from behind the nut.

These nuts need the little bit of extra torque provided by the adjustable wrench, but with only the ½ turn now applied, they can still be pulled off the tubing and reused and the tubing can be trimmed to a shorter length if it is required. If you tighten the brass ferrule nuts any tighter to start with, the brass ferrule can take a "set" on the tubing and you cannot reposition the ferrules later.

Now, as we did on the smooth ⅜ inch manifold tubing, mount the manifold to the spout connection, letting the valves hang this time. Then, carefully bend the flexible manifold tubing with the valves attached, until you can line up the valves with the holes in the sink or counter above.

I have found that in most cases, using the spirally grooved manifold tubing, I have to trim away most of the straight, smooth end portions of the flexible connections in order to make this bending procedure without kinking the tubing, near each end. If you find yourself in the same situation, trim the spiral tubing down little by little until it is the proper length.

You will discover that you can-not remove just ⅛ inch or ¼ inch of the tubing with the tubing cutter, without years of practice. This trimming might be done easier with the mini-hacksaw. I turn the blade around so that the teeth cut in a *dragging* direction. This prevents the tubing from collapsing so easily. If after trimming the manifold tubing, you should discover that the tubing is out-of-round, and you cannot get the ferrule nut and ferrule back over the end of the tubing, do not panic! Reread the section on using the adjustable wrench for reshaping out-of-round supplies, covered on page 77.

If you should happen to cut the spirally grooved manifold tubing too short, by accident, or you set the ferrules in the wrong place, you can purchase soft, rolled copper tubing of the same diameter, along with extra ferrules at the plumbing supplier. This is another good reason for doing the job in the week days.

Okay, put some plumber's putty on the bottoms of the coned escutcheons like we did for the previous design of wide-spread, on page 83. After you have both valves lining up with the holes in the sink or counter above, and the lock/mounting nuts and flange washers are threaded down the valve bodies as we did on page 85, lift the valves up through the holes from below. While holding the valves in place, thread the coned escutcheons down the male threads on the valve bodies from above, using a *counter-clockwise* direction of rotation as viewed from *below*. If your arms are too short to accomplish this by yourself, flag down a neighbor.

With the escutcheons down far enough to provide for sufficient handle movement, see page 85, get back down on your posterior and with the RIDGID basin wrench

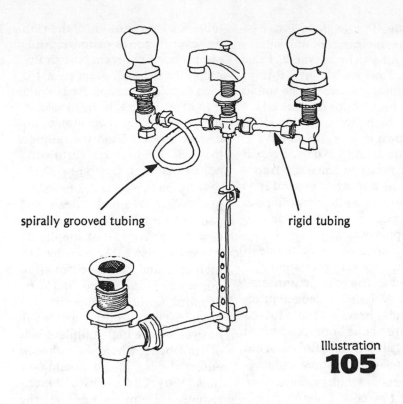

spirally grooved tubing          rigid tubing

Illustration
**105**

and safety glasses on, tighten the lock/mounting nuts up using a *clockwise* direction on the nuts as viewed from below.

Make one more final handle clearance check at the escutcheons, and then take a *very, extremely well earned break!*

## Which Faucet For Which Sink

This title is just a short one-page recommendation. It has been my experience that drawbacks and advantages exist for the two basic manifold designs we discussed in the last section. I would like to shed some light on the advantages and disadvantages in hopes of sparing you some uncomfortable hours under a cramped lavatory cabinet.

The spirally grooved tubing is not the easiest to work on for sinks and counters with holes spaced from 8 to under 10 inches.

On installations with hole spreads like these, I have often found it necessary to rotate the valve bodies so that threaded sleeves which receive the tubing are not pointing directly towards the spout connections. It is often necessary to leave the threaded sleeves pointing either to the 12 o'clock or the 6 o'clock position and then force the tubing back on itself in order to take up for its surplus length of spirally grooved tubing (which cannot be trimmed down to the most optimum length because of the grooves). See Illus. 105.

One of the advantages, however, of using the spirally grooved tubing is the use of brass ferrules and ferrule compression nuts, opposed to the rubber cone washers and friction nuts used with most of the smooth copper manifold tubing designs.

Contrary to the first two designs discussed in pages 83-88,

the MOEN wide-spread faucet is a dream to install. The flexible leads are *factory* installed (by a big gorilla with a killer-crusher handshake) to the manifold T and the faucet valves. And, the tubing bends very easily to fit almost any hole spread. Installation time and fuss-and-muss stress is reduced by 70 percent or better. I only wish that the MOEN folks would offer more spout and handle designs with their wide-spread. Listening Al? (Mr. Moen).

Other MOEN pluses are: no handle-to-escutcheon adjustment is necessary because the stems do not travel up and down; when the faucet is purchased with pop-up waste it has the male T design, which is the easiest to install and is prone to fewer leaks, and the faucet uses cartridges which are well designed and inexpensive to replace.

Attaching angle stop supplies to the 4 inch center set and to the wide-spread is the *identical* process (see pages 75-77). Just remember, always snug up the ferrule nuts onto the angle stops *first*, before snugging up the faucet connections, above. If you tighten the slip nuts on the faucet first, you can draw the supply too far up and out of the angle stops' threaded sleeve and you have a good chance for leaks.

Also, the installation of the pop-up waste is *identical* for both the 4 inch center set and the wide-spread (see pages 78-82).

● IMPORTANT NOTE: If you happen to be installing a new faucet to a new basin, I recommend that you save your body from a lot of aches and pains by installing the faucet to the sink *before* setting the sink on the wall or in the cabinet.

Well, that's that . . . hope you got something for your effort.

# Installing A New Trap

Now, we have reached the point where our angle stops, supplies, faucet and waste are installed and we can go ahead and finish up the whole ball of wax with the installation of the trap.

In this book we will be dealing with P-traps, with *unions*. There are other traps used in residential trade such as the drum trap and the S-trap. The S-trap, for practical purposes, is removed and installed with the same slip nuts and washers as we use with the P-trap. So by reading this section about P-traps, your task, if it involves S-traps, will be self-explanatory. We will *not* discuss drum traps.

In the plastic group (ABS and PVC) and the tubular brass type, the trap is composed of *two* individual pieces (J-bend and trap arm) joined together with a slip nut union. The ABS trap in Illus. 55 is made of real heavy material, designated *Schedule 40*. The trap arm for this trap is a cut-to-length piece of 1½ inch Schedule 40 ABS pipe. There is a newer, thinner, flimsy ABS trap designed for use with 1½ inch slip nut washers and slip nuts. This thinner, flimsy model comes *with* a trap arm.

The tubular brass traps are sold in one or two pieces: just the J-bend or just the trap arm. When sold together, they comprise the *complete* trap.

The ABS P-trap, whether the heavy Schedule 40 or thinner slip nut sized, are almost always solid black to a very dark charcoal shade. By the mere fact that you have an ABS plastic P-trap, it suggests the possibility that you also have ABS drains and vent piping. And, with ABS plastic drains, waste and vent systems, the trap arm is usually a piece of Schedule 40 pipe *glued* into a fitting inside the wall and not (easily for you) removable. I said usually. You can buy ABS P-traps with female threads at the union which thread onto galvanized nipples at the wall. So this all boils down to this: if you have a Schedule 40 ABS P-trap, I would suggest that you leave the trap arm alone and work around it as best you can while replacing the faucet, pop-up waste and/or rubber stopper waste.

The J-bend of the Schedule 40 ABS P-trap is removed and replaced in the exact manner as the removal and replacement of the tubular brass J-bends. To find out more about both, read on. (I know, it ain't Harold Robbins, but he ain't saving your ass either.)

Bathroom sink traps are required by code to have a minimum diameter of 1¼ inches. Kitchen sink traps are required by code to have a minimum diameter of 1½ inches. When purchasing either size of tubular brass trap, get one of *17 gauge*. This is the heavier or thicker wall design. The option remaining is a trap of 20 to 22 gauge or a lot *thinner*. The 17 gauge trap will outlive the lighter one by a long time, and in this way it is more economical.

Many bathroom lavatory sink traps will be the minimum size required: 1¼ inch J-bend and 1¼ inch trap arm. If your old trap had the 1¼ inch J-bend and a 1¼ inch trap arm, I suggest that you purchase one of the same dimensions. Depending upon the proximity of your 1¼ inch tailpiece and the drain nipple in the wall, sometimes only the smaller 1¼ inch by 1¼ inch trap will fit without substantial refitting of the old drain in the wall or moving of the sink further to one side of the drain. The larger 1¼ inch by 1½ inch trap may be used if the tailpiece is to one side of the trap by several inches or more. And even more important, the drain nipple in the wall *must* be a 1½ inch nipple to accept the 1½ inch trap arm. (If the drain nipple in the wall is a 1¼ inch nipple, no matter how far from the tailpiece it is, the 1½ inch trap arm will not fit inside it. Savvy?)

If by chance you did have the 1¼ inch by 1½ inch P-trap, and you cannot find a replacement of this size at your local supplier, you might use a 1½ inch by 1½ inch trap and buy an extra slip nut washer, one called *"a 1¼ by 1½ inch reducing"* slip nut washer. This slip nut washer will be used on the high, tailpiece side of the J-bend, where the tailpiece enters the top of the J-bend (see Illus. 106). The 1¼ by 1½ inch reducing slip nut washer has the same *outside* diameter as the 1½ inch slip nut washer, *but* the hole in the center is reduced to fit the 1¼ inch tailpiece.

Brass tubular traps are made of *thin-wall* tubing, usually with polished chrome or brushed chrome electroplating on the outside. There are other household sink traps made of *cast* brass. Because of their very expensive price, we see fewer of them used as the years go by. They are made by such folks as American Standard, Kohler and others. These traps last, figuratively speaking, forever.

Some designs of tubular brass traps use a tapered, ground-metal joint, at the union, instead of a rubber or plastic slip nut washer. I suggest that you *do not* purchase this type. It requires a most precise alignment and it is very prone to pesky drips when used by first-timers. When you go shopping for a new trap, advise the counterman or clerk that you prefer not to use this type.

The plastic P-traps also come in a 1¼ inch by 1½ inch design. I prefer the Schedule 40 ABS P-traps to the tubular brass ones. The Schedule 40 ABS P-traps outlive the brass ones and they cost less to begin with.

You will find the white, PVC P-traps traded at the home-center/hardware store level. I have neither bad nor good to say of them. Plumbers do not use them, but I know the PVC is a very tough material. However, PVC is a hot topic nowadays because of possible health situations.

## Two Most Popular Types Of Tubular Brass P-traps

This short section is going to discuss the two most popular designs of tubular brass P-traps in use today and then I am going to tell you how to install my choice of the two.

Of the two most popular types, my preference is the one shown in Illus. 107 on the next page. On this design, running around the perimeter of the trap arm, at the end with the 90 degree bend, there is a raised lip about ¼ inch from the bottom edge. Under the raised lip, the tubing continues

for about another ¼ inch. The mating side of the J-bend has a slightly belled opening to accept this lip end of the trap arm. This design, because of the male trap arm's penetration into the J-bend's female opening, leaves fewer chances for leaks.

To install a trap of this type, first slide one brass slip nut, cup end first, down the trap arm until the slip nut is well away from the end of the trap arm which enters the drain nipple or waste adapter. Next, if you wish to hide the slip nut at the wall, slide the escutcheon which is supplied with a packaged trap, down the trap arm, bell side facing the wall. Then, slide another slip nut onto the trap arm, flat side first. Follow this last slip nut with a rubber slip nut washer or beveled nylon slip nut washer. Now, put another slip nut washer onto the trap arm, *under* the raised lip, on the 90 degree bend end. Introduce the straight end of the trap arm into the drain nipple or waste adapter at the wall (see Illus. 107).

You should have one more slip nut to use on the tailpiece. So, slide this slip nut up the tailpiece with the cup side *down*, followed by the 1¼ inch slip nut washer, which will hold the slip nut on the tailpiece. Now, wrap both male threaded ends of the J-bend with Teflon tape. Go for 3 to 5 complete wraps.

While peering down into each port of the J-bend, the Teflon tape should be applied in a *clockwise* direction of wrap. Now, lift the high side of the trap onto the end of the 1¼ inch tailpiece, encasing the end of the tailpiece for at least one inch. Now, tighten the slip nut with your hands in a *clockwise* direction as viewed from above. Tighten it enough so that the trap does not fall free of the tailpiece. Next, swing the low

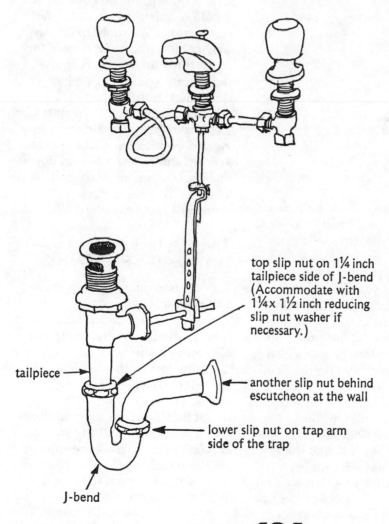

top slip nut on 1¼ inch tailpiece side of J-bend (Accommodate with 1¼ x 1½ inch reducing slip nut washer if necessary.)

tailpiece

another slip nut behind escutcheon at the wall

lower slip nut on trap arm side of the trap

J-bend

Illustration **106**

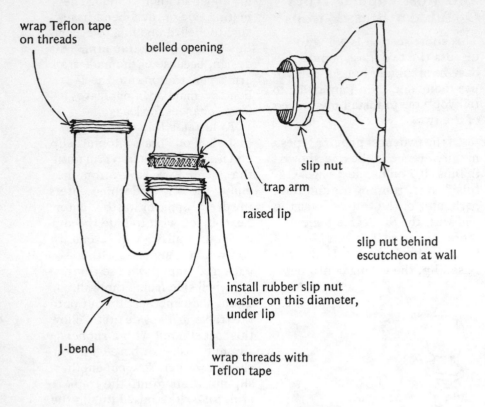

wrap Teflon tape
on threads

belled opening

slip nut

trap arm

raised lip

slip nut behind
escutcheon at wall

install rubber slip nut
washer on this diameter,
under lip

J-bend

wrap threads with
Teflon tape

## Illustration **107**

end of the J-bend under the 90 degree end of the trap arm. Pull the J-bend down a little if you have to in order for the J-bend to swing under the trap arm. If the trap arm sticks too far out for it to mate with the low side of the J-bend, pull the trap arm out of the wall and trim the length with a tubing cutter or mini-hacksaw.

We want the trap arm to be penetrating the wall nipple or waste adapter at least one or two inches when the J-bend does mate with the 1¼ inch tailpiece. When the trap arm aligns over the J-bend's lower side, lift the J-bend up to mate and start screwing the slip nut onto the lower side of the J-bend, using a *clockwise* direction as viewed from above. Snug up this slip nut with the slide-jaw

pliers, then snug up the upper slip nut of the J-bend in a *clockwise* direction as viewed from above.

If this first type of trap is not available in your locale, then your next best bet will be the following one.

We'll call it a "flush-face" or hat-brim design. This one also has a lip on the 90 degree bend end of the trap arm. The lip merely is a 90 degree upset, with *no* section of tubing continuing below it (see Illus. 108). In other words, it looks just like the brim of a man's hat. The rubber slip nut washer for this trap goes on down the trap arm *before* the first slip nut. The slip nut washer is slid all the way down until it comes to rest *on top* of the rubber

washer which in turn is on top of the little brim (see Illus. 108).

Next, shove the slip nut, cup end first, down the trap arm until it comes to rest on top of the rubber slip nut washer. Other than this, the procedure follows exactly the same steps as for the first design of tubular brass P-trap discussed.

### S-Traps?

If you have an S-trap, you still have a J-bend that attaches to the tailpiece. Instead of a trap arm which goes to the wall, your 180 degree trap arm attaches to the lower side of the J-bend and goes straight down, to the floor, to a nipple or waste adapter. All the connections use rubber slip nut washers just like we have used for the P-traps. In several respects, the S-trap is easier to replace than the P-trap.

You would undo the slip nuts in a *counterclockwise* direction as viewed from above. Lift the trap arm up and pull the J-bend down and replace one or both parts. Then reverse the process to remarry them (see Illus. 109).

### The 1¼ Inch Tailpiece — Is Yours Too Short?

This is just a quickie, so go ahead and read it.

It seems that faucet manufacturers are making their tailpieces shorter and shorter every year. Their majority stockholders are probably candy bar company execs. Those cheap . . . . You might find that your new tailpiece will not penetrate all the way through or even reach the slip nut on the female opening in the top side of the J-bend. I suggest that you measure the length of the existing tailpiece while it is still intact and working. Then, you can ask the counterman who

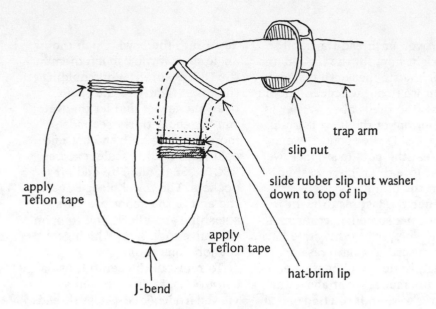

apply
Teflon tape

trap arm

slip nut

slide rubber slip nut washer
down to top of lip

apply
Teflon tape

hat-brim lip

J-bend

Illustration **108**
Hat-Brim or Flush-Face Design

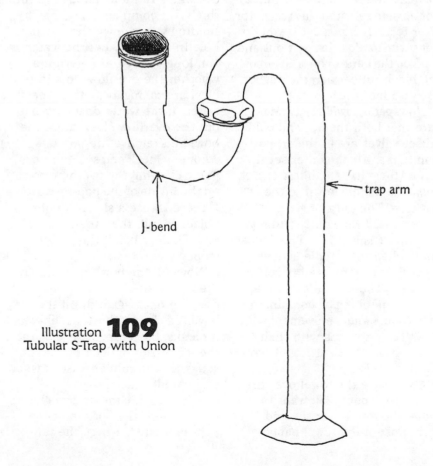

J-bend

trap arm

Illustration **109**
Tubular S-Trap with Union

serves you to compare the length of the old tailpiece to the new tailpiece that you are about to purchase. You might need to lengthen the tailpiece.

If you do indeed need an extended tailpiece to reach the new trap, you have two choices in tailpiece designs. The first one has a belled opening like the end of a J-bend and it also uses a rubber slip nut washer and slip nut to grip the existing tailpiece. They will usually come in 6, 8, 10 and 12 inch lengths.

The second choice of extension is a 6 or 12 inch long length of 1¼ inch diameter tubing with male threads at *both* ends, which match the female threads in the bottom of a pop-up waste, where the standard cheapo tailpiece threads in. I suggest that you purchase this latter type. It is more rigid once it is installed and it has no rubber slip nut washer to crack and leak with age. Also, it is more streamlined in appearance.

To install this second type, first thread one end into the bottom of the pop-up waste T, and then swing the J-bend around to one side and mark the extension tailpiece where it would be in full penetration of the belled, female J-bend. Now, take the extension tailpiece down and use the tubing cutter to sever it at your mark. When you go to rethread the new tailpiece into the waste, make sure to apply RECTORSEAL/Slic-Tite in the female threads of the pop-up waste T. These female threads are very fine and they can become cross-threaded very easily, so go *slowly* when you are threading and unthreading the tailpiece for measuring and cutting and for the final installation.

The factory shipped tailpiece and the latter type extension unthread in a *counterclockwise* direction of rotation as viewed from underneath and they rethread into the bottom of the waste T in a *clockwise* direction of rotation as viewed from underneath.

If you have a *rubber stopper* waste whose tailpiece is too short, you will have to use the rubber slip nut washer and slip nut type of extension tailpiece because the factory tailpiece is an integral part of the waste and does not unthread from the waste.

Boy! That was a real quickie, wasn't it?

## Testing The Faucet And Trap For Leaks

This is also a real short page plus of procedures, but I have included a Guidepost:

1. Remove any aerator from end of spout.
2. Place hand towel over end of spout and hold it tightly in place.
3. Turn water on *full*, both hot and cold and purge lines of all dirt, rust, scale and air pockets.
4. Reinstall aerator.
5. On pop-up wastes, lift up lift rod and fill the basin to the overflow holes and test the overflow passage.
6. On rubber stopper wastes, put cork in seat and do the same test.
7. Now drain basin and check under the sink for any gravity leaks.

Remove the aerator from the end of the faucet spout. Use a *clockwise* direction of rotation while looking *down onto* the spout, from above. There will be a little, black rubber washer used between the aerator and the inside of the spout. Sometimes this rubber washer does not come out

when you unthread the aerator. So, right now, lift the lift rod and lower the stopper onto the seat. When we turn the faucet on, you might find the rubber washer in the bottom of the bowl if it was stuck inside the spout. If we do not seat the pop-up stopper, we might lose the rubber washer down the drain.

Since the last big drought in California, some faucet manufacturers shipping to this state have been inserting a flat brass or white plastic reducing washer into the faucet spout above the aerator washer. If you find one, it will have a small hole in the center, to restrict the amount of water issuing from the spout. I personally do not care for these restrictors. They increase the pressure of the water while reducing the volume of flow. This high pressure stream has a tendency to splash out of the bowl. You do not have to reinstall this restrictor after testing the faucet if you do not want to. Just leave it out and replace the aerator after inserting the black rubber aerator washer back up into the spout.

Now, get a towel ready. Make sure that both the hot and cold faucet valves are in the off position. On a 4 inch center set that has a single handle, like a MOEN, push the handle down to the OFF position. The *only* single handle faucet that I recommend to my customers is a MOEN. This faucet is off when the handle is down, regardless of temperature setting selected. There is *no* confusing rocking, pitching or combination of both on handle movement with MOEN, like there is with their competitors. With MOEN, down is off, and on is up.

Now, place the towel over the end of the spout. You want to drape the towel over the end, with most of the towel hanging

down into the bowl. Open the angle stops if you had left them in the OFF position. While holding the towel tightly to the spout, open the faucet and let the water run for about thirty seconds or more, purging both the hot and cold lines of dirt, scale, excess RECTORSEAL/Slic-Tite and air pockets. The towel placed over the end of the spout prevents splashing and allows you to open the valve to *full on*, which gets the job done sooner.

To reinstall the aerator, use a *counterclockwise* rotation as viewed from *above*. These threads are very fine also, so take your time so that you do not cross-thread them.

After purging the system and you have the aerator back on the end of the spout, set the pop-up stopper on the seat and begin filling the bowl with water. Let the water run long enough to fill the basin completely and begin sending water down the overflow hole in the bowl. Let the water run long enough to determine whether the overflow slots in the bowl are taking away the excess water. If the water does not exit out the overflow slots, drain the bowl and remove the pop-up stopper. Check and see if there is putty clogging the overflow ports on the inside of the pop-up waste. If there is, use a slender, pointed object to pull the excess up and out. Then reinstall the pop-up stopper.

Now, fill the bowl up again and then push the lift rod all the way down to once again drain the bowl. As the bowl drains, check for leaks. Look especially close at the large friction/lock nut that squashes the rubber waste gasket to the underside of the sink. Also, check the adjustment arm gland nut. Look at the bottom of the pop-up waste T where the tailpiece threads into the waste T. Carefully inspect each slip nut on the trap system. You might have to fill the bowl and drain it several times to thoroughly check out all the points.

If you encounter a drip at any of these locations, tighten the respective nuts *slowly*, in ¼ turn increments, until the drip stops and then *stop* tightening immediately. With no leaks, you may slide the trap arm escutcheon back against the wall.

Congratulations, you just saved yourself some hard earned money and gained a lot of new self-confidence.

*Clean up your tools before putting them away*, and then go treat yourself to your favorite reward.

## Resetting The Pedestal Sink Bowl

If you are working on a wide-spread faucet or individual cocks on a pedestal sink bowl (on the floor), and have the faucet installed along with the new waste, then install the J-bend onto the 1¼ inch tailpiece now.

It is now time to place the bowl back onto the pedestal. Swing the J-bend to about the 11 o'clock or 1 o'clock position. Have the trap arm already inserted into the wall nipple or waste adapter, with the slip nut washer and slip nut on the trap arm (see Illus. 107, 108, & 110).

When the bowl is reset upon the pedestal, pull the trap arm out of the wall and lift up the J-bend so that the two components mate. Again, snug up the nuts, leaving the escutcheon away from the wall. Fill the bowl and do the same checkout as we did for the faucet and trap system for standard wall-hung and pullman mounted sinks (see preceding section).

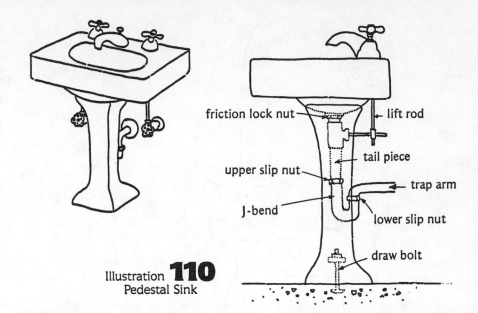

Illustration **110**
Pedestal Sink

friction lock nut
lift rod
tail piece
upper slip nut
trap arm
J-bend
lower slip nut
draw bolt

Make sure that you do not forget to refit the carriage bolts or wall brackets securing the bowl in position, on the pedestal. On wide-spread faucets, regardless of what type of sink that they are installed on, snap the hot and cold monograms on after *everything* else has been tested.

IMPORTANT NOTE: Depending upon how much of an opening you have in the backside of your pedestal, you might have to swivel it to one side in order to get the J-bend to swing under the trap arm. There were many, many companies manufacturing pedestal sinks, and no two made an identical pedestal.

## The Single-Post Lavatory Faucet

This faucet is an old design, but usually a very sturdy one. It was found mostly on pedestal lavatory sinks. The same basic design of faucet is also found in restaurants and in home kitchen sink applications; it was referred to as a pantry faucet.

The single-post faucet can prove to be a real challenge when trying to cure a drip at its under-sink draw-nut connection. How-ever, if we take our time and know going in that we will have a possible battle, it isn't so bad with yours truly showing you how.

Guidepost:

1. Remove old supplies from old faucet.
2. Unthread draw-nut and remove supply horseshoe.
3. Apply putty snake to base of new faucet.
4. Set new faucet in sink or counter hole.
5. Install new flange washer and lock/mounting nut, securing the new faucet to the sink or counter.
6. Install black, two-holed fiber washer in new draw-nut.
7. Apply RECTORSEAL/Slic-Tite into top and bottom female threads of new draw-nut.
8. Apply Teflon tape to threads of faucet bottom.
9. Install new horseshoe to new faucet bottom.
10. Install new supplies.
11. Install new spout (if loose in box) to new faucet body.
12. Remove aerator from end of spout.
13. Open angle stops.
14. Turn faucet on and purge lines and test for leaks.

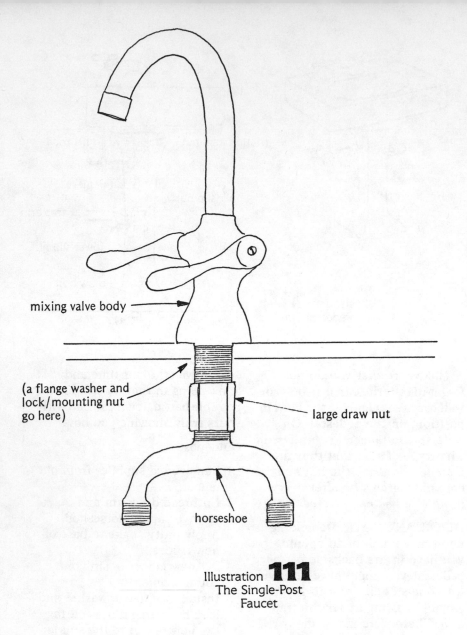

mixing valve body

(a flange washer and lock/mounting nut go here)

large draw nut

horseshoe

Illustration **111**
The Single-Post Faucet

This mixing valve faucet uses the large, thin flange washer and the thin, flat lock/mounting nut found on the other threaded faucet connections. On the bottom of the single-post faucet's threaded connection, you will find a large draw-nut, holding a cast brass horseshoe to the threaded connection (see Illus. 111). This draw-nut has right hand threads (standard) in the top half, and left hand threads (unusual) in the bottom half.

With the supplies removed from the horseshoe, unthread the big brass draw-nut from the faucet connection using the RIDGID basin wrench rotated in a *counterclockwise* direction as viewed from underneath. When you have unthreaded the nut completely off, bringing the horseshoe with it, again use the basin wrench and unthread the lock/mounting nut, in a *counterclockwise* rotation as viewed from underneath. With the lock/mounting nut off the threaded connection, you will be able to lift the faucet off the sink or counter top, from above.

To replace this type of faucet,

roll out a ⅜ inch diameter plumber's putty snake and lay it around the hole in the sink or counter. Have the new flange washer and lock/mounting nut handy, and then set the faucet into the hole. Now, fit the flange washer over the threaded connection from below and start the lock nut up the connection using a *clockwise* direction of rotation as viewed from underneath. Turn the nut up as far as you can using your fingers to start.

When you contact the bottom of the sink or counter, use the RIDGID basin wrench to snug up the lock/mounting nut. Now apply some Teflon tape to the bottom of the threaded connection. If you cannot find room to wrap the tape on, apply RECTORSEAL/Slic-Tite to the bottom one inch of threads.

Now, shipped with the faucet you will find a flat, fiber washer to insert into the bottom of the draw-nut, in the standard, right hand thread side. The washer will rest on the top of the horseshoe, inside the draw-nut (see Illus. 112).

Next, unthread the draw-nut almost off the horseshoe. To do this, you will rotate the nut in a *clockwise* direction as you look down into the nut, from above. If the nut comes completely off in your hand, start it back onto the horseshoe by rotating the draw-nut in a *counterclockwise* direction as viewed from above. Turn the nut only one or two complete revolutions onto the horsehoe.

Now, while looking at the top of the horseshoe, you will see two pegs sticking out of the flat end. There are two corresponding holes in the bottom of the faucet's threaded connection. You will have to visually align the two pegs with the two holes. Start threading the large brass draw-nut onto the faucet's threaded connection, by hand, in a *clockwise* direction as viewed from underneath, while holding the horseshoe steady with your other hand.

As you turn the nut, the two parts, the faucet and the horseshoe will be drawn together and mate (hopefully). Go slowly, using only your fingers to rotate the draw-nut. When you get to the point that you can no longer turn the draw-nut by hand, then twist, very slightly, the horseshoe one direction and then the other. You are trying to "feel" the two pegs rubbing the two holes. When twisting the horseshoe, continue trying to turn the draw-nut by hand in a *clockwise* direction of rotation as viewed from underneath.

When the pegs align with the holes, you will be able to gain another three or four complete turns on the draw-nut. Then, use the basin wrench or the slide-jaw pliers to lightly snug up the draw-nut in the *clockwise* rotation.

Now, on your new faucet, you will find two adapters on the legs of the horseshoe. Undo the slip nuts and discard the adapters. You will not need them when using the Speedway or Speed-flex supplies. The adapters are for using rigid, threaded pipe when the faucet is mounted to a thin, too easily flexible restaurant stainless steel sink. You will install your new supplies as we did for the 4 inch center set (see pages 75-77).

Now, thread the spout into the mixing valve body and remove the aerator from the end of the spout. The aerator will unthread in a *clockwise* direction as viewed from above the spout, looking down. After opening the angle stops slowly, open the hot and cold valves of the single post valve

and purge the faucet of dirt, and excess RECTORSEAL/Slic-Tite.

Now, fill the bowl and check for leaks as we did for the 4 inch center set and the wide-spread faucets. If you have a leak at the large brass draw-nut, use the basin wrench or the slide-jaw pliers if you have room and *slowly* tighten the nut further in a *clockwise* direction as viewed from underneath. If the leak does not stop, then you know that the two pegs did not find the two holes. It's sort of like being a matchmaker suffering from client divorce. Turn the angle stops off, by turning their handles in a *clockwise* direction. Then back the large draw-nut off in a *counterclockwise* direction as viewed from underneath. Back up the draw-nut for just a few complete rotations. Then again, slowly twist the horseshoe until the pegs find the holes. When you can turn the water on at the angle stops and find merely a small drip, then

use the RIDGID basin wrench to really snug up the draw-nut in a *clockwise* direction.

If you find a drip originating between the threads where the spout threads into the valve body, turn the hot and cold handles off. Unthread the spout in a *counterclockwise* direction. Apply some Teflon tape to the fine threads of the spout. Then reintroduce the spout into the valve body and start the threads *slowly*, in a *clockwise* direction as viewed from above. When the spout aligns over the sink or waste and it becomes difficult to turn anymore, stop and test for leaks. Your spout might have a female collar or male nut at the base, but they both unthread and rethread in the same direction.

Well, that's the end of the bathroom sink faucet section. I'll be referring to different parts of it throughout the rest of the book. Hope you found it worthwhile.

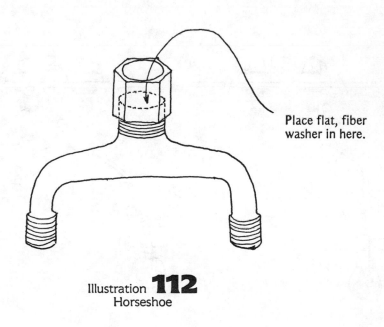

Place flat, fiber washer in here.

Illustration **112**
Horseshoe

## KITCHEN SINK FAUCETS

This section is going to take us through the process of replacing the most popular types of kitchen sink faucets. We begin by removing and installing the basic wall-hung designs after which we start again with the removal and installation of the basic deck-mount designs.

There are procedures we use in this section that we already have used for bathroom faucets and you will be referred back to those procedures when they are called for.

The kitchen sink faucet needs replacing more often than the bathroom faucet because it gets many times more use. Because of the labor cost to have a plumber replace the kitchen sink faucet, this faucet is required to stay "on-line" long after it should be retired.

## Wall-Hung Designs . . . Removal And Installation

Wall-hung kitchen sink faucets as illustrated on pages 99-102 are mounted or "hung" on the wall, above the sink. Most kitchen sinks with wall-hung faucets do not have angle stops to shut the water service off to the faucet. This is especially true for the older homes.

This absence of angle stops is due to the wall-hung's requirement for support from rigid pipe, inside the wall, to maintain the faucet's solid position above the sink. The connections of the wall-hung faucet accept threaded pipe, unlike the slip nuts and flexible supplies used in deck-mounted sink faucets (Illus. 113).

Sometimes a plumber, who had a heart, installed gate valves in the hot and cold water pipes inside the wall, under the sink. The gate valves (see Illus. 114)

themselves were plastered over leaving the handles to protrude through the plaster, plainly visible, if they did exist. The handles of the gate valves were usually painted over each time the kitchen was painted, so the handles can be overlooked if close observation is not given. You might also have what are called "screwdriver stops," not gate valves. The screwdriver stops have a stem, without a round handle. By placing the bit of a large slotted screwdriver in the slot, you can rotate the stems in a clockwise direction and shut the water off.

I still recommend to my customers who are building new homes or remodeling their existing kitchens, to seriously consider a wall-hung faucet. I do so because the height of the faucet can be adjusted to best suit the height of the homeowner. And, more importantly, the wall-hung

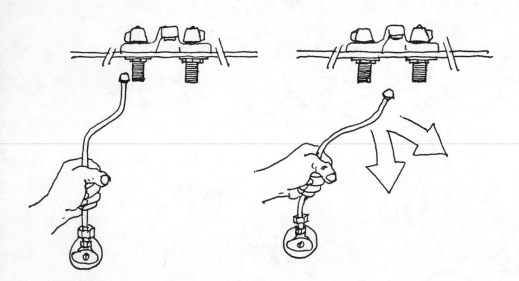
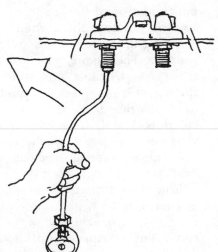

Illustration **113**
Deck-mounted Faucet with Flexible Supplies

faucet can be so installed as to best allow for the clearance necessary for washing large, cumbersome gourmet cookware, which is a feat not so practical with most deck-mounted faucets (except for the MOEN 7345 "Riser" — see Illus. 115).

I have *one* wall-hung kitchen sink faucet in mind for this type of installation: The MOEN 7400, with Delux Swivel Aerator. It is an extremely well engineered workhorse aside from being the most handsome looking of all wall-hungs (see Illus. 116).

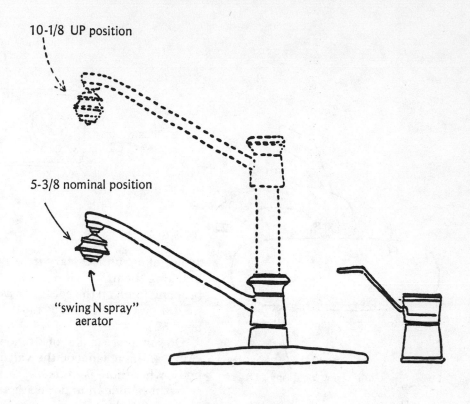

10-1/8 UP position

5-3/8 nominal position

"swing N spray" aerator

Illustration **115**
Moen Model 7345—The Riser

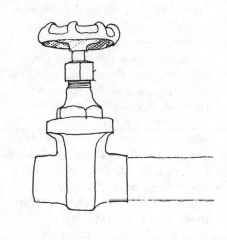

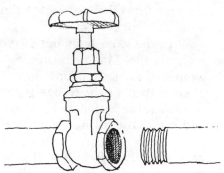

Illustration **114**
Shut-off Valves (Gate Valves)

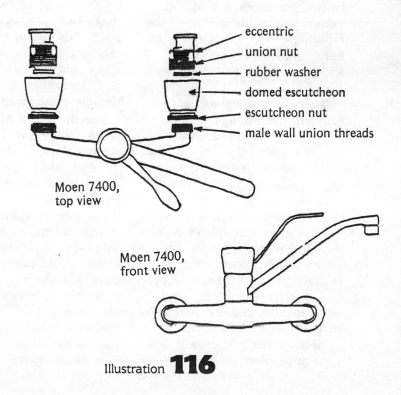

eccentric
union nut
rubber washer
domed escutcheon
escutcheon nut
male wall union threads

Moen 7400, top view

Moen 7400, front view

Illustration **116**

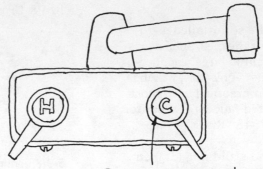

Illustration
**118**

Remove monograms and screws,
and handles and lock nuts underneath.

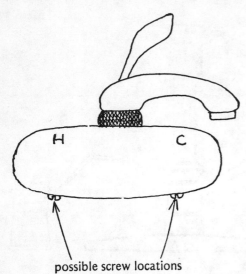

possible screw locations

Illustration
**117**

To remove the wall-hung faucet, not served by shut-off valves, you will have to turn the building's water supply off at the hand operated shut-off valve and/or the meter valve. See pages 3 and 4.

The most critical aspect of removing wall-hung faucets is getting the eccentrics (connections) at the wall, off the nipples inside the wall, without damaging the nipples. Too few plumbers ever replace the nipples when they replace the faucet. If the nipples happen to be *brass* ones, you probably will not have to worry about damaging them. However, galvanized steel nipples quite often break off the last three or so threads in the eccentric, or inside the wall fitting.

Since we do not know which type of nipples you have, and to avoid taking unnecessary risks of breaking them, we will use our propane torch on the eccentric as we did on the angle stops (see page 52).

On some rare makes of kitchen sink wall-hung faucets, the valve body, what there is of one, is sometimes hidden underneath a bulky, ugly, chrome cover (see Illus. 117). If you have such a white elephant, look for some possible machine screws on the front, bottom cover. They will hold the cover in place. Also, the knurled collar or nut at the base of the swing spout might have to be undone and lifted off in order to remove the cover. Or, you might find one or two more machine screws near the swing spout that will need removal aside from the lower ones before the cover can be removed.

For the faucet which has a spout resembling Illus. 118, remove the monograms on the hot and cold handles (try using the slide-jaw pliers to grip them and unthread them). Underneath the monograms, you will see slotted or Phillips head machine screws. Remove them by backing them up in a *counterclockwise* direction with the appropriate screwdriver. In back of the handles, you will see thin, flat nuts. Undo these nuts with the 8 inch adjustable wrench, turning the nuts in a *counterclockwise* direc-tion as viewed from in front. With the handles off, the cover will pull forward and off.

On either design illustrated in 117 & 118, you might find ⅜ inch copper tubing connecting the mixing valve or hot and cold valves without the use of the conventional eccentrics used on all standard wall-hung faucets. Instead, there will be two brass fittings with a built-in offset, which employs flare nuts (little hexagonal nuts resembling brass ferrule compression nuts). Undo these flare nuts in a *counter-clockwise* direction of rotation using the 8 inch adjustable wrench. The valve body will part from the brass flare fittings, at the wall.

With the valve body out of the way, use the 8 inch adjustable wrench if the flare fittings have wrench flats, or the 8 inch pipe wrench if the fittings are round, and rotate the fittings in a *coun-terclockwise* direction until they part from the wall nipples. If your faucet resembles Illus. 117, there will probably be a wall plate se-cured to the wall with wood screws. Remove the wood screws in a *counterclockwise* direction of rotation and the plate will part from the wall.

IMPORTANT NOTE: Before applying any tools to this task, I suggest that you lay some cardboard or several layers of old towels in the bottom of the sink.

On conventional wall-hung faucets resembling the one in Illus. 119, we will first look and see which part, the eccentric or the valve body, retains the wall union nut. To find this out, try to decide which side of the wall union nut exhibits an exposed thread or threads. When standing in front of the sink, looking at the faucet, if you see threads on the *front* side of the union nut (see Illus. 119), rotate the union nut with the 12 or 15 inch adjustable wrench in a *clockwise* direction. In this case, the wall union nut is part of the eccentric.

If you find exposed threads on the *back* side of the wall union nut (see Illus. 120), use the 12 or 15 inch adjustable wrench to turn the nuts in a *counterclockwise* direction of rotation to free the valve from the eccentrics.

When loosening the wall union nuts, regardless of which parts retain them, hold onto the faucet body with one hand. This is to prevent it from falling into the sink and causing a bad chip in an enameled, cast iron sink, or from going completely through the bottom of an old china sink (thus the reason for the cardboard or towels).

With the valve body gone, pick up the 15 inch adjustable wrench and adjust the jaws to fit the flat sides of the eccentric. Then open the jaws "just a hair" more and put the wrench down close by. With your safety glasses on, light the propane torch and direct the flame to the eccentrics from the side (one at a time). Keep the flame on the outside end of the eccentric, *away from the tile or plaster wall.* Hold the flame on the eccentric for about one minute. Then, shut the torch off and set it down safely aside. Quickly reapply the jaws of the

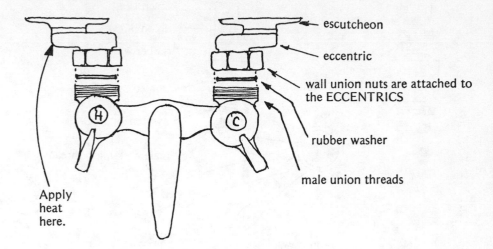

Illustration **119**
Wall Union Nuts Attached to Eccentrics

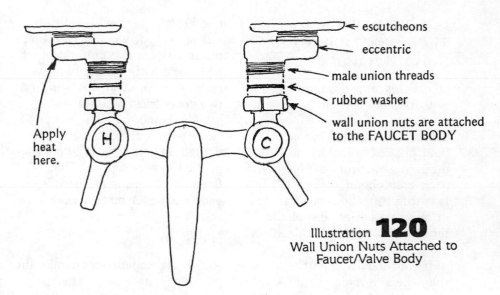

Illustration **120**
Wall Union Nuts Attached to Faucet/Valve Body

adjustable wrench to the flat sides of the eccentric and rotate it in a *counterclockwise* direction. Back off the eccentrics for three or four complete revolutions before stopping to let them cool off.

If your eccentrics come off without any damage to the existing nipples, and the nipples happen *not* to be brass, you have a decision to make:

A. Should I go after the steel nipples and remove them with the ACE EX-7, ½ inch pipe nipple back-out and replace them with new *brass* nipples? . . .OR

B. Should I just wrap the existing nipples with three or four wraps of Teflon tape if the nipples prove to be undamaged?

We discussed the procedure for using the ACE EX-7, ½ inch pipe nipple back-out before, on page 53.

Take a break!

101

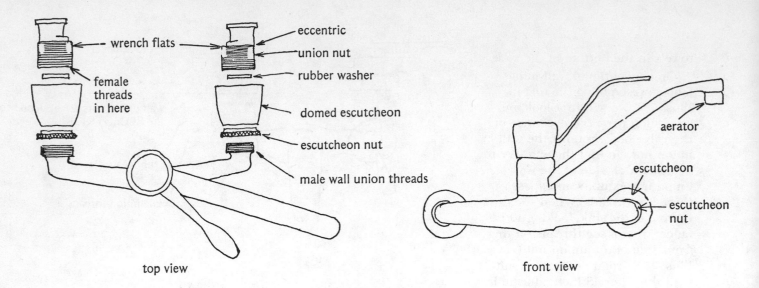

wrench flats

eccentric

union nut

rubber washer

female threads in here

domed escutcheon

escutcheon nut

male wall union threads

top view

aerator

escutcheon

escutcheon nut

front view

Illustration **121**
Moen 7400 Faucet
Wall-hung

## Installing My Choice, The MOEN 7400, With Swivel Aerator

To use this faucet, the wall nipples must not be more than ½ inch either way from being 8 inches on center. Measure the spread of your present faucet by taking a measurement from the center of each escutcheon at the wall. If it is within this allowable distance, or maybe a perfect 8 inch distance, you can install the MOEN 7400.

If your measurement is more than the allowable ½ inch either way of 8 inches on center, then you will have to choose another wall-hung faucet, preferably one from the list of Suggested Brand Names (see page 41).

Most all kitchen sink wall-hung faucets are installed in a very similar fashion, using almost identical parts. So by reading the following instructions for installing a new MOEN 7400, you will also understand how to install other models.

Inside the MOEN faucet box, you will find several cellophane and kraft paper packets. Inside one packet you will find two thin, chromed escutcheon nuts, which are round with knurling on the outside edges. Also, you will find two eccentrics, with unions attached, and included will be two rubber union washers. The domed escutcheons will be loose-packed in brown paper. The faucet body has male threads on each end which mate to the union nuts.

Guidepost:

1. Thread eccentrics (hand tight only) onto wall nipples.
2. Adjust eccentrics so as to make sure a level, easy mating with the faucet body occurs; and, mark the location of eccentrics with a lipstick, on the wall.
3. Take eccentrics back down and apply RECTORSEAL/Slic-Tite to the female pipe threads of eccentrics.
4. Install rubber union washers into large recesses of eccentrics' union nuts.
5. Reinstall eccentrics, this time using 8 inch pipe wrench.

6. Wrap Teflon tape on the faucet body's male threads (both ends).
7. Slide escutcheon nuts onto faucet body, followed by domed escutcheons.
8. Mate faucet body to eccentrics.
9. Remove aerator and test for leaks.
10. With no leaks, slide escutcheons into place and secure with the escutcheon nuts and replace aerator.

First, let's wrap the wall nipples with several wraps of Teflon tape. Now, by hand, start the eccentrics onto the wall nipples just two complete revolutions, in a *clockwise* direction. Adjust the eccentrics so the union nuts (round, threaded sleeves with wrench flats on the back edge) easily mate to the threaded ends of the faucet body. You will notice that the adjustable spread of the wall unions will mate to the faucet either above or below the height of the wall nipples. Now, with a lipstick or grease pencil, make a mark on each eccentric and on the wall so that you can find the same positions again after we take down the eccentrics. Next, remove the eccentrics using a *counterclockwise* direction of rotation.

Now, put some RECTORSEAL/ Slic-Tite in the female threads of each eccentric and then insert the rubber union washers into the larger female recesses of the round union nuts. There are wrench flats on the back side of the externally threaded union nuts (see Illus. 121). Shove the union washers all the way to the back, inside. You may carefully use the slotted screwdriver to push the washers to the back by going around and around the edge of the rubber washer, pushing a little at each point until the washer is flat against the flat inside back of the union nut. Use the 8 or 12 inch pipe wrench to reinstall the eccentrics to the wall nipples.

With Teflon tape wrapped on each end of the faucet body's male union threads, slide the round escutcheon nuts, flat side first, onto the faucet, far up each side. Next, slide the domed escutcheon onto the faucet body, with the belled side *trailing*.

Move these towards the center of the faucet to keep them out of the way.

Now, mate the wall union nuts to the male union threads of the faucet body. This time, use the 12 inch adjustable wrench to snug up the wall union nuts to the faucet body, using a *counter-clockwise* direction of rotation as viewed from in *front* of the faucet. Leave the round escutcheon nuts and the domed escutcheons where they are for now.

Next, turn the aerator with your fingers in a clockwise direction as viewed from *above* the spout and you will remove it from the end of the spout. Check to make sure that the rubber washer with the fine mesh in the middle came free with the aerator (see Illus. 122).

Now, lift up on the handle. We are ready to resume water service to the building and check for leaks.

On most conventional wall-hung designs, the domed escutcheons are much flatter and usually thread onto the outside of the eccentrics before they are in turn threaded onto the wall nipples. But just about everything else is the same procedure as we followed here, for the MOEN 7400.

## Testing The New Wall-Hung For Leaks

The title says it all. It's real quick, straightforward, and too short for a Guidepost. So, just dive in why don't you.

With the aerator off the end of the spout, we are ready to return the water service to the building. We left the faucet handle of the MOEN 7400 *up*, so the water coming back into the building will not produce a shock for the water piping and cause a new leak at the weakest link in the fresh water system. On older, conventional faucets, we would have left both the hot and cold valves open, just a bit.

Now, go turn the water back on and do not waste time in coming back to the sink. If you had to leave the lowest hose bib open during the installation, turn it off *slowly* when the water once more starts coming out the spout.

Back at the sink, slowly push the handle down and off. When the handle is in the full OFF position, look for leaks around the eccentrics where they thread onto the wall nipples. Also check the wall unions for leaks. If you have a drip at the wall unions, place the 12 inch adjustable

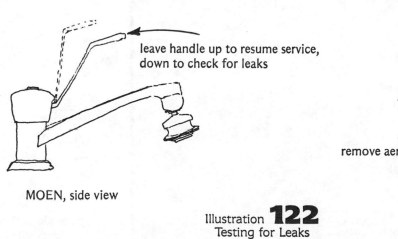

leave handle up to resume service, down to check for leaks

MOEN, side view

remove aerator

OFF

Illustration **122**
Testing for Leaks

wrench on the wrench flats on the back side of the union nuts and tighten them in ¼ turn increments in a *counterclockwise* direction as viewed from in *front*, until the drip stops.

If you have a drip at the eccentric and wall nipple, you will once again have to turn the water off to the building, remove the faucet body from the wall unions and further tighten the eccentrics onto the wall nipples. Then reinstall the faucet body and check for leaks again.

With no drips, you can then slide the domed escutcheons back against the wall, followed by the round escutcheon nuts. Thread the escutcheon nuts onto the fine threads protruding out the hole in the domed escutcheon. Use a *clockwise* direction of rotation on the knurled escutcheon nut and tighten it to finger tight limits before putting just a half-turn more on it with the slide-jaw pliers.

If you managed to turn the cold inlet valve to the water heater off, you will have to turn the valve back on *before* testing the new faucet for leaks on the hot side.

With the aerator still off the end of the spout, place a hand towel over the end of the spout and hold it there with one hand. With the free hand, lift the handle all the way *up*. On other conventional faucets, we would open both valves, hot and cold. With the MOEN 7400 handle all the way up, swing the handle from side to side *slowly*, purging the hot and cold lines of excess debris and RECTORSEAL/Slic-Tite.

If you have a friend present, and you can explain or demonstrate to him or her how to shut the building's water off, I have this suggestion: After removing the old faucet and either having replaced the old wall nipples with new *brass* ones, or having wrapped the old nipples with Teflon tape, purge the water pipes *before* you begin to install the new faucet. You do this by holding one large towel over each wall nipple and have your friend turn the water back on and then count to five slowly. At the count of five shut the water back off and proceed to install the new wall-hung faucet. This will remove most all loose scale, grit and other line debris left in the pipes *before* it gets trapped in the faucet's internal filter, inside the MOEN cartridge.

If you are afraid of getting a bath while holding the towels over the nipples, you could instruct your friend to do so and just tell them to stand there holding the towels until you return (I didn't say that).

You may rethread the aerator back onto the end of the spout in a *counterclockwise* direction as viewed from *above* the spout, *after* purging the hot and cold lines.

You are now back in business! As with all MOEN single-handle faucets, you may select the water temperature before turning the faucet on. Over the years, this could represent a big savings in water bills and heat energy.

Take a well earned rest!

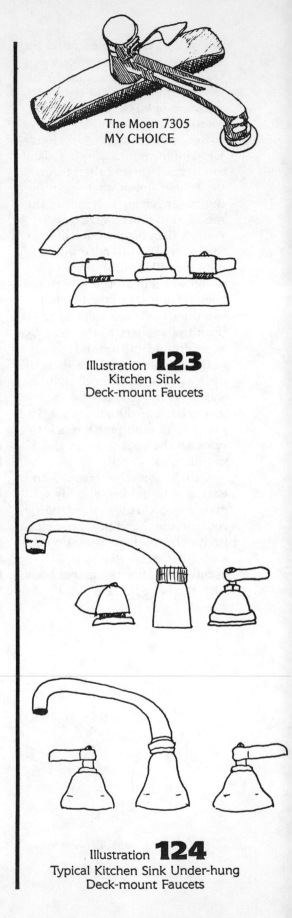

The Moen 7305
MY CHOICE

Illustration **123**
Kitchen Sink
Deck-mount Faucets

Illustration **124**
Typical Kitchen Sink Under-hung
Deck-mount Faucets

## Deck-Mount Designs . . . Removal And Installation

Kitchen sink deck-mount faucets can be divided into two major types: those having the valve itself on *top* of the sink, with the connections hanging down below the sink, and those having the valves underneath the sink with the handles and trim *only*, on top of the sink. We will refer to this latter type as under-hung deck-mount faucets. Illus. 123 is the typical deck-mounted faucet. Illus. 124 depicts the under-hung deck-mount faucet (handles and spout only above the sink).

If you have a single-post faucet on your kitchen sink, it will be removed and installed just as we did the bathroom lavatory single-post faucet (see pages 95-97).

Removal and installation of the typical deck-mount faucet (Illus. 123) is the same one we followed for the 4 inch center set, in pages 69 & 74-77, so we will not have a Guidepost for this faucet.

If your deck-mount kitchen sink faucet has a dish spray hose to be mounted in a separate, fourth hole, be careful! Take extra care when snugging up the cheap, pressed steel lock/mounting nut for the spray-head base. It can have sharp edges and it will collapse when a good torque is applied to it. It is ironic, but even the most expensive faucets can be found with this cheapo nut supplied. However, lately there has been some improvement in the design used with a number of companies making the dish spray hardware. The improved nut is made of ABS plastic and has a wide flanged diameter, eliminating the need for a flange washer (usually made of steel and ready to flake off into your eyes when you try to remove it). Who knows how long it will take though

for the cheapo pressed steel nut to go the way of the Dodo.

If you have a three-hole sink or four-hole sink and an air gap for the dishwasher already occupies the fourth hole, you may purchase a deck-mount faucet that has the dish spray as part of the faucet's mounting base. The MOEN model having the dish spray in the base is number 7831.

I personally dislike dish sprays; they are time bombs for leaks and ruin many a cabinet, yearly. Besides, the MOEN Delux Swivel Aerator does an equally fine job cleaning dishes and shampooing.

When removing old faucets with the dish spray hose, which will not again be used, I do not waste any time trying to unthread the hose from the valve body. I just pick up my trusty pocket knife and cut the hose in two. You can then yank the spray head out of the flange or base on top of the sink, leaving you a clean shot at the faucet lock/mounting nuts.

## Under-Hung Deck-Mount Types . . . Removal And Installation

For under-hung deck-mount kitchen sink faucets, those that mount under the sink or counter and have only the hot and cold handles and the swing spout showing above the sink (see Illus. 124), removal and installation is very similar to the wide-spread bathroom lavatory faucets (see pages 70-71 & 83-88).

This is a short, "quickie" title, so just plow through it — it won't take you but five minutes, or less.

Start by removing the handles, escutcheon nuts, and the escutcheons from the sink or counter (remember, this is covered in the bathroom lavatory wide-spread removal). With the 12 or 15 inch adjustable wrench, unthread the thin, brass top lock/mounting nuts at the base of each valve, above the sink (see Illus. 125 & 127). Undo these nuts in a *coun-*

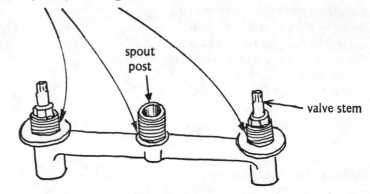

Illustration **125**
One-Piece/Integral Spout Under-hung Faucet

105

*terclockwise* direction as viewed from above. Sometimes the basin wrench will grip these large diameter nuts, using the wrench in the inverted position.

The spout is fastened to the faucet manifold either above or below the sink or counter (see Illus. 125, 126, 128 & 129). Look under the sink or counter; if your faucet manifold has a small nut in the bottom center, the spout connection is joined to the manifold in the same manner as spouts for lavatory wide-spread faucets.

If you undo this little nut in a *counterclockwise* direction as viewed from underneath, and have the top lock nuts removed, the faucet will part from the sink, from *below*, leaving the spout base left in place. Watch your head! Make sure to have your safety glasses on!

With the valves and manifold gone, undo the lock/mounting nut holding the spout to the sink or counter and then lift it off the sink or counter from *above*. You undo the spout lock/mounting nut in a *counterclockwise* direction as viewed from below.

If you have a type of under-hung faucet that resembles Illus. 125, the spout connection is an *integral* part of the manifold. After undoing the top lock nuts at the base of the valves and the one at the base of the spout post, the faucet will part from the sink or counter, from *underneath*.

To get at the lock/mounting nut for the spout post, first unthread the knurled collar or thin nut that secures the swing spout to the post. Turn this collar or nut in a *counterclockwise* direction as viewed from above. You may also use the slide-jaw pliers for this task. Lift the spout up while slowly swinging the spout from one side to the other. When the spout comes free, lift off the

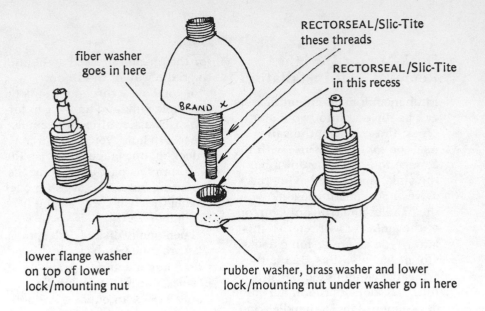

fiber washer goes in here

RECTORSEAL/Slic-Tite these threads

RECTORSEAL/Slic-Tite in this recess

BRAND X

lower flange washer on top of lower lock/mounting nut

rubber washer, brass washer and lower lock/mounting nut under washer go in here

Illustration **126**
Under-hung Faucet with Separate Spout Base

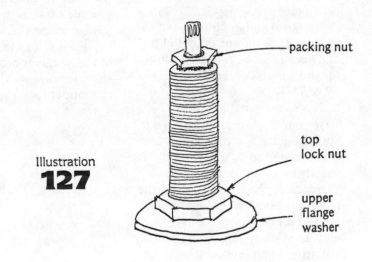

packing nut

Illustration **127**

top lock nut

upper flange washer

BRAND X

Illustration **128**
Separate Spout Base

106

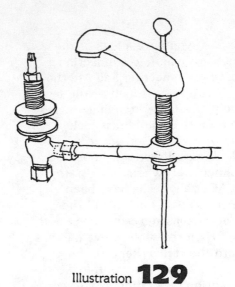

Illustration **129**

escutcheon and the *top* lock/mounting nut will be visible on top of the sink or counter. Undo this nut also in a *counter-clockwise* direction.

The faucet should now drop into the bottom of the sink cabinet.

Take a break!

---

**See Important Notice
on page 88.**

---

## Installing The Under-Hung Kitchen Deck-Mount Faucets — Separate Spout Base

We will first install the separate spout base model of under-hung faucet. Again, because of the almost identical procedure to the installation of lavatory wide-spreads, we will refer you back to that section for some of this instruction.

At least for kitchen under-hungs (compared to lavatory wide-spreads) you have a larger cabinet to work in with manifold connections that, for the most part, are in straight lines.

Guidepost:

1. Apply plumber's putty to spout base and install in center hole (or appropriate hole if you have a four-hole sink, with air gap).
2. Thread lower lock/mounting nut down threaded exterior of each valve, followed by a large flange washer.
3. Lift valves up from underneath and nest spout connection in manifold recess (after inserting fiber washer into recess).
4. Apply another washer to the bottom of spout connection, protruding through manifold, followed by brass washer and brass lock/mounting nut.
5. Turn the lock/mounting nuts *up* the valves until they contact the bottom of the sink or counter.
6. Wrap putty snakes around the base of each valve where they protrude through sink or counter.
7. Drop flange washers down valves and then thread remaining top lock/mounting nuts down valves to top of sink or counter.
8. Further tighten lower lock/mounting nuts under sink or counter.
9. Apply final torque to top lock/mounting nuts.
10. Install spout and remove aerator.
11. Install supplies.
12. Open angle stops and valves and check for leaks.

Look at Illustration 126. Now, unpackage all the parts in the box. You will find the spout base separated from the swing spout, in most cases. There are usually four large flange washers (metal) and maybe four large, thin, flat rubber washers; the lock/mounting nuts (four for the valves and one for the spout), and the faucet slip nuts for the supply connections. The flat rubber washers are for slipping over the valves above and below the sink, supposedly eliminating the need for plumber's putty. You can use the rubber ones too, but *still* use the putty as directed.

On a three-hole sink or counter, set the spout base in the center hole, on top of a putty snake (if it would not adhere to the bottom of the spout base). From underneath, place one flange washer (it might be cup-shaped; cup side is to be installed *up*) over the threaded connection of the spout. Then, thread the lock/mounting nut *up* the spout connection, using a *clockwise* direction of rotation as viewed from underneath. Now, thread the nut up as far as you can, using just your fingers. Some manufacturers test their faucets with water, instead of air, before shipping them. In this case, there might be a fiber washer stuck to the bottom of the spout connection. You will have to peel the fiber washer off before you can start the lock/mounting nut up the threads. Don't lose the washer, you will need it later.

If possible, I will always turn the spout base so that any name of the manufacturer is facing out and centered. Snug up the lock/mounting nut on the spout connection, tightly, using a *clockwise* direction of rotation.

Next, thread the lower lock nuts down the threaded exterior of the valves (see Illus. 126). Thread them down almost to the last thread for now. Then, drop the two large flange washers, one on each valve, down the valves so that they rest upon the lock/mounting nuts already threaded down. If there are any differences between the diameter and thickness of the lock/mounting nuts, put the larger ones on the valves first, for the underside.

Now lift the valves up, from underneath, with the fiber washer in the top, female recess of the manifold, like we did for the wide-spread lavatory faucet (see page 84). Now, nest the spout connection in the female recess on top of the manifold. I would suggest that some RECTORSEAL/Slic-Tite be put in the top female recess of the manifold.

Out the bottom hole in the manifold, some smaller diameter male threads will protrude. And, again we have another small rubber washer to slide up this male thread, followed by a flat washer (brass) and finally the small lock/mounting nut (as discussed for the wide-spread, on page 84).

Now, snug up the small brass spout lock/mounting nut using a *clockwise* direction of rotation as viewed from underneath. The 6 inch adjustable wrench is a very comfortable tool for doing this. While still under the sink or counter, turn the lower lock/mounting nuts *up* the valves by using your fingers, all the way until they contact the bottom of the sink or counter.

Next, make some small putty snakes and lay them around the base of each valve protruding up through the sink or counter. Now, drop the other two flange washers, one on each valve, down to rest on the top of the sink or counter. Using your fingers, chase the other two lock/mounting nuts down the valves from above, using a *clockwise* direction of rotation (see Illus. 130). Now, go back under and rotate each lower lock/mounting nut one more complete revolution in the *clockwise* direction using the basin wrench. At last, again from above, snug up the top lock/

mounting nuts using the 12 or 15 inch adjustable wrench or the basin wrench (inverted) until the plumber's putty has all but squished out from underneath the flange washers.

Take a break!

•

Left in the box is the spout with the knurled collar or the thin nut with wrench flats on the outside. If you have the small tin of stem grease, you can use your "pinkie" to spread some grease around on the inside of the spout connection and some around the male end of the spout that marries into the female.

With the faucet set upon the sink or counter, it is now time to install the supplies. It is the same, exact procedure we followed for the bathroom 4 inch center set on pages 75 to 77. Leave the faucet escutcheons and the escutcheon nuts *off* the valves, *for now*. Remove the aerator from the end of the spout by rotating it in a *clockwise* direction of rotation as viewed from *above*.

Whew! Hang in there! Almost got it. Now, open each faucet valve slightly by just setting the handles on the stems, without inserting the machine screws. Also, open the valves under the sink (angle stops) slightly. With the hand towel placed over the end of the spout, turn the water service to the building on or have a friend do it for you if it is not already on. Open the faucet valves *full* when water starts issuing out the spout and purge the faucet of excess crud and RECTORSEAL/Slic-Tite. Then, open the angle stops all the way.

Then begin to look for leaks at the spout-to-manifold connection and at your supply connections: angle stop ferrule nuts; angle stop packing nuts; and the faucet slip

nuts. If you have a leak at the spout-to-manifold connection, leave the faucet on and use the RIDGID basin wrench or the 6 inch adjustable wrench to further tighten the small brass lock/mounting nut, you got it, in a *clockwise* direction. Stop immediately when the drip stops.

After any leaks have been checked, you may install the escutcheons and escutcheon nuts and then screw the valve handles onto the stems. Replace the aerator using a *counterclockwise* direction of rotation as viewed from *above*, and finally snap the hot and cold monograms in place. CONGRATULATIONS!

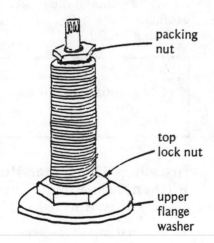

Illustration **130**
Wide-spread Valve

packing nut

top lock nut

upper flange washer

## Installing The Under-Hung Kitchen Deck-Mount Faucets — Integral Spout Post

This section comprises the second design of under-hung deck-mount faucet that we deal with in this book. It is an easy procedure to follow, so let's put one foot in front of the other. Note Illus. 131.

Guidepost:

1. Thread larger diameter lock/ mounting nuts down valves and spout post, followed by flange washers.
2. Wrap plumber's putty snakes around holes on sink or counter top.
3. Lift valve *up* through holes in sink or counter, from underneath.
4. Drop remaining flange washers down valve and spout post followed by threading the remaining lock/mounting nuts down to contact the sink or counter top.
5. Set escutcheons over valves and spout post and adjust valve height for proper penetration of escutcheon nuts into packing nuts with escutcheons in place.
6. From under sink or counter, thread lower lock/mounting nuts *up* the valves and spout post until contacting the underside of sink or counter.
7. Remove escutcheons and tighten top lock/mounting nuts until the plumber's putty has stopped oozing out from under flange washers.
8. From underneath, once again tighten lower lock/mounting nuts, applying final torque to these nuts.
9. Put finish torque on top lock/ mounting nuts and then snug up the packing nuts on top of the valves.

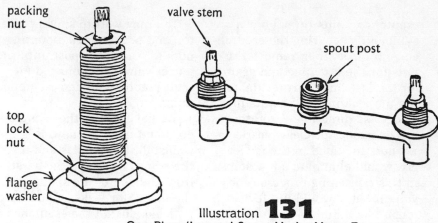

**Illustration 131**
One-Piece/Integral Spout Under-Hung Faucet

10. Install supplies, remove aerator from end of spout and install spout.
11. Open valves and test for leaks.
12. With no leaks, install escutcheons and handles and any hot or cold monograms.

Congratulations!

First, take a look at Illus. 131 again. This second type of under-hung, with the spout post as an integral part of the manifold, will now be installed. So, unwrap all of the parts. Then, thread the larger of the lock/mounting nuts down the valves and spout post, followed by the large flange washers. *Clockwise* direction on nuts.

Make three plumber's putty snakes and roll them around the holes in the sink or counter top. Now, lift the faucet *up* through the holes in the sink or counter from underneath. While holding it in place, drop the remaining flange washers down over the valves and spout post to rest upon the putty snakes (see Illus. 130).

Then thread the top lock/ mounting nuts down the valves and spout post so that you can put the escutcheons over the valves and have the proper amount of valve protruding up, allowing you to thread the escutcheon nuts into the packing nuts, with the escutcheons in place. Whew!

Now, from underneath thread the lower lock/mounting nuts *up* the valves and spout post in a *clockwise* direction using your fingers. When you make contact with the bottom of the sink or counter, then unthread the escutcheon nuts and lift the escutcheons off the valves and spout post.

Then, tighten the top lock/ mounting nuts using the 15 inch adjustable wrench or the RIDGID basin wrench (inverted) in a *clockwise* direction until the plumber's putty has squished out from under the flange washers. Get down again, and from underneath, tighten the lower lock/ mounting nuts in a *clockwise* direction, applying the finishing torque on these lower nuts. Even more plumber's putty will have squished out from the flange washers above. Use the basin wrench this time.

Now, set the escutcheons over the valves and spout post to double check for proper penetration of the escutcheon nuts into the packing nuts. You want the escutcheon nuts to rest *flat* on top of the escutcheons, securing them firmly in place. If the

109

escutcheon nuts thread down sufficiently securing the escutcheons in place, then remove the nuts for the last time and again for the last time, further tighten the top lock/mounting nuts in a *clockwise* direction of rotation.

The rubber or clear plastic washers included in the faucet box would eliminate a few steps in this tightening process (and you probably would not feel so much like a human yo-yo) but in time they tend to crack, dry out and begin letting splash water seep under the valves and cause splash leaks. So, thus the plumber's putty and a little extra exercise.

You may wait to snug up the top and bottom lock/mounting nuts for the spout post until the faucet valves are adjusted for their escutcheons and escutcheon nuts.

We have left off the escutcheons and nuts, for now. It is time to install the supplies and install the spout. Unthread the aerator from the end of the spout. Test the faucet for leaks. If you have no leaks, install the escutcheons and nuts *for the last time*. Replace the aerator, install the handles and put any hot and cold monograms in place, for good.

Congratulations! Sit down for a good spell and rest your knees.

---

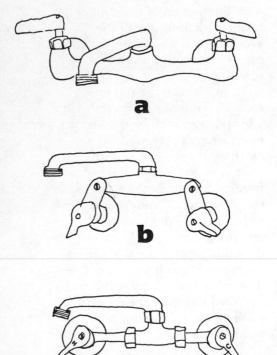

**a**

**b**

**c**

Illustration **132**
Wall-hung
Laundry Tray Faucets

## LAUNDRY TUB/ TRAY FAUCETS

### Removal And Installation Of Wall-Hung Faucets

This section is a fairly long one because we are dealing with three wall-hung designs, two of which I wish to warn you about. The complete section will cover the three wall-hung versions and one deck-mount which is discussed further on (see page 113).

The first version of wall-hung faucets (Illus. 132a) is very similar to the wall-hung kitchen sink faucet. For this design removal will be the same as is discussed in the kitchen sink faucet section on pages 98-101.

In the second type of wall-hung faucet (see Illus. 132b) the hot and cold valves are separate, each having a long, round "tongue" which is cast 90 degrees to the valve itself. The valves have ½ inch female iron pipe threads in the back, which thread *directly*

onto the wall nipples. Unless the valves are shipped with handles already fastened to the valve stems, with visible hot and cold markings or monograms, you could install the wrong valve onto the nipples. *Cold* is always on the *right* and *hot* on the *left*. I mean should be. Many times the water has been "roughed in" with the hot and cold water lines crossed.

The standard travel for the handles is *lift* for *on* and *down* for *off*. If you install the valves onto the wrong nipples, this travel will be reversed.

When I replace the faucet in Illus. 132b I remove it in this manner: Pick up the mini-hacksaw and saw the round tongues in two, on each side of the swing spout's manifold barrel. Then, with the 15 inch adjustable wrench, placed on the wrench flats of the valves, rotate the valves in a *counterclockwise* direction of rotation as viewed from in *front* of the faucet.

The faucet depicted in Illus. 132b is one of two that I never did care for, and I confess to feeling a slight enjoyment when I cut this "turkey" free. There! Now you are ready to install a new tray faucet, and hopefully it will not be this one.

If you presently have this design of faucet, and it leaks at these manifold-to-tongue connections, you might first want to try repairing it before replacing it with a new one.

To try to stop these joints from leaking, back up the slip nuts with the 8 inch adjustable wrench, using a *counterclockwise* direction of rotation as viewed from the *flat*, backside of the slip nut. Unthread the nuts all the way off the male threads of the manifold barrel. Then, cut away any remaining rubber cone washer present on the round tongues. After doing this, wrap the male threads of the manifold barrel with Teflon tape, going around for six complete wraps. Now, liberally apply some RECTORSEAL/Slic-Tite in the female threads of the slip nuts. Then, wrap some graphite string packing around the valve tongues, where they enter the manifold barrel. Tighten the slip nuts back onto the barrel, turn the faucet on and check for leaks.

To install a new faucet of the same design, you hot-shots may use the following Guidepost. It is followed by the thorough text for the rest of us cowards, greenhorns, etc.

Guidepost:

1. Wrap the old or new wall nipples with Teflon tape.
2. RECTORSEAL/Slic-Tite the female threads of the valve bodies. (Apply the pipe joint compound in the female threads.)
3. Hand tighten the valves onto the wall nipples for four to six revolutions (whichever is possible) in a *clockwise* direction.
4. Leave the tongue of the COLD valve pointing *down,* to the 6 o'clock position. Leave the tongue of the HOT valve pointing *up,* to the 12 o'clock position.
5. Install the cone washers, friction rings, and slip nuts onto the valve tongues.
6. Slide manifold barrel onto hot valve tongue.
7. Bring valve tongues horizontal.
8. Center manifold barrel on both valve tongues.
9. Tighten the slip nuts onto the manifold barrel.
10. Install the spout (if it is not already installed on the barrel).
11. With aerator removed, test faucet for leaks. Then replace aerator.

The center manifold barrel, which secures the base of the swing spout, uses rubber cone washers on each side to make a watertight seal on the valve tongues. Friction rings and slip nuts compress the cone washers just like the rubber cone washer angle stops.

Make sure that you wrap the wall nipples with Teflon tape, laying the tape on in a *clockwise* direction. Apply three wraps of the tape. Then, put some RECTORSEAL/Slic-Tite in the female iron pipe threads of the valves. Try to use the brush (inside can) to "drag" the RECTORSEAL/Slic-Tite across the threads from the bottom to the outside. This will pack the valleys of the female threads, lubricating the way for the male nipples.

By checking the handle movement, choose the proper valve for the cold nipple (if the handles are not marked hot and cold). Start the valve onto the cold nipple by threading it on in a *clockwise* direction as viewed from in front.

You should be able to turn the valve onto the nipple for a good four to six complete revolutions, by hand. Leave the tongue of the cold valve pointing down, to the 6 o'clock position. Then, start the hot valve onto its nipple trying to again get from four to six complete revolutions by hand before using the 15 inch adjustable wrench to get one more turn and leave the tongue pointing up, to the 12 o'clock position. Remember, the cold valve is on the right and the hot valve is on the left.

Now, slide one cone washer nut (or slip nut) cup end up, *down* the tongue of the hot valve, followed by the friction ring and the rubber cone washer (beveled side up). Slide the other cone washer or slip nut, cup side down, *up* the tongue of the cold valve, followed by the friction ring and the rubber cone washer, beveled side down. Slide these nuts, rings and washers well onto the tongues, taking them down as close to the base of the tongues as you can (see Illus. 133).

Now, wrap some Teflon tape on the male threads of the center manifold barrel, doing both sides. Wrap the tape on in a *clockwise* direction of wrap as you look down, into the hole. Then, slide one end of the barrel onto the tongue of the HOT valve, pushing it down as far as you can take it. Make sure that the swing spout is going to be on top when it is horizontal. Now, put the jaw of the 12 or 15 inch adjustable wrench on the wrench flats of the hot valve and bring the tongue down to a horizontal position. Do so by following a *clockwise* arc. Next, slide the jaws of the 12 or 15

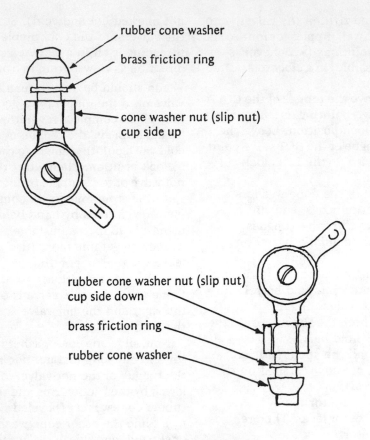

rubber cone washer

brass friction ring

cone washer nut (slip nut)
cup side up

rubber cone washer nut (slip nut)
cup side down

brass friction ring

rubber cone washer

Illustration **133**
"Oakland Pattern"
Laundry Tub Faucet

inch adjustable wrench onto the cold valve and swing the tongue *up,* to a horizontal position, by following a *clockwise* arc.

If the tongue of the cold valve collides with the manifold barrel attached to the hot valve *before* reaching a full horizontal position, mark the tongue of the cold valve where it overlaps (actually underlaps) the swing spout's manifold barrel. Use the mini-hacksaw to cut off this excess length of tongue. If you want the manifold barrel to be centered on the valve tongues, divide the measurement you have just taken in half. Then saw that amount off of *both* tongues.

Now, bring the cold tongue up to the full horizontal position

using the *clockwise* swing. Slide the manifold barrel onto the tongue of the cold valve and center the manifold barrel as best you can. Then, slide the cone washers, friction rings and cone washer nuts down the tongues and start them onto the male threads of the manifold barrel. (I always put some RECTORSEAL/ Slic-Tite in the female threads of the cone washer nuts.)

Use the 12 inch adjustable wrench to snug up the cone washer nuts using a *clockwise* direction of rotation as viewed from the flat sides of the nuts.

You want to have the threaded sleeve for the swing spout (which is part of the manifold barrel) pointing straight up; or if your

swing spout is already connected to the barrel, make sure to have the spout lying in a horizontal position.

If you are installing one of these faucets onto a wall which happens to be set back from the edge of the sink, you might want to cock the swing spout up a bit to give the issuing stream of water a further projectory into the sink.

If your faucet has the sleeve on the manifold barrel, put some RECTORSEAL/Slic-Tite or better yet, some stem grease inside the sleeve and some on the female threads of the nut or collar at the base of the swing spout. Insert the male O-ring end of the spout into the hole of the sleeve, on the top of the manifold barrel and tighten the collar or nut in a *clockwise* direction as viewed from above.

Take a break!

Make sure to leave the valves open just a crack when you return the water service to the building to prevent pressure shock on the piping system. When you return the water service, and have no leaks after shutting the valves completely off, your task is complete.

If you do have a leak at the nipples, where the valves thread on, turn the water back off. Undo the cone washer nuts so you can slide the manifold barrel off the end of one tongue. Then, use the 15 inch adjustable wrench and turn the leaking valve or valves onto the nipples a further turn or two. Recenter the manifold barrel and retighten the cone washer nuts on the male threads of the barrel once again. If you have a leak at the cone washer nuts, use the 12 inch adjustable wrench and tighten them in a *clockwise* direction in ¼ turn increments until the drip stops.

Congratulations!

The third version of wall-hung laundry tray faucet discussed in this book uses a form of an eccentric; rather than a wall union nut to mate the valve body to the eccentric, a machine screw or bolt and flat fiber washer is used (see Illus. 132c). This is the one design that I find most troublesome and I advise you to choose the laundry tray faucet that looks just like a kitchen sink wall-hung but without the aerator (see Illus. 132a).

On the faucet in Illus. 132c the face of the eccentric and the faucet manifold are machined flat, and a fiber washer is sandwiched between the eccentric and the manifold and held tight when a machine screw is inserted through a hole in the faucet body and threaded into a tapped hole in the eccentric. (Lately you might find a bushing that has a tapped hole for the machine screw. This bushing is slid into the eccentric from behind, with its own plastic washer.)

A Phillips head screw or a hex head screw is usually used here so that you can really achieve a high degree of torque when snugging up the screw. A slotted head screw would probably break.

This design might require that you use both hands to give you the added strength to tighten the screw sufficiently enough to achieve a watertight seal at this joint.

I personally do not recommend this design because of pesky drips that show up at these sandwiched joints. The spout is usually shipped loose, and you will have to install it into the familiar male sleeve on top of the manifold as we did for the earlier designs. The same method of positioning the eccentrics as mentioned in the process of wall-hung kitchen sink faucets,

on pages 102-104 is applied here also.

If you are replacing this design of faucet with an identical one, first remove the screws and the spout and manifold will part. Then, remove the eccentrics with the 15 inch adjustable wrench or the 12 or 18 inch pipe wrench by rotating the eccentrics in a *counterclockwise* direction as viewed from in front.

The installation of this type is the reverse. First wrap the wall nipples with Teflon tape, making three wraps minimum in a *clockwise* direction. Put some RECTORSEAL/Slic-Tite in the female threads of the valves and then thread them onto the wall nipples in a *clockwise* direction, trying to get four to six complete revolutions onto the nipples. Again, if the handles are not already threaded onto the valve stems, you will have to check handle movement to decide which valve you want on which side (see page 110).

This faucet should have the manifold and spout mounted above the height of the nipples (see Illus. 132c). Adjust the off-set of the valves to mate with the spout and manifold. Then, insert the small plastic or fiber washers into the female recess on the back side of spout manifold. Now, install flat plastic or fiber washers over the machine screws that secure the manifold to the valves. Then insert the screws through the holes in the manifold and start them into the tapped holes or bushings in the eccentrics. Tighten these screws *very* tightly. Now resume the buildings's water supply and then open the valves and check for leaks.

When installing this faucet, put RECTORSEAL/Slic-Tite in *every* female cavity you find and on all male whatevers.

## The Deck-Mount Laundry Tray Faucet And Plain Ole Hose Bibs

The fourth faucet design is the deck-mount laundry tub faucet. It mounts to the sink or counter *exactly* like the deck-mounted kitchen sink faucet and the 4 inch lavatory center set, using cupped flange washers, typical lock/mounting nuts, faucet slip nuts and the flexible supplies (see pages 74-77).

As a rule, all laundry tray faucets are not a smooth, shiny chrome on the outside. Most are what is called "satin" chromed, or just plain dull chrome. Some are even left in the natural brass, without any plating at all. The swing spouts on laundry tray faucets should have male hose threads on the end. Being able to have hot water at the end of a garden hose, outside, is a great aid in cleaning garbage cans, filling waterbeds inside, etc.

In some very old homes, you might find hose bibs above a cement wash tub (leftover of WW II). A pedestal, cast iron laundry tub is a very common sight in the old, old home. If you do have hose bibs over such sinks, they are the same type installed on the exterior of the building. They unthread in a *counterclockwise* direction and rethread to the nipples or wall fittings in a *clockwise* direction. Some hose bibs are female, having female iron pipe threads on the back. Male hose bibs have external iron pipe threads on a short shank. Regardless of which type you have, both unthread with a *counterclockwise* direction and rethread with a *clockwise* direction.

If you remove the female type, wrap Teflon tape on the nipples and put RECTORSEAL/Slic-Tite in the new female hose bib prior to installing them. On the male type of hose bib, wrap Teflon tape on the male pipe threads and put some RECTORSEAL/Slic-Tite in the female pipe threads of the wall fitting.

Also, check to make sure the packing nuts are tight. These nuts are right below the handles and tighten in a *clockwise* direction of rotation as viewed from above. Most of these packing nuts are loose when you buy them. If you have leaks coming out around the stems when you turn the water back on, these nuts need tightening.

Well, that's it for laundry tray faucets. Let's go have a beer.

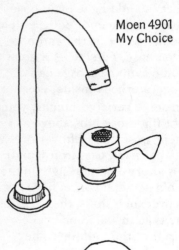

Moen 4901
My Choice

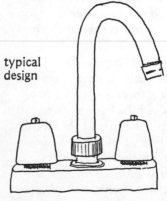

typical design

Illustration **134**
Bar Sink Faucets

## BAR SINK FAUCETS

### Removal And Installation

Bar sink faucets that have individual handles are almost identical to the bathroom lavatory 4 inch center set. The bar sink faucet differs in that it usually has a high-loop spout (see Illus. 134). Sometimes a high-loop spout is designed to swing from side to side, and sometimes not.

The faucet will use the crimped, cupped flange washers and the typical lock/mounting nuts like other deck-mounted faucets and mount in the exact same manner (see pages 74-77). Sometimes you will find the single-post bathroom lavatory faucet used in place of the typical bar sink faucet. Or, it might be the single-post "pantry" or kitchen sink faucet found here.

My personal choice for bar sink faucets to be used on the modern *stainless steel* bar sinks is the MOEN faucet, model 4901 (see Illus. 134). I like this one because of its superior nondrip performance and water-saving action. *However,* MOEN could have made better use of this faucet. *It will only mount to a thin, steel sink.* The threaded connections for the valve and the spout are too short to pass up through the thicker, enameled cast iron and porcelain basins, not to mention a custom tiled counter top.

If the connections were also of a smaller diameter, this faucet could be mounted (to the joy of millions of plumbers and home-owners alike) to the old cast iron wall-hung lavatory basins that use individual cocks, and *only* individual cocks because *nothing* else will fit. A plumber could splice the ⅜ inch copper manifold tubing and have the valve in one hole and the spout moved over to the other hole. There are nice qualities to the old lavatory wall-hung bowls, and a lot of them are condemned to the scrap pile because few modern day Americans want the old, drippy, single cocks of limited design.

This model 4901 MOEN bar sink faucet is similar to under-hung deck-mounted kitchen sink faucets in that the valves and the spout connections hang underneath the sink, out of view.

This faucet also has the soft copper "pig tails" or drop leads. (See Illus. 87, page 75.) If you have a stainless steel sink, you couldn't do better than this faucet.

## SINK STRAINERS

Over the years the diameters of basket sink strainers have changed along with sink design and preference. In the days before garbage disposers, when most kitchen sinks were porcelain, strainers were usually 2 or 2¼ (small) inches in diameter. Replacement strainers of this size are still available, but it is increasingly more difficult to find ones of any quality.

Some bar sinks have a 1½ to 2¼ inch strainer with a cute little lift-out basket with a bail handle. Some of the more modern stainless steel kitchen sinks have integral basket strainers, which means they should never be pestering you with drips such as those from a loosely installed strainer in a conventional sink.

Most sinks made for today's kitchens use the larger diameter basket strainer (see Illus. 135) which permit you to install a garbage disposer in its place.

Sink strainers are a common source of gravity leaks. Strainers may leak at one or two places and

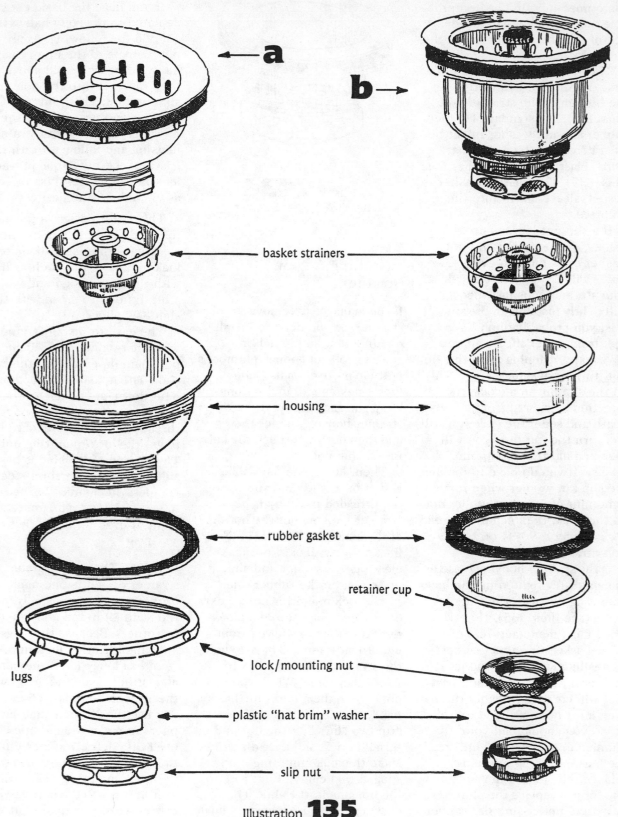

**a** ←

**b** →

basket strainers

housing

rubber gasket

retainer cup

lock/mounting nut

lugs

plastic "hat brim" washer

slip nut

Illustration **135**
Two Kitchen Sink
Basket Strainers

sometimes at both. The first probable source is a loose or dried out bed of plumber's putty under the strainer's lip.

The second major leak source is at the slip nut connection on the bottom of the strainer (see Illus. 135). The standard 1½ inch rubber slip nut washer might be used here or instead the "hat brim" plastic nesting washer (see Illus. 135). This plastic washer is nested, sleeve down, into the tailpiece.

If a slip nut loosens up or cracks, or the rubber slip nut washer dries out and breaks, water will escape. First check your strainer housing to see if it is still tightly installed in the sink. If it is, you probably don't have a leak from under the lip. If you have water dripping from the slip nut, turn *very slowly* and evenly on the slip nut in a *clockwise* direction as viewed from underneath and see if the leak stops. If you turn the nut fast, you will break an old rubber slip nut washer. If you *do* have to replace the slip nut washer when further tightening of the slip nut does not do the trick, then be sure to read pages 56-59 & 90-94 on tubular brass traps.

Is the strainer housing loose in the sink? Try tightening the lock/mounting nut with the slide-jaw pliers (see Illus. 135). However, since most manufacturers of these basket strainers (except names like KOHLER) produce such *crap,* using pot metal parts that will corrode so badly that they must be sawed and chiseled apart, you should call your plumber unless you *can* unthread the lock/mounting nut and replace the old strainer for a new one (or just replace the plumber's putty and under-sink flat rubber gasket).

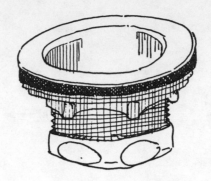

Illustration **136**
Bar Sink Basket Strainer

## Installing A New Strainer

If you managed to remove the old strainer, or you need to install one in a new sink, read on.

First, roll out enough plumber's putty to make a "snake" about ½ inch thick and 12 inches long. Wrap the snake around the strainer housing, under the lip and then push it through the hole in the sink bottom.

Then, lift up the flat rubber gasket or washer and slip it over the threaded portion of the strainer hanging out the bottom of the sink (see Illus. 135). Now, lift up the cardboard or maybe clear plastic washer and slide it up to rest on the rubber one.

The lock/mounting nut is next. Start threading it up in a *clockwise* direction as viewed from underneath. You will have to hold the strainer housing still with your other hand. When you cannot tighten the nut any further by hand, use the slide-jaw pliers to grip two "lugs" on the nut and turn it in the *clockwise* direction. Make the lock/mounting nut as snug as you can without rotating the housing in the sink. The excess plumber's putty will squish out from under the lip.

If you have the basket strainer depicted on the *right* half of Illus. 135, do the following: Apply the putty snake to the lip of the basket housing as we did above and then insert it into the hole in the sink bottom. Then, lift the retainer cup up and over the hanging portion of the strainer housing and follow up with the friction/lock nut. Snug up the lock nut in a *clockwise* direction as viewed from underneath.

This latter design is the easier to install because you are not working with a large diameter lock/mounting nut such as used with the first design and which is a bit difficult to grasp with the slide-jaw pliers.

The easy-to-install strainer with the retainer cup will *not* fit a porcelain on cast iron (the best) sink. The housing is too short to hang down far enough for the cup to go on and still have enough threads out the bottom of the cup to get the lock/mounting nut on. This design of housing is best suited for an enamel-on-steel or stainless steel sink. But because it has steel parts, I do not recommend it even for sinks that can accept it.

NOTE: The most durable strainer design is one made of *all brass parts,* which usually means the KOHLER brand and maybe a few others. Because the "lugs" on a KOHLER friction/lock nut are *round* (a lousy idea) they are almost impossible to grasp with the 10 inch slide-jaw pliers. You can use the 18 inch slide-jaw pliers to grasp the *outside* edges of a KOHLER friction/lock nut, but the larger tool is more frustrating to handle under the sink. However, it is worth the battle to have a strainer of this quality at work for you.

116

# ABOUT WATER HEATERS

This section is just what the title states: about water heaters. Not the installation or the repairing of, but facts about the one plumbing appliance that affects our lives more than any other and one which we give the least thought. This one section and the knowledge you derive will be worth the price of this book, alone.

We shut the cold water inlet valve to the water heater off prior to the replacement of the angle stops and wall-hung kitchen sink faucets. This prevented the siphoning off of the holding tank. We also turned the burner control to the PILOT position, or killed the electrical service to an electric water heater. This measure assured us that no harm would come to a partially filled tank.

Many customers have asked me how the rust and debris gets into their water lines when we turn the water back on when all of their piping is copper. Some debris is scale (bits of hardened chemicals) and some of the rust flakes off the inside of the steel nipples. The rust can also originate from inside the water heater.

Unless your water heater has a *very* visible emblem or decal on the front of the tank, near the top, which states that the holding tank is made of *copper* or *Monel*, the tank is then constructed of hot-rolled steel. This steel tank is not electroplated with any non-ferrous metal. In time, rust begins to form on the inside walls and bottom of the tank, and any heavy solids or water-borne rust in the cold water supply also falls to the bottom of the heater, accelerating the rusting process on the tank bottom. This stuff becomes a layer on the bottom of the tank.

In effect, it becomes an insulating barrier to the flame of the burner (requiring more energy to heat the water).

When we shut the water off to the entire building to do our replacements, and then drained the residual hot and cold water off, we created a void in the water piping. When we resume the hot water service to the building by reopening the cold water inlet valve (after returning service to the building), some of the rust and scale on the bottom of the tank can become dislodged by the incoming blast of water and then be carried up through the hot water pipes as the void is again refilled. This rust then shows up at the faucet when we purge the system of excess air and RECTORSEAL/Slic-Tite. However, most of the rust is a result of disturbing the old angle stops and replacing the old nipples.

One of the last residential water heater manufacturers producing a copper tank water heater (on the West Coast) was the Hoyt Company of Oakland. This company ceased producing the residential copper heater in the early sixties. At this time, the copper tank heater sold for a small ransom.

If you have one of these copper or Monel tank water heaters, proper maintenance will allow it to serve you longer than you could believe possible (40 to 50 years).

●

On today's water heaters, those of recent manufacture, you may see a decal or emblem on the top, outside front of the tank. This decal or emblem may say *"Glass Lined."* You would be surprised how many people believe that this means that the inside of the tank has a *real* glass lining, similar to a thermos bottle. It means

no such thing. And the manufacturer takes no pain to tell you otherwise!

The term Glass Lined refers to a very thin *enamel* coating on the inside of the tank (which all too soon cracks, and flakes off).

One way to get more miles out of your water heater is to drain off one gallon of water each month. This should be done from the very first month that the water heater is installed. By doing this, you carry off the rust and chemicals that settle on the bottom of the tank *before* they can cause any damage.

If your heater is already four or five years old, the battle for a 30 year heater is lost. But, by draining the heater completely and flushing the rust and scale out of the drain cock, and then following the one gallon a month drain off, you would probably eek out some additional years. Even if you buy a water heater with only a one year warranty, by taking the gallon a month out and maintaining the lowest acceptable temperature setting, you can easily get 10 to 15 years on the appliance.

One of the greatest enemies to the water heater is excessively high water pressure. If your water pressure is pushing 90 to 100 pounds or more, have a plumber install a reducing valve (regulator) in the building's main line. Everything will last longer, including the piping system itself.

The older water heaters had a drain cock very similar to a hose bib. It was made of *brass* and had a faucet washer on the end of a stem. This rubber stem washer, because of its close proximity to the burner, at the bottom of the tank, would become hard and brittle. Once you opened the drain cock, it quite often cracked and failed to shut off all the way again.

If your present heater has a brass drain cock, and you wish to drain and flush the tank and begin the monthly one gallon drain off, make sure that you purchase a small assortment of stem washers before you drain the tank. You can replace yours if it fails to shut off all the way.

To drain the tank, you first must have a means of getting the water to the outside of the building. Use a *heavy duty* garden hose opposed to the "cheapie" because of the hot temperature of the water. The female end of the hose will thread onto the drain cock. If the heater is lower than the outside ground level, and you have no floor drain, you will have to use a bucket to drain the heater, in repeated trips to the outside or to a possible laundry tub close by. Do not pour or drain the heater onto a lawn or flower bed; the hot water will kill them very quickly.

Another aspect of today's water heaters is the *joke* that the manufacturers call a drain cock. It might look like a white plastic donut, with a male sleeve in the center. The sleeve has male hose threads on it. To open the valve, you turn the donut in a *counterclockwise* direction. You will also have to rotate the hose in the same direction while turning the donut or the twist in the hose will turn the donut back in the opposite direction or unthread the hose from the donut. I suggest that you also do not open the donut for more than about five complete revolutions. If you exceed this number, and you leave your burner setting on a high temperature mark, you stand a good chance of having the donut shoot out of the heater, in your hand. Besides scalding your hand, you will have from 20 to 50 gallons of hot water ruining your floors.

Some new water heater manufacturers are installing a high quality plastic drain valve, which resembles the shape of the old brass ones. This valve is actually an improvement in one way, over the brass one. In this case, the stem never becomes so stationary that you need a pair of pliers to turn it.

Regardless of which type of drain cock you have, first turn the burner control to the *pilot* position or kill the electric service to an electric water heater. Then, close the cold water inlet valve to the heater. Next, go to the hot faucet at the highest level in the building and open it. This will break the air-lock on the hot water piping system and allow the heater to drain much faster. With the hose attached to the drain cock, open the cock and "let her go."

Usually you will find no telltale color until the water level in the tank nears the bottom, where the rust has settled. Then the water may come out between a brown and a purplish red in color. Once all the water has drained out, leave the drain cock *open* and open the cold inlet valve. This will send a cascade of water to the bottom of the tank and possibly dislodge some of the rust. Let the water run for a minute or so and then close the inlet valve, letting the remaining water in the tank drain out and then repeat this process several more times before closing the drain cock until next month.

When the service is returned to the hot side of the heater and you have water issuing out the faucet that you opened up to break the air-lock in the piping system, let the water run for several minutes purging the system of air.

With the heater full of water and all the faucets off, return the burner control back to the ON position or turn the electricity back on for an electric heater. Now check for drips at the drain cock and at the packing nut if you have the brass variety. If the packing nut is letting water escape at the stem, tighten the nut with the 12 or 15 inch adjustable wrench in a *clockwise* direction until the drip stops and then stop turning the nut.

If you operate your water heater at the lowest temperature setting that you can be satisfied with, the life of the heater is greatly extended. On the water heaters of newer manufacture, there is a plastic dip-tube that nests inside the threaded connection on the cold inlet to the water heater. This dip-tube is about 36 to 40 inches long, and it hangs down into the tank. The purpose of the dip-tube is to introduce cold water into the heater at the lower level of the tank, where it will be warmed more efficiently by the burner and also so the incoming cold water does not dilute the heated water at the top of the tank, exiting out into the hot water line.

When a heater of a newer manufacture is operated at the high and highest setting, this plastic dip-tube becomes brittle and cracks. Then it begins to crumble and fall off into pieces which fall to the bottom of the tank. As more of the tube falls away, it becomes shorter and therefore introduces cold water at higher levels into the holding tank. The symptoms of such tube break down is realized in less hot water produced by the heater and lower temperatures of the heated water that you do produce. Another warning may be a slight plastic "aftertaste" to the water. If your water heater all of a sudden produces a lot less hot water, and you have even moved the temperature setting to the highest point, to no avail, there is a good chance that your heater has this plastic dip-tube and it has failed.

Whenever I install a new heater for a friend, I will sometimes pull the plastic dip-tube out and throw it away. I then make a copper dip-tube like the manufacturers *used* to provide and like plumbers *used* to be able to buy for replacement. I peen the edge of a ⅝ inch inside diameter piece of copper tubing, 36 inches long. I then drill a hole about ⅛ of an inch in diameter, through one wall of the tubing, 6 inches down from the top, peened edge. The peened top edge prevents the tube from falling down into the bottom of the tank. The peened edge nests in the ¾ inch female iron pipe threads on the cold inlet side.

MANY AN EXISTING WATER HEATER IS JUNKED FOR A NEW ONE SIMPLY BECAUSE THIS PLASTIC DIP-TUBE HAS FAILED.

If you have an electric water heater, you will have to kill the electrical service to the heater in order to drain it. Some electric heaters have a very visible switch to turn off the service; others will not have this switch. If yours does not have the switch, look for a possible water heater listing on the door of the fuse box or on the identification tag under each circuit breaker.

If you accidently turned the burner control (in the case of a gas fired water heater) to the *off* setting instead of the *pilot* setting, when we first began to replace the angle stops and you feel too insecure to try following the relight instructions yourself, do not feel embarrassed. If you do not have a neighbor who can help, then call your local gas utility and request that a service

person come out and relight your heater. The utility company is usually more than happy to save both of you a possible agonizing incident.

Well, that's it for water heaters. I hope you found the section worth your time.

NOTE: If your hot water ever begins to take on an unpleasant oily or "plastic" aftertaste, there is a good chance that the dip-tube has failed and the parts on the bottom of the heater are being burned by the burner flame, thus the flavor.

# ABOUT AUTOMATIC WASHERS

## —Clothes And Dish—

Today's variety of household clothes and dish washers are offering more features every year. However, one thing that never changes is the requirement of a minimum, constant water pressure. It varies a little between makes, but an average would be about 35 pounds per square inch.

Water pressure also plays another role in automatic washer operation. Any *excessively* high water pressure (90 pounds and over) is an enemy of your machine (along with all your faucets, toilets, water heater and supply piping system in your home).

The reason for this is the punishment that the solenoid valve (automatic, electrically operated) in both types of washers, takes. These valves do not shut off progressively, like the travel on a faucet stem when activated. The solenoid valve controls the water flow into and through the inside of the machine

during its operation. When the valve closes, the excessive pressure causes it to "slam" shut. After many such "slams," the valve is vibrated into malfunctioning. Either the valve is stuck in the open or closed position. In most cases, the machine will fail to admit additional water for a cycle when the valve has gone bad.

If you have had the service man out more than once to work on your automatic washer, he might be repairing or replacing solenoid valves. Most repairmen are conscientious and will recommend that a "reducing valve" (regulator) be installed in the home or building water line when this excessive pressure condition exists.

The reducing valve steps down the water pressure *before* it enters the home's plumbing system. You can rent a water pressure gauge from most tool rental agencies. You merely thread the test gauge onto an outside hose bib and then turn the valve on. The needle on the face of the test gauge will indicate the pressure. I would suggest that you attach the gauge to the hose bib closest to the main water line, usually in the front of the house or building. You should take *two* readings, one in the mid-day and the other late at night. Your pressure could be as much as 20 pounds higher late at night, when there is a reduced demand for water in the community.

If you find the water pressure to be 90 pounds or more, I would suggest that you have a reducing valve installed. Also, I would recommend that you have a plumber do this. It is a job that I feel few merely "handy" people could do.

Automatic clothes washers will have a fine, wire-mesh screen *inside* the hose connection on the back of the *appliance* and or inside the hose connection on the rubber supply hoses. Any time you *all-of-a-sudden* have a loss of hot or cold water entering the machine, when it is supposed to be filling, then turn off both hoses and check the inside connections for debris clogging fine, wire mesh screens. Also, it is a good idea to turn the water supply off when the machine is not in use. The hose connections unthread in a *counterclockwise* direction. You can use the slide-jaw pliers to get a good grip on them.

# ABOUT GARBAGE DISPOSERS

There is one Cardinal Rule about garbage disposers: *Do Not* put stringy, tough, or fibrous food scraps in your machine. The particular demons that come to mind are:
   a.  celery
   b.  banana peels
   c.  artichoke leaves
   d.  corn husks
   e.  string beans
   f.  asparagus bottoms

When your disposer comes to a halt as a result of introducing such products, it will usually be futile to try restarting it. You will probably have to call a plumber to remove the unit from the sink, separate the case and retrieve the compacted debris.

If you do not wish to pay the plumber's fee to work on an old appliance, maybe you should consider having him install a new one. The cost of repairing the old one (labor time) and installing a new one would be just about the same. The following are my recommendations for a replacement:

   a.  IN-SINK-ERATOR (stainless steel models)
   b.  KITCHEN-AID (stainless steel models)
   c.  MAYTAG (stainless steel models)

Another bit of good advice: *Never* introduce any chemical drain cleaning agents into a sink which has a disposer in it; if you do, you might be replacing it all too soon.

There are two sections following:
1. The Red Button Rescue, and
2. The Broomstick Start.

These are two strategies you may employ if you're caught in a pinch. There is a third one, but we'll wait until we cross that bridge before diving into that one.

## The Red Button Rescue

A typical call for help might go like this: "The disposer stopped after it had been running for just a few seconds—it's been in the sink for a long time and never acted like this before."

If you find yourself in this situation, and it is not the result of the stringy demons, mentioned at top, then get down on your hands and knees and look on the bottom of the garbage disposer for a little *red button*. This little button might be a different color, but it will be plainly obvious that it has a purpose. Push *in,* hard on the little button. You might hear a little "click" noise when you do so. If you forgot to turn the switch off, the disposer might startle you when it starts up, so don't bump your head trying to get out from under the cabinet.

Once the disposer starts up again, leave it running and turn the kitchen sink faucet to full on, and let the water run for a full minute or two. The little button on the bottom of the disposer is a circuit breaker. When the electric motor inside the disposer reaches a temperature where damage to the appliance is imminent, the circuit breaker automatically cuts the electrical power to the motor.

When the little red button is pressed in, it reconnects the electrical contacts inside the disposer. If the motor became *real* hot before stopping, it will not start up again until it has had a chance to cool down sufficiently. You might have to wait a while before pushing the button does any good.

When your disposer starts behaving like this often, it is probably due to the cutters in the unit becoming dull, thus requiring more time and energy output to do its job, (sort of like human machines, no?) so much energy that the motor cannot deliver it. You better plan on replacing it.

If you will use lots of water while operating the disposer, regardless of which brand it is, the unit will last a lot longer than if little water is used. Also, I recommend that you turn the water on to full flow, *before* turning the disposer on and *before* introducing the food scraps.

## The Broomstick Start

If your disposer stopped when one or two hard objects were introduced, or it stopped while it was working on a diet of okay stuff, you might try what I call a Broomstick Start, *before* calling for help.

After trying the Red Button Rescue to no avail, pick up your household broom (pending it has a *wooden* handle). Although I have never heard of anyone having an electrical shock doing this with a metal broomstick, if yours is made of metal, I would not use it. The disposer being an electrical device, some water, a metal shaft and 110 volts could give you a new hair-do, the cost being the space between your ears.

As you peer down into the hole in the sink, the grinding chamber lies underneath the rubber, fingered skirt. The cutters are fastened to the bottom of the rotating chamber. Some brands have the cutters rotating in a clockwise direction and others in a counterclockwise direction. The ones that I recommend have models that change directions after each cycle, thus greatly reducing the chance of becoming jammed.

Now, introduce the end of the *wooden* handle at about the 7 o'clock position and move it around the inside perimeter of the chamber until you can find a point at which the stick "catches upon something." While pushing down on the stick, pull backwards and to the right on the vertical portion of the handle, pulling towards the 4 to 5 o'clock position, trying to budge the cutting chamber. It could take as many as six or seven attempts until the cutting chamber will move (if it is going to). Try reversing the procedure by inserting the handle at the 4 o'clock position and pulling back to the *left* towards the 6 o'clock position.

Once the chamber gives a bit, flip the on-off switch. If the disposer tries to start up but immediately stops again, turn the switch off *quickly*. You don't want the disposer to heat up again. When the disposer starts up and continues to run, then turn the sink faucet on full and let it run for a minute or two.

## Split The Case Time

This is the section that I bring up when your first two "bridges" were burned. It is a more drastic measure, one which few laypersons could perform, and one which is required when the Cardinal Rule is ignored. It usually requires about an hour to an hour-and-a-half to do the job; or, about one-third the cost of a new disposer.

So, if your machine does not respond to the Red Button Rescue, nor the Broomstick Start, then solly pal, it's Split the Case Time.

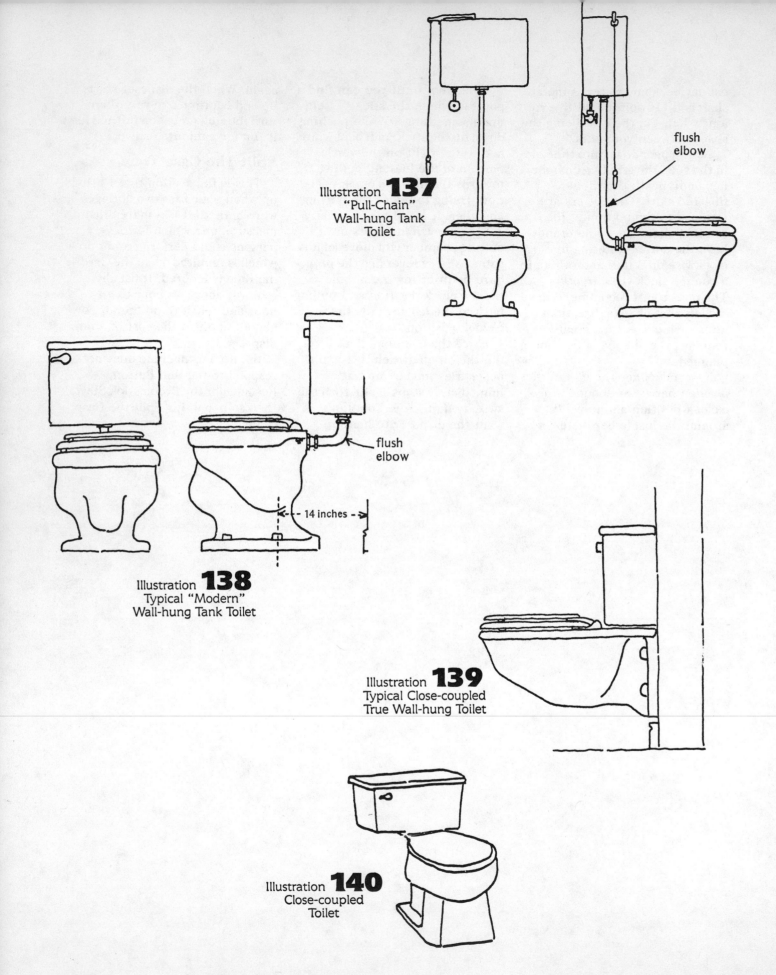

flush
elbow

Illustration **137**
"Pull-Chain"
Wall-hung Tank
Toilet

flush
elbow

— 14 inches —

Illustration **138**
Typical "Modern"
Wall-hung Tank Toilet

Illustration **139**
Typical Close-coupled
True Wall-hung Toilet

Illustration **140**
Close-coupled
Toilet

# Part III
# Toilets

## OUR MAN CRAPPER

Have you ever wondered how many folks ever stop and ask themselves who they have to thank for making our modern flush toilet a reality?

In 1848 a young British lad of eleven walked 165 miles from Yorkshire to London in search of gainful employment in the plumbing trade. His name was Thomas C. Crapper, the son of a poor, maritime sailor. At the age of twenty-four, after thirteen years' employment as a plumber, Thomas Crapper established his own business, a true sanitary "engineering" firm.

Because the Board of Trade feared the total drainage of metropolitan London reservoirs due to the wasteful, inefficient, excremental waste removal systems of the time, the Metropolis Water Act of 1872 was passed.

There were at this time a good number of indoor flush toilets in existence, but of a very poor design. The Metropolis Water Act prompted Thomas to devote his attention to its new regulations, and develop a toilet which would perform within those regulations.

As a result, Thomas C. Crapper unveiled a most remarkable new version of the "unmentionable" at the Health Exhibition of 1884. It was titled "Crapper's Valveless Water Waste Preventer." Thomas's new toilet still holds a record to this day. At the unveiling, he successfully sent ten apples, one flat sponge, three balls of rolled paper, a handful of grease, and one by-stander's cap all down the drain with one pull of the chain.

The old saying "They Don't Make Them Like They Used To" is very apropos in this instance. How many modern day toilets could flush even one apple, let alone all the other debris?

Oddly enough, it is the USA that pays foremost tribute to this great inventor by our dubious use of the term "crapper" in reference to that great indoor luxury. And luxury it is. We could possibly see the day that the water consuming toilets go the way of the dinosaur, with the world supplies of fresh water diminishing yearly.

For those interested parties, a book titled "Flushed With Pride" authored by Wallace Reyburn and published by Prentice-Hall in 1971, gives full and humorous account of Our Man Crapper.

## Choosing A New Toilet

In this section, we will be dealing with residential toilets only. I have grouped residential toilets into two groups:

a. Wall-hung tank, and
b. Close-coupled. There are several distinctions within each group which we will now note.

Wall-hung tank toilets include those designs where we find the tank mounted to the wall and the bowl set upon the floor, with a flush pipe or flush elbow connecting the two components. Illus. 137 is a wall-hung tank toilet facsimile found to this day in many of the older homes. Illus. 138 illustrates the modern, later model of wall-hung tank toilet. Illus. 139 represents a true wall-hung toilet, having both the tank and the bowl mounted to the wall. Illus. 140 is a facsimile of the more common, modern close-coupled toilet, having the tank coupled to the bowl itself.

When you consider replacing a toilet of either group, except the true wall-hung, it is prudent to answer several questions prior to performing any labor.

Toilet bowls are manufactured today in three sizes: 14 inch rough, 12 inch rough, and 10 inch rough. This measurement criteria is the distance from the center of the waste line, in the floor, to the finish wall behind the bowl (see Illus. 138).

The wall-hung toilet bowls are usually the 14 inch size, where the majority of the modern close-coupled units are of the 12 inch size. The 10 inch bowl comes into play where a bathroom or toilet alcove is *very* small and every inch of space must be utilized to its fullest.

To determine the rough (size) of your toilet bowl, look at the

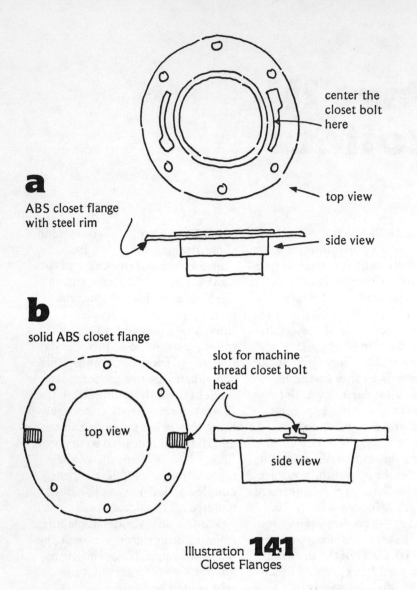

**a**

ABS closet flange
with steel rim

center the
closet bolt
here

top view

side view

**b**

solid ABS closet flange

slot for machine
thread closet bolt
head

top view

side view

Illustration **141**
Closet Flanges

base or "foot" of the bowl. It is held in place by bolts called "closet bolts." The toilet is referred to as a "closet" by the plumbing fixture and warehouse industry. The older toilet bowls and a few of the present day manufacturers have a four-bolt pattern (four bolts holding the bowl to the floor). Most of the late model and new toilets have only two bolts holding them to the floor.

Using your yardstick or tape measure, measure the distance from the bolts nearest the *back* of the bowl, over to the wall (see Illus. 137). If your bowl has only two bolts, all the more simple. This measurement will tell you which rough (bowl size) you have. Example: If your measurement is, say, 13 inches, the larger 14 inch bowl could not fit in this space and it will have to be a 12 inch bowl (with a little space behind the tank and the wall). If your measurement is 14 to 15 inches, then you have the larger, 14 inch rough.

A 10 inch rough will have a measurement from 10 inches on-the-money to maybe 11 inches. You will want to know your present bowl size when telephoning suppliers, asking how much new "closets" cost.

• IMPORTANT NOTE: If you are only going to lift your old bowl to reseat it with a new bowl wax, you will not have to bother with any measuring. This is only for those intending on replacing their closets.

The close-coupled, true wall-hung design (see Illus. 139), having both the tank and the bowl mounted to the wall is not restricted in size by the closet bolt criteria. This design uses a drain inside the *wall*, not in the floor and the entire toilet is mounted to a special bracket, called a "carrier," inside the wall. This toilet, like the back-shelf faucet in the faucet section, is a design which I feel is beyond most of you first-timers and I am not going to delve into this particular unit, other than telling you how to replace the tank components, which we discuss further on.

Aside from bowl size, our second question for which we need an answer is knowing the type and condition of waste line, under the bowl.

When our ancestors first moved the "johnnie" inside the house, the waste lines were hand fabricated from lead sheet. If your home is pre-turn of the century, or up to the late 1930s, you stand the chance of finding a lead waste line in the floor. These lead waste lines or *closet bends* require extra care when working with them and require a different procedure in setting a new bowl upon them. We will delve into this procedure further on.

In more modern construction, the closet bend is either cast iron, copper or ABS plastic. Underneath the toilet bowl, attached to the top of the modern waste line or closet bend, you will find a *closet flange* (see Illus. 141 & 142). This flange is attached

124

securely to the waste pipe or closet bend and should also be screwed to the floor. On each side of this flange, there are two slots, at 180 degrees to each other. This flange is what holds the toilet bowl to the floor, employing a closet bolt in each slot.

The flat heads of the *machine thread* closet bolts slide under the slots in the flange, and draw the toilet tight to the floor. Between the underside of the toilet bowl and the closet flange, a *bowl wax* or *wax ring* is placed to make a watertight seal (see Illus. 143).

This wax ring used to be made of real bee's wax years ago, but nowadays it's made from either vegetable wax or petroleum. Prior to the development of the wax ring, plumber's putty and plaster of Paris was placed on the floor just before setting the bowl, which afforded a somewhat good water seal.

If your toilet has only two holes in the base for closet bolts, you can be fairly certain that your waste line has this closet flange. I said fairly certain. Older wall-hung tank toilets having four holes in the foot might have the old lead closet bend without a flange. We won't know for certain until we have lifted the old bowl.

For installations having the lead closet bend and no closet flange, the toilet bowl was held to the floor with closet bolts which had wood screw threads on the bottom half which penetrated down into the wooden subfloor. The top half of these bolts had machine threads which accept the solid-dome closet bolt nuts or "Acorn Nuts."

Without a closet flange, it requires two more bolts of the wood screw variety to securely hold a four-bolt bowl to the floor—thus the two extra front

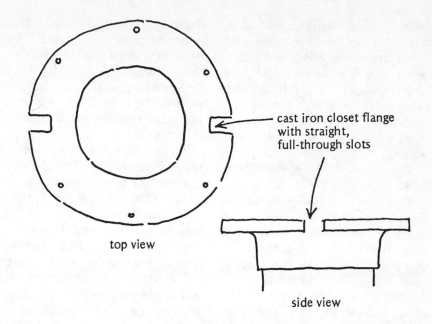

top view

side view

Illustration **142**

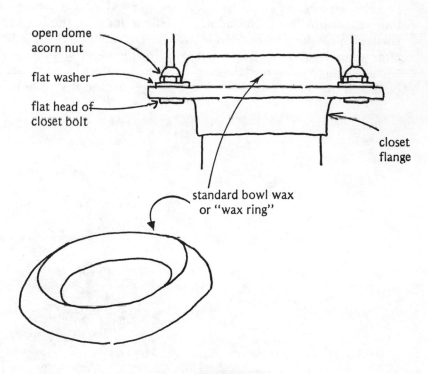

open dome acorn nut

flat washer

flat head of closet bolt

closet flange

standard bowl wax or "wax ring"

Illustration **143**

bolts. In place of the closet flange, the old lead closet bend has a lip which merely overlaps onto the wood floor. If you have a four-bolt toilet bowl and the two back bolts have acorn nuts with threads protruding out the top, it usually means that you *do* have a closet flange.

You are no doubt wondering what is the big "ta-do" about having or not having a closet flange. Well, it means a great deal when selecting a new toilet. Most new toilet bowls will have only two bolt holes in the foot since most houses now have iron, copper or plastic drains with closet flanges. Another consideration is this: toilets which do not have the closet flange and rely upon the wood screw type of closet bolt often suffer from a soggy or rotten subfloor due to seepage over the years, under the toilet bowl.

After many years of blissful bottoms kissing the seat, the toilet may shift just a bit and a small seepage leak begins. And, after several years of undetected leakage, the wood screw closet bolts will no longer continue

drawing the bowl tight enough to maintain a watertight seal. If you have asphalt tile or linoleum on the bathroom floor, and it is buckling or lifting in front and/or around the toilet bowl, it usually indicates seepage and a possible rotten subfloor.

In this case, new wood screw type closet bolts will not be able to draw the toilet bowl down tightly to the floor because the wood screw bolts pull out of the wet wooden subfloor. This poor floor condition might be the very reason that you desired to replace the existing toilet to begin with, not because you might be tired of its appearance or dated design.

This is not to say that you cannot have seepage problems with closet flanges. Many times I have found the sides of the closet flanges to be broken loose due to over-tightening of the acorn nuts or someone failing to screw the flange to the floor. When this happens, the bolts are no longer pulling down on the bowl and seepage occurs.

In this toilet section of this book, I am not going to get into piping repairs. If you do have

serious problems in this area, get in touch with your plumber. If you fear that you do indeed have such problems, after the bowl is removed you can better assess any real damage. And, removing the existing bowl will save you some money in plumber's time. So, if you have more than one toilet in the house and can live without one for a few days, you might want to use this book and lift your leaking bowl.

Today, many folks prefer to keep their old wall-hung tank toilets instead of setting new close-coupled ones because of the higher flushing velocity of the old wall-hung type (better performance). Also, many younger homeowners in vintage homes are striving to maintain the "bygone years" theme of pedestal sinks, full length, cast iron, legged bathtubs and wall-hung tank toilets. As a result, some of you might have wall-hung tank toilets in very good shape but need to reset the bowl, or replace a corroded flush el or replace some of the tank components. Well, it's all here, in this book . . . read on!

# Tool Chart
## The Tools You Need For Each Job

Just as we did for the sections dealing with faucets, angle stops, wastes, traps, etc., on page 11, below you will find the cross-reference for the Toilet Section. I will use the same tool list that appears on page 5, and add just a few new tools as noted at the bottom of the page.

*Note: The letters in parentheses refer to illustrations on pages 5 to 10.*

| TO REPAIR | YOU NEED— | | | | | |
|---|---|---|---|---|---|---|
| WALL-HUNG TANK | adjustable wrenches (6 inch only) (A) | standard hacksaw (E) | 15 to 16 inch slotted screwdriver (F-1) | 15 to 16 inch slide-jaw pliers (I-1) | | |
| WALL-HUNG TANK TOILET BOWL | adjustable wrenches (A) | mini-hacksaw (D) | 10 inch slide-jaw pliers (I) | 15 to 16 inch slide-jaw pliers (I-1) | 7/16 inch open-end box wrench (Z) | |
| BOWL SPUD | pipe wrenches (B) | standard hacksaw (E) | 15 to 16 inch slide-jaw pliers (I-1) | spud wrench (Z-1) | Teflon tape (Q) | |
| FILL VALVE (BALLCOCK) | adjustable wrenches (A) | mini-hacksaw (D) | 10 inch slide-jaw pliers (I) | Teflon tape (Q) | pipe joint compound (S) | |
| FLUSH VALVE | pipe wrenches (B) | standard hacksaw (E) | 15 to 16 inch slotted screwdriver (F-1) | 15 to 16 inch slide-jaw pliers (I-1) | Teflon tape (Q) | plumber's putty (R) |
| TWO-PIECE FLUSH ELBOW | pipe wrenches (B) | standard hacksaw (E) | 15 to 16 inch slotted screwdriver (F-1) | tubing cutter with 2⅛ inch capacity (H-1) | Teflon tape (Q) | pipe joint compound (S) ... spud wrench (Z-1) |
| STRAIGHT FLUSH PIPE | pipe wrenches (B) | standard hacksaw (E) | 15 to 16 inch slotted screwdriver (F-1) | tubing cutter with 2⅛ inch capacity (H-1) | Teflon tape (Q) | pipe joint compound (S) ... spud wrench (Z-1) |
| CLOSE-COUPLED TANK | adjustable wrenches (6 inch only) (A) | 10 inch slide-jaw pliers (I) | plumber's putty (R) | pipe joint compound (S) | penetrating oil (T) | 5/8 inch box wrench (Z-2) |
| CLOSE-COUPLED BOWL | adjustable wrenches (6 inch only) (A) | mini-hacksaw (D) | 10 inch slide-jaw pliers (I) | 7/16 inch open-end box wrench (Z) | | |
| LIFT WIRES | mini-hacksaw (D) | 10 inch slide-jaw pliers (I) | | | | |
| **TO REPLACE** TOILET SEAT | adjustable wrenches (6 inch only) (A) | mini-hacksaw (D) | #2 slotted screwdriver (F) | 10 inch slide-jaw pliers (I) | penetrating oil (T) | |

Added Tools:
- F-1   15 to 16 inch slotted screwdriver
- I-1   15 to 16 inch slide-jaw pliers
- H-1   tubing cutter with 2⅛ inch capacity
- Z-1   spud wrench (see Illus. 149 on page 130)
- Z-2   5/8 inch box wrench (looks just like a 7/16 inch box wrench, but is just a bit larger)

# Replacing The Modern Wall-Hung Toilet

## Removing the Tank and Bowl

This book will kick off the removal/replacement procedures for the modern wall-hung tank toilet first (see Illus. 144).

Immediately following this instruction, this book will include a Tank Renovation section which we can refer back to for the close-coupled and the true wall-hung designs.

Guidepost:

1. Turn off the angle stop.
2. Undo the supply's slip nut at the fill valve's connection.
3. Flush toilet and empty tank; then sponge out until dry.
4. Remove old flush elbow's slip nut from tank's flush valve connection.
5. Remove tank from the wall.
6. Remove flush elbow from bowl.
7. Remove closet bolt cover caps.
8. Remove closet bolt nuts and washers.
9. Lift bowl from floor.
10. Scrape closet flange clean of old wax ring and/or plumber's putty.
11. Remove old spud from bowl.

Our first step to removal is turning off the angle stop under the toilet tank. Turn the handle in a *clockwise* direction as far as it will go (see Illus. 145). Next, flush the toilet tank while continuing to hold the flush handle or "trip-lever" down, or up, as the case may be. We want to drain as much water out of the tank as possible. Then, use a large sponge or old towel to get all of the remaining water from the tank.

Following this, use the sponge again and remove as much of the residual water from the *bowl* as you can. I use a plastic marine bilge pump (Thirsty Mate) for this job. It has a long discharge hose which I stick in a convenient sink or tub. If you happen to be a boat owner in possession of one, try it out. Now, remove the supply's slip nut at the fill valve (ballcock) connection on the tank bottom. If possible, remove the supply tube entirely. Pages 47-55 cover this procedure for faucets, which is the same for toilets.

Now it is time to remove the flush elbow (if you are going to replace it with a new one or trash your old wall-hung tank toilet for a new close-coupled). Take the 12 inch hacksaw and sever the one-piece flush elbow in two (see Illus. 146). If you should happen to have a two-piece flush elbow,

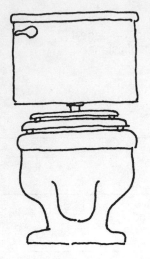

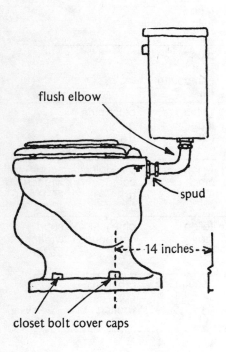

flush elbow

spud

← 14 inches →

closet bolt cover caps

**Illustration 144**
"Modern" Wall-hung Tank Toilet

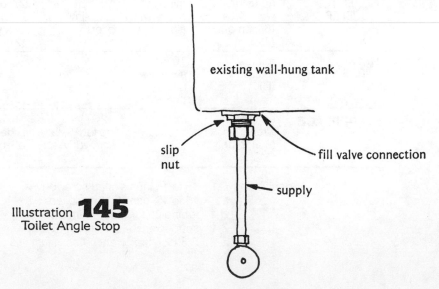

existing wall-hung tank

slip nut

fill valve connection

supply

**Illustration 145**
Toilet Angle Stop

this is not necessary (see Illus. 147). In this case, just undo the union nut in the center of the two-piece elbow and read on. If you need only to reseat the bowl and the flush elbow is new or rather new, by lifting the tank *up* off the top of the flush elbow, you can salvage it for reuse.

Now back to those trashing their old design. When you have almost severed the one-piece flush elbow completely in two, the weight of the tank might pinch the hacksaw blade. You can use the mini-hacksaw and finish the cut from the *backside* of the elbow.

With the flush elbow severed, undo the bolts or screws which are holding the tank to the wall. They are at the top, inside back of the tank (see Illus. 148). I suggest that you have a friend present to help hold onto the tank as you undo these screws or bolts. This will prevent the tank from falling and possibly breaking itself or the bowl.

Now, with the tank safely lying on the floor, use the 15 to 16 inch slide-jaw pliers to unthread the slip nut holding the elbow to the bottom of the tank. Back the nut off in a *counterclockwise* direction as viewed from behind the nut. Then, use the same pliers to remove the slip nut holding the

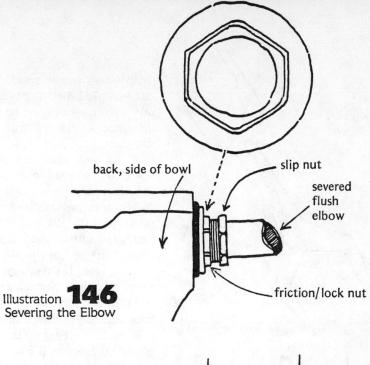

back, side of bowl — slip nut

severed flush elbow

friction/lock nut

**Illustration 146**
Severing the Elbow

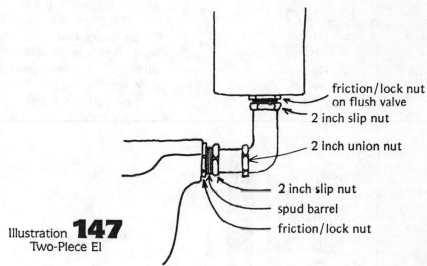

friction/lock nut on flush valve

2 inch slip nut

2 inch union nut

2 inch slip nut

spud barrel

friction/lock nut

**Illustration 147**
Two-Piece El

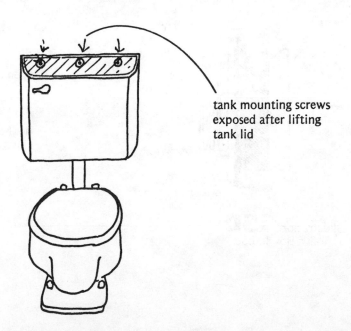

tank mounting screws exposed after lifting tank lid

**Illustration 148**
Removing Tank

129

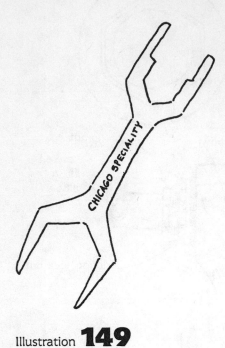

Illustration **149**
Spud Wrench

flush elbow to the spud, in the back of the bowl. Turn this slip nut also in a *counterclockwise* direction as viewed from behind the nut.

If the large slide-jaw pliers will not budge the slip nuts, try using the 18 inch pipe wrench.

When removing the severed portion of the flush el from the spud, the entire spud might rotate, instead of the slip nut coming free. If this happens, place the spud wrench (see Illus. 149) on the flats of the spud's friction/lock nut (see Illus. 150).

Now, place a rag on the severed elbow to prevent it from cutting you. Hang onto the elbow keeping it stationary and rotate the spud wrench in a *counterclockwise* direction as viewed from behind.

When the friction/lock nut is backed up until it rubs the slip nut, try wiggling the flush el

around in a circular motion while *pushing in* on the elbow. The spud will travel inward into the hole in the back of the bowl. Then, using a sharp pocket knife or utility knife, cut the black rubber spud gasket free of the spud. With the gasket cut free, the spud will then *pull out* of the bowl.

If the elbow did part from the spud by loosening of the slip nut, then again loosen the spud's friction nut and cut the rubber spud gasket free and remove the spud. If you are going to keep the wall-hung tank toilet, we will replace the old spud with a new one as instructed on page 137.

With the old flush el removed from both the tank and bowl, and with the old spud removed from the bowl, we are now ready to tackle lifting the old bowl from the floor.

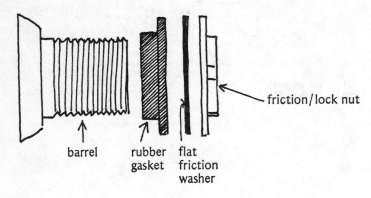

barrel  rubber gasket  flat friction washer  friction/lock nut

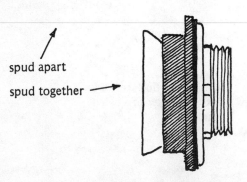

spud apart
spud together

Illustration **150**
Toilet Bowl Spud

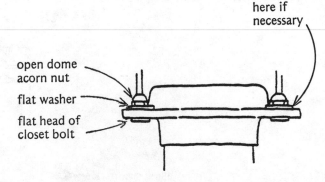

saw here if necessary

open dome acorn nut
flat washer
flat head of closet bolt

Illustration **151**

130

## Lifting The Old Bowl

If you have ceramic or plastic caps covering the closet bolt nuts, use the slide-jaw pliers to grip the caps and wiggle them free. Do not panic if you break one, you can purchase individual caps at your local plumbing supply or complete hardware. *However,* if you have a colored bowl with matching caps, it is a different story. If you break a ceramic colored cap your chances of finding one of identical color will be slim. If you do have matching colored caps, several days prior to doing any work, I would squirt penetrating oil around the base of the caps to soften the old plumber's putty or plaster of Paris used to adhere the caps to the foot of the bowl. This is of course only for those who wish to keep and reuse your old bowl.

Now, place the 7/16 inch box or open end wrench on the acorn nut of the closet bolt. It doesn't matter which one you choose first. (Some real old "rounded top" closet nuts were 1/2 inch instead of the 7/16 inch size of the present day nuts. You can use the 6 inch adjustable wrench on these nuts if the 7/16 wrench is too small.) Unthread the nut in a *counterclockwise* direction. If the nut unthreads off the bolt, do the remaining bolt or bolts. If the entire bolt rotates without the acorn nut coming free, pick up the mini-hacksaw and place the blade flat on the washer underneath the nut and saw the nut off, completely. It is not at all uncommon to find this necessary on one or all of the old closet bolts (see Illus. 151).

If the closet bolts are so loose that you can lift them up a ways, you will have to grip the nut in the jaws of the smaller slide-jaw pliers so that the mini-hacksaw

blade cuts through the bolt instead of just rotating it in place when you try to sever it. When you have sawed the bolts or managed to unthread the acorn nuts, it is then time to lift the bowl.

To separate the bowl from the floor, straddle the bowl, grip the edges of the bowl in the middle, squat down until your butt rubs the rim and then lift with your LEGS, *not with your back*. While lifting, apply force in a circular motion.

A few hard pressed cases, when my 240 pounds could not lift a most stubborn bowl, and the toilet was being junked anyway, I have laid a heavy canvas over the bowl, completely draping it all the way to the floor. Then, swinging a 10 pound sledge hammer (head hanging down) struck the bowl and broke it into many small pieces. This is done *only* with a long sleeve shirt on, and eye goggles in place. *Gloved* hands remove the rubble.

With the bowl off the flange or lead bend, take a putty knife and scrape clean the area around the flange or lip of the lead bend. If you had to saw the front bolts in the case of a four-bolt bowl, pick up the 10 inch slide-jaw pliers and try gripping the remaining portion of the bolts jutting from the floor. Try to rotate them in a *counterclockwise* direction until they part from the floor. If you cannot extract the front bolts using the slide-jaw pliers, the 4 inch pipe wrench will do the job.

If the back two closet bolts are not attached to a closet flange, but also thread into the floor, remove them in the same manner. If the back two closet bolts were sawed in two and they mate to a closet flange, we will also have to remove them. If there is no additional acorn nut at the base of the bolts, securing them tightly to the

flange, grip them with the slide-jaw pliers and wiggle them while pulling them to the outside of the flange, and out from underneath the flange.

If these two back closet bolts do have acorn nuts at the base (a sign that a conscientious plumber installed the bowl), undo this second nut with the 7/16 inch wrench using a *counterclockwise* direction of rotation and then pull the bolts also to the outside of the flange.

If your old closet bolts were corroded and broke off at the level of the floor, you've got a few problems, but they're *not* insurmountable. Read On! We will get you out of this one a little further on.

Many times I have found that the linoleum man or the tile man ran his flooring over the edge of the closet flange or lead bend lip, up against the original closet bolts. If you have linoleum, you can take a screwdriver and hammer and chisel away the linoleum or asphalt tile away from the bolt and free it from the flange. If you have ceramic tile up against the bolts, and had to saw the nuts off, you will have to *very* carefully chip away the tile from the bolt using the 1/4 inch cold chisel with the eye goggles *on*.

If the back bolts did not require sawing to remove the acorn nuts, and they were not trimmed off close to the top of the acorn nut so that the caps would cover them, you *might* be able to reuse them. Let them be, for now.

Wanna take a break?

•

With the tank and bowl out of the way, go to pages 47-55 and read the procedure for installing a new 1/2 inch IPS by 3/8 inch compression angle stop, if you do not have one already.

If you are going to reseat your existing bowl, and you did find a bowl wax under it, scrape as much of it away as you can from the closet flange or lead bend and from the horn on the bottom of the toilet bowl. Clean away any remains of plaster of Paris from the floor, if you should find any.

During the last ten years or so, a new design of wax ring or bowl wax has become popular. It has a plastic skirt or sleeve that protrudes out the flat, bottom side of the wax. This skirt slips down inside the waste line (see Illus. 154 & 155).

Your new wax ring might have a brand name like "Cant-Leak" or Never-Leak, or No-Seep or the such. You might find this plastic sleeve still stuck in place in the waste line if this type had been previously used. Also, it may be stuck to the horn, on the bottom of the bowl. If it is present at either location, peel it free. That is why it is important to clean the waste's closet flange or lead bend.

I am going to assume that you had to saw the nuts off your old closet bolts, or that the old ones broke off when trying to remove them so that you will know how to install new ones properly.

Closet bolts are made in two lengths, Standard and Long. You will find these two lengths for both the wood screw and the machine thread type of bolt (see Illus. 152). I always carry the extra long variety for all occasions and then trim them to length later. Read on, you'll find out why.

We now have to make a determination which bowl wax to use with your waste line. Measure the *inside* diameter of the waste line. If it is 3 inches in diameter, you should purchase a 3 by 4 No-Seep or anti-leak type. The numbers 3 by 4 mean that this type will fit both the 3 and 4 inch waste lines. If your waste line is 4 inches, you should purchase the straight 4 inch bowl wax.

I never use the 3 by 4 in a 4 inch waste line. This wax is necked-down so that it can be used in the 3 inch waste line. By installing it on a 4 inch waste line, it further slows down the water and "deposits" exiting the toilet into the line. The straight 4 inch wax should be used with the larger 4 inch line.

One word of caution: The male horn on the bottom of some older toilet bowls is of a greater girth

and depth than the new toilets. It is possible to break the foot or base of your very old bowl when using the 3 by 4 bowl wax. When you begin to tighten down on the closet bolts, the larger horn can bottom out on the necked-down plastic portion of the wax when you still have from ½ to ¼ inch to go before resting flush on the floor. With continued tightening of the acorn nuts, the foot suddenly pops.

I would suggest that if you do indeed own a very old bowl and a 3 inch waste line, only purchase the No-Seep type if you find one *already* under the bowl when you lift it, or buy a standard wax ring without plastic sleeve. Then, when you set the bowl again, flush the bowl using a bucket a half dozen times, checking for seepage around the edge of the foot, before going any further with the installation.

If you removed the wood screw type of closet bolts from two, or all four holes, and the wood flooring is sound, you can rethread new bolts of the same type back into the floor, when we go through the resetting of the bowl.

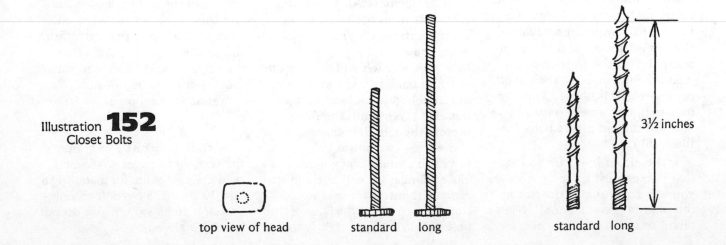

Illustration **152**
Closet Bolts

top view of head     standard  long     standard  long

3½ inches

## Reseating Your Bowl With Wood-Screw Closet Bolts

We are going to use ONLY the *long* closet bolts, as opposed to the standard, shorter one. Our long one is 3½ inches overall, with 1¾ inch of wood screw threads on the bottom and ¾ inch of machine threads at the top with ¾ inch of smooth space in between (see Illus. 152).

Thread a solid domed acorn nut onto the machine threads of each bolt, until it "bottoms out" in the last thread. Now, using the 6 inch adjustable wrench or the ⁷⁄₁₆ box or open end wrench, rethread the bolts back into the existing holes in the floor. If you are putting back the same bowl, you can include the front two bolts (those well in front of the waste hole in the floor). The bolts will rethread in a *clockwise* direction. Turn them in until you reach the last thread.

Then, grip the smooth portion of the bolts with the slide-jaw pliers and use the 6 inch adjustable wrench or open end wrench to unthread the acorn nuts off the bolts using a *counterclockwise* direction.

Next, disregarding the instructions on the bowl wax box, set the wax on the *lead bend*. If your bowl wax is a No-Seep type, the sleeve (see Illus. 155a ) will drop into the waste opening. If it is the standard type (see Illus. 155b), it will lie flat, entirely on the top of the waste opening.

Usually the closet bolts gouge a groove in each wall of the wax ring, but don't worry about it. After you have put the final torque on the closet bolt nuts with the bowl in place, the wax ring (if you could see it under the bowl) spreads out and the closet bolts actually protrude up through the middle of the bowl wax's wall.

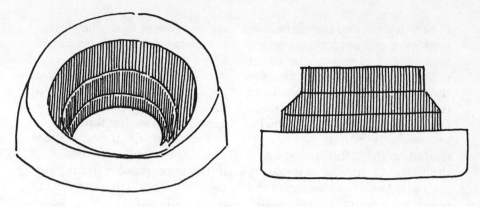

Illustration **153**
3 Inch by 4 Inch No-Seep Bowl Wax

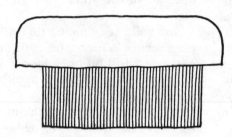

Illustration **154**
Straight 4 Inch No-Seep Bowl Wax

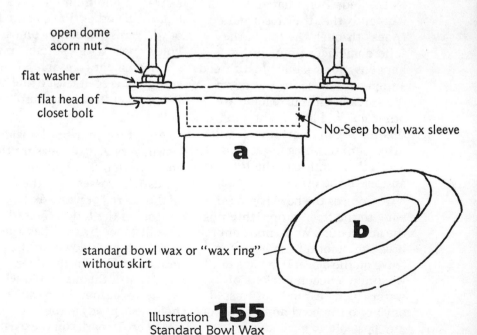

open dome acorn nut

flat washer

flat head of closet bolt

No-Seep bowl wax sleeve

**a**

standard bowl wax or "wax ring" without skirt

**b**

Illustration **155**
Standard Bowl Wax

Now it's time to carry the bowl back over and set it down on top of the wax and waste. The closet bolts will act as locating pins for the holes in the foot. Slowly lower the bowl down onto the wax ring. *Do not* push down on the bowl unless the bolts have not protruded up through the holes in the foot. You only need about ¼ inch of threads sticking out of the holes to get both the washers and acorn nuts on and started.

Preferably, you should use brass or stainless steel flat washers on top of the closet bolts. If you use *steel* or *any* kind of *plated* steel, you will have bad corrosion, and soon.

After the washers are dropped over the protruding closet bolts, then rethread the solid dome acorn nuts back onto the machine threads on top of the closet bolts. Now using the 7/16 open end or box wrench, tighten each nut three or four complete rotations before going to the next one, and so on, until the bowl is snug to the floor.

You might find that the acorn nuts drive the closet bolts all the way down until the bowl does rest on the floor. But, what also might happen is that the closet bolt "pops" through the top of the solid dome acorn nut. If this happens, don't panic. Just thread an open dome acorn nut down the threads until it reaches the other nut and keep tightening this top, open dome nut. It will drive both down as far as you want, then unthread the top nut and leave the other one alone.

As soon as the bowl is nice and snug to the floor, stop tightening the acorn nuts. We do not want to break the foot off the bowl. We'll leave off the closet bolt caps until we dump a dozen buckets of water (being careful not to spill any) into the bowl and check for any possible seepage out from

under the foot of the bowl. If there are no leaks, you can trim down the extra closet bolt length with the mini-hacksaw and then pack the inside of the caps with plumber's putty. Now, push the caps down over the nuts.

For those of you who had corroded closet bolts that broke off in the floor, thank you for your patience. We will now get you out of your dilemma.

It is almost impossible to drill out the old bolts using a drill bit and electric drill, let alone a hand-cranked one. The drill bit invariably skids off the remaining bolt and makes a bigger hole to one side or the other. So we'll make new holes.

You will need an electric drill, preferably a ¼ inch motor and an extension drill bit of ⅛ inch diameter (a 6 inch long bit is the optimum length).

With no closet bolts sticking up out of the floor acting as locating pins, we will have to use a yardstick to mark the floor with a crayon so you can position the bowl properly.

Lay the yardstick down forming a straight line from one broken bolt to the other. Have one edge of the yardstick center on each hole or bolt. With a suitable marking implement (erasable), draw a straight line so at least 6 inches of line goes out past each broken bolt.

Now, turn your bowl upside down, very gently. Measure the total width of the bottom, as the yardstick crosses over the *center* of the "horn" or waste exit, on the bottom of the toilet. Next, divide this distance by two. Lay the yardstick back down on the crayon marks, on the floor. Center half the measured width of the toilet foot, over the waste hole (lead bend) in the floor. Now, make cross marks on the existing

crayon lines, indicating the outside edges of the toilet bowl.

If you're faint of heart, it's a good time for a shot o' whiskey.

Now, pick up your bowl and move it over the waste and line up the outside edges of the bowl to the marks on the floor. Use the holes in the foot as a gauge. The original, long straight lines crossing the center of the waste should be passing through the center of the closet bolt holes in the bowl's foot.

Now, with drill in hand, make a pilot hole to either the inside or the outside of the old bolt hole. In either case, the new long bolts will be threading in at an angle.

Pick up the bowl and put the bowl wax down, in place. Then again carefully set the bowl down onto the wax. You can again use the marks on the floor to assure you that the bowl is indeed going back down in the proper location.

With a solid domed acorn nut and washer on each bolt, go fishing and find your new holes. Then, very slowly use the 7/16 inch wrench to draw the bowl down onto the floor. As you will read in the section for the machine thread type closet bolts used with closet flanges, we can fasten that type to the closet flange and then use them for locating pins. But in our case now, because the new wood screw type bolts will be on such angles, we would be unable to lower the bowl onto our angled bolts and still find the holes in the foot of the bowl.

One problem with using the wood screw type closet bolt is their failure to grip in wet and rotten wood flooring. The bolts in this case merely pull up and out of the wood when you attempt to thread them in. If you discover that you have a bad case of rot, you will have to replace this rotten portion of flooring with new material before the wood screw type closet bolts can once again draw the bowl down tightly to the floor.

However, if the bolts should pull free and the rot is not too substantial (or you need your toilet until you can schedule the floor repair), you can try this last ditch measure:

Purchase two 5/16 inch diameter by 4 inch long brass lag bolts and two flat washers for the bolts. Try threading these larger diameter bolts into the existing holes. Since these bolts have hex heads, the bowl will already have to be setting on the wax ring; the heads will not pass up through the hole in the foot of the bowl. If you are able to draw the bowl down tightly to the floor, you might be out of the woods for some time. We will know for certain after you bucket flush the bowl a dozen times and then check for seepage like we did on page 132.

### Reseating Your Bowl With Machine Thread Closet Bolts

If under your bowl you should find a closet flange (see Illus. 156 & 157) and the bolt slots are still existing, we will now properly install new flat head, long machine thread closet bolts. If your flange is composed of either cast iron or brass, we will slide the head of the new bolts under the slot and center the bolt shank in the length of the slot. Now drop a new flat washer (brass or stainless steel) down over the bolt and follow the washer with an open domed acorn nut. (Be very careful if you purchase these items at a hardware store. Many will sell prepackaged parts which are *steel* but plated to look like brass. And for heaven sakes, do not buy *anything* that is not brass.)

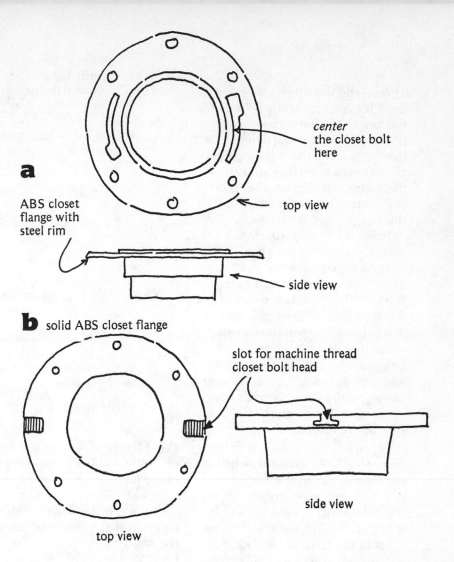

**a**

ABS closet flange with steel rim

*center* the closet bolt here

top view

side view

**b** solid ABS closet flange

slot for machine thread closet bolt head

side view

top view

Illustration **156**
ABS Closet Flanges

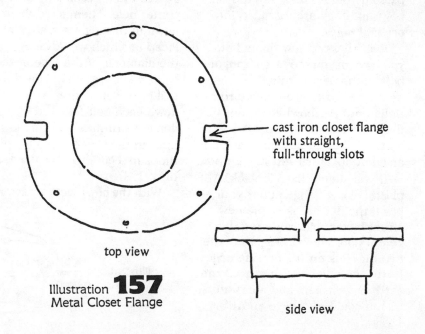

cast iron closet flange with straight, full-through slots

top view

side view

Illustration **157**
Metal Closet Flange

Thread the nut all the way down until it snugs up against the flat washer at the bottom, securely holding the bolt to the flange. Use the 7/16 inch or the 6 inch adjustable wrench to further snug up on the acorn nut. Repeat this procedure for the remaining slot in the flange.

Next, set the appropriate bowl wax down upon the flange. The outside edge of the wax will be gouged as we mentioned earlier. With the bolts attached to the flange, you may now pick up the bowl and set it upon the wax ring, using the closet bolts as locating or guide pins. Again, drop a stainless steel or brass flat washer over the top of the closet bolts as they protrude out through the holes in the foot of the bowl.

If you have a four-bolt bowl, the rear closet bolts (those attached to the flange) will now get open domed acorn nuts threaded down the bolts until they contact the flat washers. If you have another two bolts in the front of the foot, you will use wood screw type bolts which can be threaded into existing holes at this time. You could also have them already threaded in place if you are resetting the same bowl and they are threaded into original holes.

Regardless of how many bolts you have in your bowl, go from one bolt to the next turning the acorn nuts three or four complete rotations until the bowl is flat on the floor and resists any rocking motion. Then *slowly* turn each nut an additional turn and stop for now.

If you should have a black, ABS plastic closet flange under your bowl, the flat heads of the new closet bolts might slide into horizontal slots which are a part of the two big slots on the outside edges. In this case you will not need the extra flat washers and acorn nuts.

You could also have an ABS

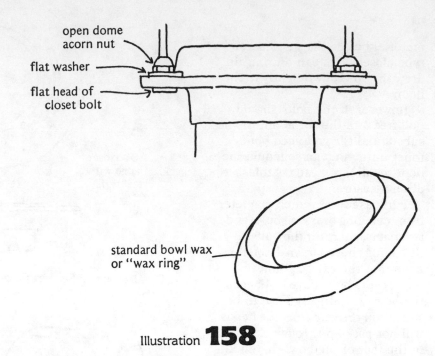

open dome acorn nut

flat washer

flat head of closet bolt

standard bowl wax or "wax ring"

Illustration **158**

closet flange with the center made of plastic and the outside portion of the flange made of steel. (These are usually orange or blue in color.) This outer metal flange will rotate on the center plastic portion until the wood screws secure it to the floor. With this type of closet flange, you would slide the flat head of the long machine closet bolt into the *larger* opening in the slotted arc on each side of the center hole. Then, slide them down until they are resting at a location which would represent the diameter of the hole in the center. Then, as we did for the iron and brass flange, drop a flat washer down each bolt followed by open dome acorn nuts and thread the nuts all the way down and snug them up securely to the flange (see Illus. 158).

With the bowl securely set upon

the floor, we can perform a test which will tell us if we will have a leak between the bowl and the floor. With a standard sized bucket, filled in a possible convenient tub or shower, pour the contents into the bowl, one bucketful after another. Do this a dozen times, being careful not to spill any water on the floor which could be mistaken for a leak of the closet bowl wax.

If you do have a leak at the bowl wax, water will seep or flow out from underneath the bowl. If after dumping these dozen bucket loads through the bowl, you have no leak, you can be relatively certain that a good seal has been achieved.

If we did have a leak, we would lift the bowl once more and reseat it before proceeding to the tank installation. If you have no leaks . . . Take A Break!

Illustration **159**
Spud Wrench

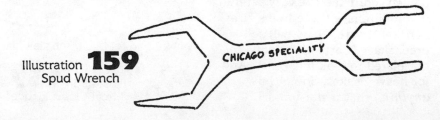

CHICAGO SPECIALITY

## Installing A New Spud
## In The Bowl

The spud (see Illus. 160) has two locations which are possible leak sources. One is between the rubber spud gasket and the porcelain bowl. The other is the threads of the spud barrel, where the flush elbow's slip nut threads on.

Aside from seepage from under the bowl, a leaking spud is one of the most common leak sources on wall-hung tank toilets. Usually the spud gasket dries out and cracks after many years of service and is no longer resilient, allowing water to sneak by.

The rubber slip nut washer under the slip nut attached to the spud suffers the same fate. So, it's very possible you might be reading this material because you have a spud related leak, not a waste related one.

If you do have a slip nut leak, at the spud, and can unthread the nut off the spud without rotating the spud in the back of the bowl, try wrapping the old dried out slip nut washer with Teflon tape, going around the elbow in front of the washer, over it and onto the threads of the spud. Then liberally apply RECTORSEAL/Slic-Tite to the female threads of the slip nut and then rejoin the two components. The slip nut will unthread from the spud in a *clockwise* direction as viewed from in *front* of the bowl.

To replace the spud, the flush elbow must be removed first. And on a newly reseated bowl, it is a very good idea to install a new spud or at least a new spud gasket if the old lock/mounting nut unthreads (most are corroded together so badly, it's a lost cause trying to reuse them) from the spud, and is still in good shape.

So, here we go — we are going to install a spud in a naked bowl.

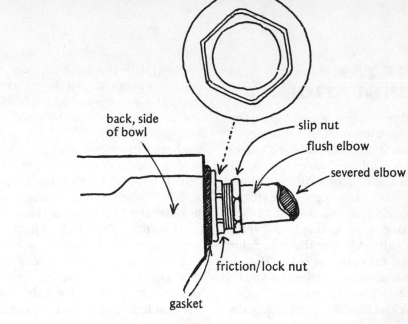

back, side of bowl

slip nut

flush elbow

severed elbow

friction/lock nut

gasket

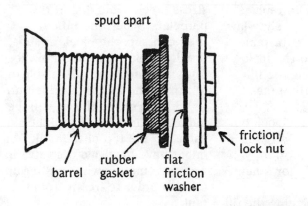

spud apart

spud together

barrel

rubber gasket

flat friction washer

friction/ lock nut

Illustration **160**

First, consult the spud illustrations above. A spud is composed of four parts:

1. a brass barrel
2. a rubber spud gasket
3. a flat friction washer, and
4. a friction/lock nut

Begin by backing up (unthreading) the friction/lock nut until the rubber gasket moves freely. Then insert the belled end of the brass barrel into the hole in the back of the bowl, using two or more fingers inserted inside the barrel. Now, shove the spud into the hole until the rubber spud gasket contacts the bowl. (Sometimes the hole in the bowl is a bit oblong and it takes a bit of wiggling to get it in.)

While holding it there, use your other hand to finger tighten the friction/lock nut. You should be able to count five or six threads on the backside of the friction/lock nut when the spud is installed good and tight.

Now use the large opening of the spud wrench (Illus. 159) to further tighten the friction/lock nut. The modern wall-hung tank toilet (1920 to 1930) will usually have the 2 inch spud, while the older pull-chain wall-hung will usually have a 1¼ inch spud. The spud might also be mounted to the *top* back of the bowl.

137

## THE TANK RENOVATION

In this section, we will gut your old existing tank of its components (ballcock and flush valve) and install new components. If both the ballcock (fill valve) and the flush valve were behaving properly and you do not wish to replace them at this time, you can skip ahead to the rehanging of the tank, on page 141. But, for those of you with true grit and the necessity, trudge onward!

With the tank lying safely on the floor, or still on the wall for those who need only to replace the fill valve, pick up the slide-jaw pliers or the 12 inch adjustable wrench and unthread the lock/mounting nut securing the fill valve to the tank bottom (see Illus. 161).

Then, pulling the ballcock out of the open tank, while wiggling it around in a circular motion, you will have a clean hole for a new valve.

For those just replacing the fill valve, now go to page 140.

Next, with the 15 or 16 inch slide-jaw pliers, adjust the jaws to grasp the lock/mounting nut holding the flush valve to the tank bottom (see Illus. 161). Try to unthread this nut off its threaded sleeve using a *counterclockwise* direction of rotation. If the large slide-jaw pliers will not budge the nut, use the 18 inch pipe wrench.

The entire flush valve might begin to rotate inside the tank. If this happens to you, place a block of wood or an old shoe between the base of the overflow tube and the inside back or front wall of the tank to prevent a possible stress crack occurring in the porcelain. When the tube base then contacts the block or shoe, it will check the rotation of the flush valve and you will be able to unthread the lock/mounting nut.

With the nut all the way off the male threaded sleeve, pull the old valve out the top of the tank. You might have to wiggle the valve in a circular motion while pulling up on it in order to free it from the tank.

Now that we have a naked tank, take a break!

## Fill Valves And Flush Valves

A very good, modern fill valve called the FLUIDMASTER 400A replaces the old ballcock designs in both close-coupled and wall-hung tanks. The ballcocks are inferior because of all the linkage and hinge-points in their design, and the float many times rotates on the float arm, thus not maintaining its adjustment.

Wall-hung tanks are deeper and hold more water than the close-coupled toilets. The FLUID-MASTER 400A *telescopes* to fit most all toilet tanks.

As for flush valves, the best one you can buy is the AMERICAN STANDARD #3158.078 "tilt-back." This model is made only for modern, low water level toilet tanks. But, with a little Yankee ingenuity, we can adapt it to also serve the wall-hung tank.

We will first go through the process of installing the old flush-ball type flush valve and then I will explain the little tricks enabling us to use the far superior AMERICAN STANDARD tilt-back design in the old wall-hung design.

When shopping for a flush-ball flush valve for your wall-hung tank, you must remember to tell the counterman or store clerk that you want one for a wall-hung tank. (Most hardware store clerks won't know the difference.) It would be a good idea to take the old, defective one with you or measure from the bottom of the tank to the top of the overflow tube.

Before installing the flush valve in the tank, we want to adjust the wire guide while the valve is still easily handled and a good side view is still possible. The wire guide is the little arm that clamps around the overflow tube (see Illus. 162). On the end of the wire

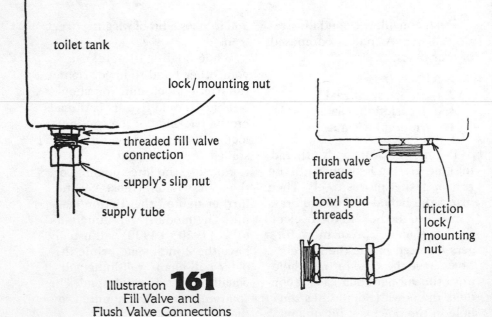

toilet tank

lock/mounting nut

threaded fill valve connection

supply's slip nut

supply tube

flush valve threads

bowl spud threads

friction lock/mounting nut

Illustration **161**
Fill Valve and
Flush Valve Connections

138

guide arm is a hole for the lift wire to slide through. The hole in this arm should be so situated as to be as close to center as possible above the flush ball seat (see Illus. 162). This guarantees that the flush ball will drop onto the seat as vertical and as level as possible, thus providing trouble free action and a watertight seal.

The wire guide will have a split in the circular portion that grips the overflow tube. This split will have a screw on one side which, when tightened, draws the ring tightly to the overflow tube after being set in a desired position.

Your wire guide might be loose in the box or it might be already secured to the overflow tube. Get the new flush ball out of its package and set it on the seat of the flush valve. If your wire guide is loose on the overflow tube, drop the lift wire with the male threads on the end, down through the hole in the arm and try threading it into the top of the flush ball. You might have to swing the wire guide a tiny bit one way or the other before the lift wire is vertical enough to be threaded into the flush ball.

The eye on the top of the lift wire should protrude out the top of the hole in the wire guide by 1½ inches or so. You may have to raise or lower your wire guide from its present position.

When you have set the guide to provide 1½ inches of lift wire out the top of the wire guide, make one final check for plumbness, or true vertical centering of the wire guide into the flush ball (see Illus. 162).

One way to do this is to view the flush valve from the vantage point which visually places the lift wire in front of the overflow tube. The lift wire should travel directly up the visual center of the overflow tube. Now, we are

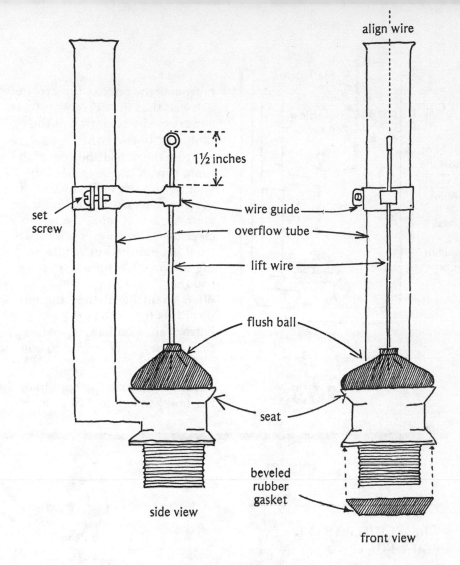

align wire

1½ inches

set screw

wire guide

overflow tube

lift wire

flush ball

seat

beveled rubber gasket

side view

front view

Illustration **162**
Flush Valve

ready to insert the flush valve into the tank, after tightening the set screw on the wire guide.

Aside from the overflow tube and flush valve itself, you should also have a rubber gasket and a large, thin friction nut. Usually, you have to purchase two lift wires and the flush ball separately. Before we install the new flush valve, remove the one lift wire and the flush ball and be careful not to bump the wire guide.

Now, slide the beveled rubber gasket, flat side up, up the threaded sleeve at the bottom of the flush valve (see Illus. 162). Shove it all the way up until it

reaches the top of the threads and cannot go any further.

Next, try cutting a piece of cardboard from an old box so that you can lay it on top of the bowl and then place the tank flat side down, on top of the cardboard. I find this elevation much easier to work at than trying to do it on the floor. Also, the finished tank will be closer to its final destination.

Now, apply liberally some RECTORSEAL/Slic-Tite to the *entire* beveled surface of the tank gasket and to the threads of the sleeve on the bottom of the flush valve. Once this is done, insert the valve into the hole in the

139

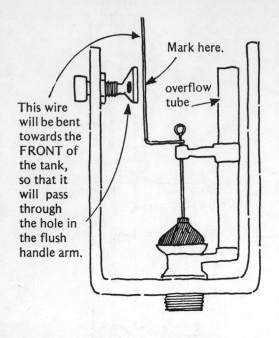

This wire will be bent towards the FRONT of the tank, so that it will pass through the hole in the flush handle arm.

Mark here.

overflow tube

Illustration
**163**

bottom of the tank and rotate the valve so that the overflow tube is closest to the back wall of the tank (see Illus. 163).

From the outside bottom of the tank, thread the large friction/lock nut up the male threads of the sleeve as far as you can using your fingers, turning the nut in a *clockwise* direction when viewed from behind the nut. While holding the overflow tube stationary, use the 15 or 16 inch slide-jaw pliers to further tighten the nut until it is flat against the tank bottom and you have squashed the rubber gasket inside the tank.

Once the large friction/lock nut first contacts the bottom of the tank, you should be able to

make two further revolutions on the nut. If the nut should still turn fairly easily, go slowly and try for an additional revolution or stop when you feel stiff resistance. When you finish tightening the nut, the overflow tube should still be close to the back wall of the tank.

We will do the final installation of the lift wires and flush ball when the tank is again rehung upon the wall.

NOTE: On some cheapo, low-boy designs, the flush valve is cast as an integral part of the tank bottom, in porcelain. For these types, you will have to use the FLUID-MASTER Flush Valve Replacement Kit.

## The FLUIDMASTER 400A Fill Valve

Now it is time to install the new fill valve. My choice is the FLUID-MASTER 400A because I can adapt it to almost every toilet tank made. It is easy to remove the valve top and clean it out if it ever becomes necessary. It is a simple design, well made, and provides years of trouble-free service. It is a little bit noisier than brass ballcocks, but well worth the trade-off.

Open the box and remove the valve and any cellophane bag containing the extra parts. Also inside the box is a section of black, vinyl tubing. Inside the cellophane bag you will find a black rubber gasket which has a deep circular groove about halfway in from the edge and in the very center is a small hole. Often you will find a black, right angled

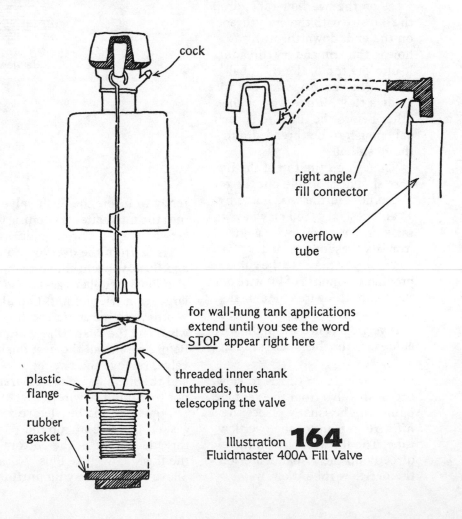

cock

right angle fill connector

overflow tube

for wall-hung tank applications extend until you see the word <u>STOP</u> appear right here

plastic flange

rubber gasket

threaded inner shank unthreads, thus telescoping the valve

Illustration **164**
Fluidmaster 400A Fill Valve

140

fill connector shoved through the hole. Pull it free.

With one pair of slide-jaw pliers (10 inch), grip the *outside* portion of the gasket. Now, with a second 10 inch slide-jaw pliers, grip the inner circle portion of the gasket and pull the two pieces apart. That deep groove was made so we could thus separate the two parts.

The larger, outside gasket will slide *up* the threads of the fill valve's base, with the raised lip of the gasket pointing down. Shove the gasket all the way *up* until it contacts the plastic flange (see Illus. 164).

The FLUIDMASTER 400A telescopes to fit almost any height of toilet tank. By gripping the post in the center with one hand and by using the other hand to unthread the *lower* portion, using a *counterclockwise* rotation as viewed from the bottom, unthread and *extend* the height of the fill valve until one inch of the fill valve protrudes out the top of the tank, when the valve is inserted into the hole in the tank bottom.

Rotate the entire valve in the hole until the little cock on the top of the valve (see Illus. 164) points directly towards the overflow tube of the flush valve. Then, with the slide-jaw pliers, tighten the friction/lock nut in a *clockwise* direction until the fill valve is held rigidly in place.

Now, another content of the cellophane bag is a black, right-angled piece of plastic with a stainless steel clip attached to the short side. This clip slides down the side of the flush valve's overflow tube, the side *closest* to the fill valve. If you put it on the wrong side of the tube, the water will fall into the tank instead of going down the inside of the tube. (This puts water back into the bowl after flushing.)

Pick up the flexible, black vinyl tubing and shove one end onto the barbed end of the right-angled plastic clip. Shove the stainless steel clip down over the overflow tube, and cut the vinyl tube to a length enabling you to shove the other end onto the fill valve's cock, without kinking the plastic tubing.

Congratulations! That's that.

## Rehanging The Tank

Reusing the old screws that you removed from the tank, which held it in place, or using new screws, rehang the tank in its original location. The standard, or shorter length of wood screw type closet bolt and solid domed acorn nuts are often used in place of common, roundhead wood screws for this application. And, since the closet bolts are brass, they will never rust. I suggest that you have a friend present to help hold the tank in position as you start the screws into the wall. With the tank secured, we can proceed to replumb the tank to the bowl, this time using a *two-piece* flush elbow.

## Two-Piece Flush Elbow

The two inch, two-piece flush el or closet elbow has a union in the middle which allows us to have already set the bowl and hung the tank back in position, prior to installing the el. With the standard one-piece flush el, we would have to attach the tank to the flush el while simultaneously hanging the tank on the wall. This is no great challenge to a plumber, but for the do-it-yourselfer I fear that it would be a real headache (see Illus. 165).

Inside the box containing the two-piece flush el, you will find three slip nuts, two brass friction rings, a flat rubber union washer

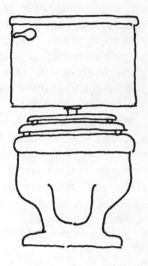

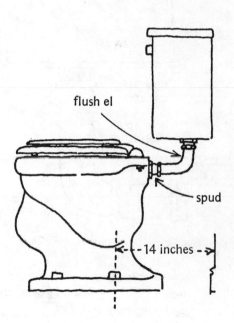

flush el

spud

- 14 inches -

Illustration **165**
Typical "Modern"
Wall-hung Tank Toilet

141

and two, 2-inch rubber slip nut washers (see Illus. 166).

First, we will assemble the two-piece flush el so that we can measure, cut and fit it to the tank and bowl, prior to its final installation. The bent half of the two-piece flush el will have a lip on the bend end and the straight half will have male threads on the end.

Now, pick up the bent half, with the lip (see Illus. 166). Slide the slip nut on, cup side down, down from the smooth end until it comes to rest over the lip. Next, insert the *flat* rubber union washer into the union nut attached to the bent half.

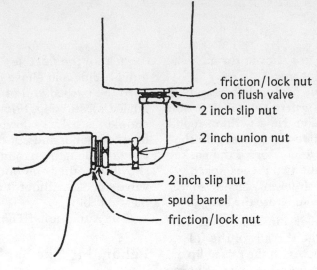

Illustration **167**

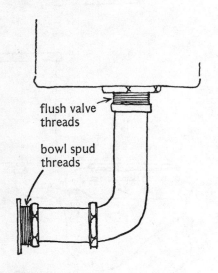

flush valve threads

bowl spud threads

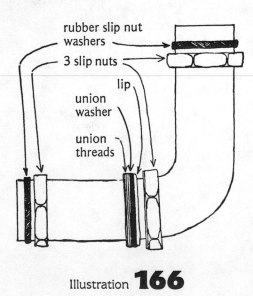

rubber slip nut washers

3 slip nuts

lip

union washer

union threads

Illustration **166**

Next, pick up the straight half and thread the slip nut onto the male threads using a *clockwise* direction of rotation on the nut as viewed from *above* the flat, backside of the nut. We want to join the two pieces to form a 90 degree bend. Tighten the nut only finger tight for now.

Now, insert the end of the bent half of flush el into the threaded sleeve on the bottom of the flush valve, on the bottom of the tank. While holding it there, swing the el to one side or the other so that the bottom end lays up against the side of the bowl spud (see Illus. 168). This end of the flush el might be several inches below the level of the spud. If it is, we will make further adjustments further on. For now, taking in account the depth of the hole in the back of the bowl spud, mark the flush el where it would be in full penetration into the spud. A lipstick or a grease pencil works well. You could also use the mini-hacksaw to lightly cut through the chrome plating.

If you should find that the length of the tubular elbow is okay as it is, so much the better. To trim the el to length, open the jaws of the tubing cutter far enough so that you can slide it over and down the tubing to your mark. Close the jaws, bringing the cutting wheel into contact with your mark. (Take time to read page 75 which discusses the use of tubing cutters.)

After trimming the bottom half, again insert the top half back into the flush valve and again swing the bottom up against the side of the bowl's spud. Now with a ruler or tape measure, measure from an imaginary center line of the flush el to an imaginary center line of the bowl spud (see Illus. 169). This measurement will tell you how much to trim off the top portion of the flush el, the half that is now inserted into the flush valve. With a ruler or tape measure, measure down from the top of the flush el and mark the distance that you must trim off. Again, use the tubing cutter to trim the top half of the flush el to this length plus ¼ inch.

On very rare occasions I find it unnecessary to do any trimming of the flush el, or maybe just to one end. (The tank just happens to be at the right height and the bowl is just the right distance from the wall. You could conceivably find yourself in this rare position, but the odds are slim.)

142

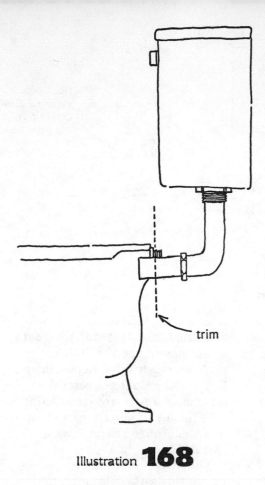

trim

Illustration **168**

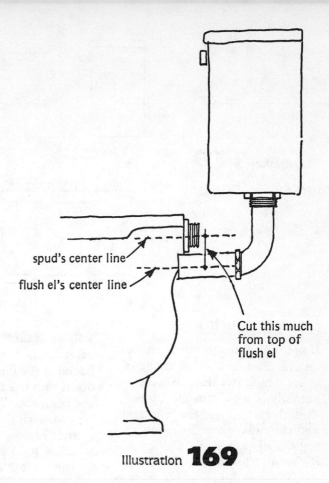

spud's center line

flush el's center line

Cut this much
from top of
flush el

Illustration **169**

With the top section of flush el trimmed, we can now make a final installation. Make a mark 'T' on the tank end and 'B' on the bowl end of the flush el. This will save you any confusion from putting the wrong end of the el in the wrong place.

Now, undo the union nut joining the two halves together and be careful not to lose the flat, rubber union washer that's inside the slip nut. Next, slide another slip nut, cup end *up*, down the top, tank side of the el, followed by a rubber slip nut washer (see Illus. 166). Now, wrap some Teflon tape on the toilet bowl spud's threads, following the *clockwise* direction of the threads.

Now, slide the last slip nut, cup side out, onto the straight spud side of flush el, followed by the other rubber slip nut washer (see Illus. 166). After doing this, insert the smooth end into the bowl spud, and slide the slip nut back bringing with it the rubber slip nut washer. Thread the slip nut onto the spud's threads by rotating the slip nut in a *counter-clockwise* direction as viewed from in *front* of the bowl. Use only your fingers for now.

Next, wrap the threads of the flush valve, which protrude out the bottom of the tank, with Teflon tape. Again, make sure to follow the upward, *clockwise* direction of threads on the valve. We can now insert the bent end of the tank half of the flush el into the flush valve and slide the slip nut *up*, bringing with it the rubber slip nut washer and thread the slip nut onto the flush valve threads using a *clockwise* direction of rotation as viewed from below. Again, use only your fingers for right now (see Illus. 167).

Now, reinsert the flat, rubber union washer into the middle slip nut if it has fallen out. Then, thread the slip nut onto the male union threads using a *counter-clockwise* direction of rotation as viewed from in *front* of the bowl.

When all three slip nuts are finger tight, use the big opening on the spud wrench or the jaws of the 15 or 16 inch slide-jaw pliers to snug up each connection.

You might have to pull down on the tank half of flush el or pull out on the bowl half of flush el to mate the two halves, if the two pieces are trimmed a little short. If the two pieces will not both fit into the tank and bowl and allow you to join them with the union slip nut, then one or both pieces of flush el are still too *long* and must be trimmed down further.

Use a mini-hacksaw to do this further trimming if the tubing cutter is too wide to accomplish the feat.

Take A Break!

143

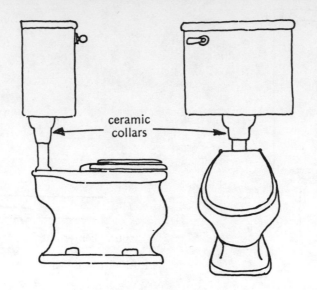

ceramic collars

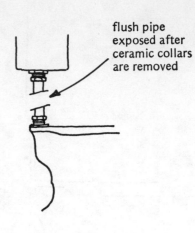

flush pipe exposed after ceramic collars are removed

Illustration **170**
Wall-hung Toilet
with Straight Flush Pipe

## Straight Flush Pipe

If you are so fortunate as to own an old CRANE, or other make of toilet which has the flush el actually being a *straight* pipe directly connecting the bowl spud and the tank, your flush valve replacement task is a slight bit different. The straight flush pipe has only one dimension to trim to length: the vertical height. Removal of the flush valve from the tank is identical to page 138.

Installation of the AMERICAN STANDARD #3158.078 Tilt-Back flush valve is a bit different. If the tank bottom is so thick as to prevent enough of the flush valve's threads to protrude out the bottom far enough to thread the upper 2 inch slip nut fully and tightly in place, then discard the beveled, rubber tank gasket and make a putty snake of plumber's putty ½ inch in diameter and wrap it around the base of the flush valve, up against the bottom of the lip (see Illus. 174).

If the top of the overflow tube is too far below the old water level (in most cases it will be), read pages 147-148 on *Hot Rodding Your Wall-Hung Tank Toilet*. It will instruct you on how to heighten the overflow tube and modify your existing flush handle to accept the new flush valve.

On some of the straight pipe wall-hung tank toilets, the fill valve inside the tank does not fasten to the tank at all, but hangs down into the tank, from above the back rim. With this type of "over-the-rim" ballcock, you cannot replace it with the FLUID-MASTER 400A fill valve.

The same 2 inch rubber slip nut washers and slip nuts are used on the straight pipe as we used on the two-piece, 90 degree flush el. Your only difference here is that you must hold the tank in place, up against the wall as you refit the straight flush pipe into the bowl spud, and flush valve.

Also, you will find (probably) a porcelain collar, in one or two pieces, which hides the flush pipe when in place. The top half of the collar might unthread from a bracket which in turn is threaded to the flush valve's threads.

When you install the new flush valve, any such bracket will probably not thread back onto the new flush valve. (The old flush valve had a good deal more threads protruding out the bottom of the tank for this purpose.) So, use plumber's putty packed between a two-piece collar which is taped together until the putty becomes stiff enough to hold the two pieces securely. A one-piece collar can be cemented in place.

Because of these collar brackets, this is one instance where it would pay to use the FLUID-MASTER Flush Valve Replacement Kit. This product converts the flush mechanism from the old lift wire/flush ball system to a stainless steel hinged flapper valve (Kit 555).

I have seen just a few occasions where this kit would not fit because of an oversized overflow tube. Ask your supplier if you may return the kit if it doesn't fit, before you purchase it. I would say that it is a safe 90 percent chance that the kit will fit your flush valve.

Congratulations. Take a breather.

NOTE: It is sometimes possible to replace the flush elbow on a wall-hung tank *without* removing the tank from the wall. I said *sometimes*. By undoing the lock/mounting nut on the flush valve and lifting the flush valve out the top of the tank, you can then, maybe, lift the old flush elbow up and out the same hole in the tank bottom. Then, reintroduce the new flush elbow into the bowl and replace the flush valve.

I went through the process of removing the tank because for many an installation, it is the *only* way to install a new flush elbow.

144

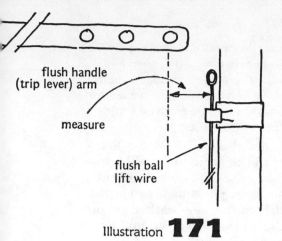

flush handle (trip lever) arm

measure

flush ball lift wire

Illustration **171**

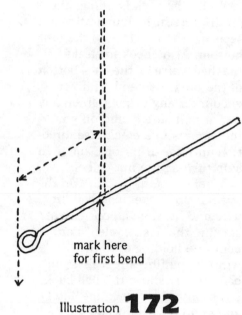

mark here for first bend

Illustration **172**

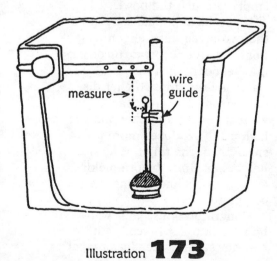

measure →

wire guide

Illustration **173**

## Installing The Lift Wires, Flush Ball And Supply Tube

Now it is time to finish the tank plumbing. Set the new flush ball back on its seat. (We removed it and the wires before installing the valve in the tank.) Then insert the lift wire with the male threads on the end down through the hole in the wire guide and thread the end into the top of the flush ball. Using a tape measure, measure the distance from the lift wire to the underside of the flush handle arm (see Illus. 171). It will probably be somewhere about one inch to actually having one directly above the other.

Next, pick up the remaining lift wire, the one without the threads on the end. Measure from the eye end and make a mark at the same distance that you measured already, from the flush ball lift wire to underneath the flush handle (trip lever). At this mark, grip the smooth ended lift wire with one pair of slide-jaw pliers, so that the wire lays in the first groove near the front of the jaws.

Now, with the second pair of slide-jaw pliers, grip the wire on the far side of your measured mark and bend the wire into a 90 degree bend (see Illus. 172). Next, unthread the lift wire which is threaded into the flush ball and remove it from the wire guide. Then set the eye of our newly bent, 90 degree wire over the hole in the wire guide.

We now want a vertical measurement, where we will be level with the closest hole in the flush handle arm (see Illus. 173). Mark the wire again at this point. We are going to use the 10 inch slide-jaw pliers again to make a 90 degree bend in the wire. However, we first must determine which direction to bend the wire, towards the back of the tank or

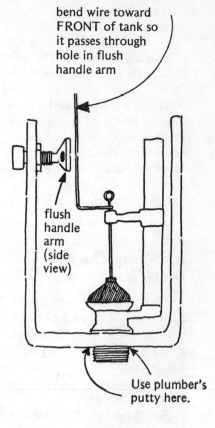

bend wire toward FRONT of tank so it passes through hole in flush handle arm

flush handle arm (side view)

Use plumber's putty here.

Illustration **174**

towards the front of the tank. The direction will be determined by which side of the flush handle arm the vertical wire passes (see Illus. 174).

In the appropriate direction, bend the wire again in the 90 degrees. With the mini-hacksaw, cut the wire's end so that only 1½ inches stick out the hole in the flush handle arm (trip lever arm).

With the eye of our bent-formed lift wire placed on the hole in the wire guide, drop the straight, flush ball lift wire down through both holes and thread the end back into the top of the flush ball. Now, send the end of the bent-formed wire through the closest hole in the flush handle arm if you haven't done so

145

already. Use one pair of slide-jaw pliers to bend the last 1½ inches down.

So much for that design. One of your lift wires might be a different shape from the one we bent-formed in the above exercise. If you have a smooth end wire which already has a 90 degree bend at the eye end, you may need to bend-form the flush handle arm, moving it closer to the overflow tube.

Congratulations, take a break!

•

## Installing The New Wall-Hung Tank Supply Tube

You have already read pages 47-55, on angle stops and supplies and have a new ½ inch female iron pipe by ⅜ inch brass ferrule compression angle stop (or other type) installed . . . correct? Now for the supplies.

Toilet fill valves are the *one* location where I employ any rubber cone washers with a new supply. I also use the "faucet" supply with the acorn head (BRASS CRAFT/EASTMAN) sized for faucet connections, and I want to tell you why.

The acorn head of the faucet supply will slide up the inside of the larger diameter connection of the fill valve. When you fit the supply to the angle stop and the fill valve, slide the acorn a full 1½ inch up the fill valve connection. You will notice that you can insert the acorn up at least this far on the FLUIDMASTER 400A before it bottoms out on a reduced diameter.

By doing this, you can then drop the supply back down and insert the other end into the threaded sleeve on the angle stop after trimming it to length. You do not have to further bend the supply to make it fit. After doing

this "fitting-up," remove the supply and then slide the ⅜ inch rubber cone washer up to within 2 inches of the acorn, followed by the hard, red plastic friction washer followed by the amber colored plastic slip nut included in the cellophane bag.

Then, install the ⅜ inch brass ferrule compression nut onto the supply, cup side down, followed by the brass ferrule. Once again, shove the acorn up into the fill valve connection and then drop the other end into the angle stop. As you read in the angle stop section, start the threads of the ferrule nut first (see page 77).

Wrap Teflon tape on the male threads of the fill valve and then thread the upper slip nut onto the fill valve connection using a *clockwise* direction of rotation as viewed from below. Then, snug up both nuts.

The only options to the faucet supply are poor choices. There is a closet supply designed for ballcocks which has a flat head, surfaced in hard plastic which resembles the brim of a hat. This flat surface mates flush to the bottom of the fill valve connection upon installation (supposedly) of the slip nut.

This type of supply is *very* unforgiving if absolute accuracy is not attained on fitting-up, and the threaded plastic connection of the 400A is softer than that of a brass ballcock and does not offer a real good resistance to the hard plastic brim; thus, the leaks.

Your other choice is the spirally grooved supply with a rubber cone washer on top. We sometimes use this type when a close-coupled toilet replaces a wall-hung toilet, and the angle stop is too close to the bottom of the tank to successfully bend the smooth ⅜ inch faucet supply. However, when there is room to

use the smooth faucet supply, I do so because we get a better seal with the acorn up inside the fill valve connection and we cannot always trim the grooved supply to the optimum length.

Are you ready? We can now open the angle stop and begin filling the tank. Have a pair of slide-jaw pliers handy to further tighten the cone washer nut on the fill valve connection if it produces a leak.

While the tank is filling, check for drips at the lock/mounting nut securing the fill valve to the tank bottom. Also check for leaks at the flush valve on the back bottom of the tank. Remember, if you encounter any drips, tighten any nut or bolt *slowly* and only in ¼ increments in a *clockwise* direction until the drip stops, and then *stop* turning the nut or bolt.

When the tank is full, grip the eye on top of the flush ball lift wire and lift the ball off its seat, starting the flush cycle. Then, continue holding onto the lift wire. If you find any leaks, you can quickly shove the ball back down onto the seat immediately and end up with a whole lot less water on the floor than if you activated the flush handle and let the entire contents of the tank empty through the bowl.

If you have no leaks, even in the two-piece flush el connections, then concentrate on observing the foot of the toilet bowl. The water is dropping a higher distance from the tank than when we tested with a bucket and the higher fall produces more pressure. Flush the toilet at least a half dozen times before picking up your tools and calling the job complete.

Congratulations, your wall-hung tank toilet is ready for another several decades of loyal service.

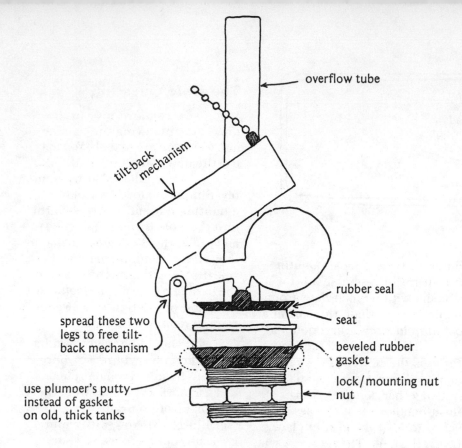

overflow tube

tilt-back mechanism

spread these two legs to free tilt-back mechanism

use plumber's putty instead of gasket on old, thick tanks

rubber seal

seat

beveled rubber gasket

lock/mounting nut nut

Illustration **175**
American Standard #3158.078 Flush Valve

## How To "Hot Rod" Your Wall-Hung Tank Toilet

If you can muster the patience to follow through with the following section (having a second toilet helps) you can make your existing wall-hung tank toilet out-perform any new one on the market. It requires a little bit of creative work, but it is really quite simple.

The AMERICAN STANDARD #3158.078 flush valve (in this plumber's opinion) is the best one on the market, bar none (see Illus. 175). It will fit almost all toilets, save some of the "low-boys" and the original "pull-chain" designs. The #3158.078 is the *only* valve that I can install and *know* that it will perform its job year in and year out without any trouble.

Around 1978 California mandated that new toilets being sold within its boundaries be limited to a much smaller tank capacity, due to recent drought conditions. On the new toilets that do have a smaller tank, you find that the overflow tube on the flush valves have been trimmed in height by about 1½ inches. Thus, any attempt to raise the water level in the tank is foiled by the water runoff down the shorter overflow tube. However, if they can cut the tube down, we can put it back and even higher so that you can use this excellent product in your old wall-hung tank toilet.

By purchasing a ¾ inch PVC coupling (solvent by solvent sockets), about 6 inches of ¾ inch PVC pipe, and some PVC solvent/cement, we can extend the height of the overflow tube.

Installation of the valve is exactly the same as for the flush ball type that we have already installed on pages 138-140 except that we do *not* have any lift wires to fuss with. You might have to purchase the matched AMERICAN STANDARD #3525.011 Tilt-Back flush handle (trip lever) assembly. You *will* have to purchase approximately 6 inches of heavy duty, brass rubber stopper ball chain and two couplers (see Illus. 176).

After you have installed the new flush valve and the new FLUIDMASTER 400A fill valve, rehang the tank to the wall and install the new two-piece flush elbow as discussed on pages 141-143.

Now it is time to tackle the removal of the old flush arm and handle (trip lever). On these older toilets, you will probably find two types of flush handles. If you have a lock/mounting nut on the *inside* top of the tank, it will probably be a *left hand* thread (see Illus. 177 on next page). Use the 12 inch adjustable wrench, if it will fit, or one of the smaller adjustable wrenches and try to rotate the nut in a *counter-clockwise* direction as viewed from in *front* of the tank, not from in back of the nut. Loosen

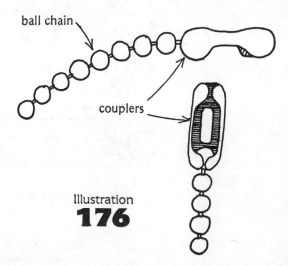

ball chain

couplers

Illustration **176**

147

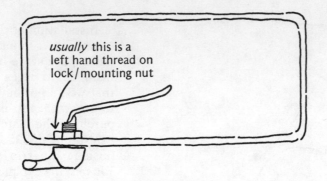

Illustration
**177**

*usually* this is a
left hand thread on
lock / mounting nut

## The Hole Question

If you see a *square* hole in the tank after removing the handle and arm, you are in luck. You may use the new AMERICAN STANDARD #3525.011 handle and arm assembly. Simply remove its lock/mounting nut and insert the arm into the hole (from the outside) and make the 90 degree turn and then slide the nut up the arm, flat side first, and thread the nut onto the handle base using a *clockwise* direction of rotation as viewed from in *front* of the tank.

the nut all the way off the threads and then slide it all the way off the flush arm.

Once the nut is off, try wiggling slightly the handle as you pull out on it. If it will not budge, squirt some penetrating oil from inside the tank into the visible space around the threaded handle base. Now go have a cup of coffee or a shot of Irish and come back in fifteen minutes. If the handle still won't budge, use the slide-jaw pliers and grip the handle in the jaws and pull out *slowly* and steadily to free it, and keep wiggling the handle.

If your tank has a handle held in place by a screw on the top front of the handle, remove the screw using a *counterclockwise* direction and slide the handle off. Behind the handle, you will see a

different type of lock/mounting nut. It might resemble a little volcano with wrench flats around its perimeter. Undo this nut in a *counterclockwise* direction and you will be able to pull the arm in towards the center of the tank and it will part from the tank wall.

One other common design of flush handle assembly uses a set screw to hold the arm in place, inside the tank. The set screw will be on top of the arm, securing it to the handle. Undo the set screw and the arm will slide free. Now, using the slide-jaw pliers, rotate the lock/mounting nut holding the arm bracket to the tank in a *clockwise* direction as viewed from in *front* of the tank. Then the bracket will part from the tank wall. KOHLER toilets use this later design.

If you should happen to find a *round* hole, we will reuse your existing handle. Using a ruler, make a mark 4¼ inches from the axle or pivot point of your arm (see Illus. 178). Now, with a mini-hacksaw, cut a groove in your flush arm ⅛ inch deep. Next slide a standard paper clip down the end of the arm and make sure that it drops into the saw cut. It is time to reinstall the arm and handle back into the tank.

Now, pick up one of the two ball chain couplers you bought and attach one to the end of the ball chain already attached to the tilt-back valve. You might have to squeeze the end of the coupling once it is in place if the coupling is sized for a larger ball. Insert the end of the ball chain that you purchased into the other end of the coupler.

If you were able to use the #3525.011 handle, hold the chain in an almost direct line to the end of the flush arm, allowing a bit of slack in the chain, and then lay the chain in the slots of the flush arm. You do *not* want the tilt-back seal to be raised off the seat of the flush valve when the handle is at rest, or the tank will flush.

For you paper clippers, send one end of a chain coupler over the outside leg of the paper clip,

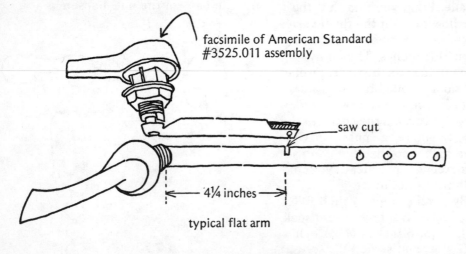

facsimile of American Standard
#3525.011 assembly

saw cut

◂— 4¼ inches —▸

typical flat arm

Illustration **178**
Flush Handles

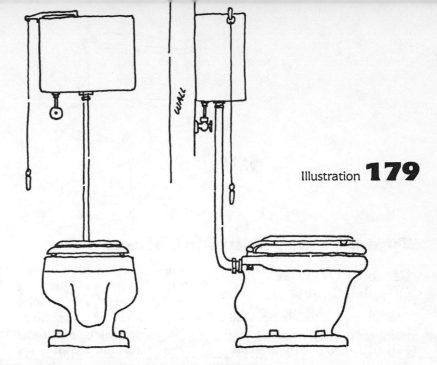

Illustration **179**

bringing it down to rest at the bottom curve of the clip. Again as we did above, attach the end of the tilt-back chain to the second chain coupler. To this coupler, attach the end of the chain you purchased. Now, lifting the chain up until it is almost a direct line to the coupler hanging in the paper clip. Again allow for a little slack in the chain. Slip the appropriate chain ball into the open end of the coupler. You will have to cut off the excess length of chain, so start long and work up to the exact length needed. You might also need to saw off the excess length of flush arm, ¼ inch from the saw cut. If the end of the arm now completes its travel without lifting the tilt-back valve off its seat, then proceed with cutting it down.

Our last operation is to extend the height of the overflow tube. Pick up the ¾ inch PVC coupler and using the solvent cement, glue it onto the short piece of PVC pipe that you purchased. Now, measure the distance from the top of the overflow tube on the flush valve to about 1 inch below the flush handle hole. Cut your PVC pipe to this measurement and cement the other side of the coupling to the top of the overflow tube. You might have to force the coupling on a bit but it will slide onto the overflow tube for a good ¼ inch.

Open the angle stop and fill the tank. Do your check-out as described on page 146.

Task completed, take a breather.

NOTE: In time, the paper clip will rust away and need replacing. If you could get ahold of some stainless steel tying wire or some brass wire to wire the coupler to the notch in the flush arm, it would make for a more lasting repair.

## Pull-Chain Wall-Hung Toilets

If you still have one of the real old pull-chain wall-hung toilets, finding tank components is almost impossible. Salvage dealers specializing in old building supplies would be your best bet. This toilet (see Illus. 179) had a lead lining inside the wooden, wall-mounted tank. After many years, the lead would spring a leak and the water would come cascading down from the sides and bottom of the wood tank.

If you remove the tank from the wall and then remove the flush valve and fill valve just as we did for the modern wall-hung tank toilet, you can take the remnants of the old lead liner to your local sheet metal shop and have them fabricate a new one from galvanized steel, or copper.

The flush valve on this old toilet tank unthreads from the tank the same way the more modern version does. Your fill valve might be the "Over The Rim" type. If you need a new fill valve, I suggest that you telephone the plumbing suppliers in your area and ask if they know where you can order one. Instead of a rubber flush ball, or a tilt-back design of flush mechanism, the old timers had a cast iron or brass tubular "horseshoe." When lifted vertically off its seat, the falling water escaping down the flush elbow then siphoned the remaining contents of the tank even after the heavy elbow fell immediately back into place on the seat.

There are several manufacturers producing reproductions of this old style toilet and they use modern fill valves and flush valves. If your present tank has a water supply *below* the tank (instead of the "Over The Rim" ballcock), you might want to consider scrapping the old tank for a newer design.

The bowl will be installed exactly like the more modern wall-hung tank toilets. You might find that your bowl spud is on the top rear of the bowl, instead of on the back like the more modern designs.

It's been my experience that whenever the bowl is lifted for reseating with a new bowl wax, the old waste in the floor needs a good bit of doctoring. Unless yours is seeping, my advice would be to leave it alone.

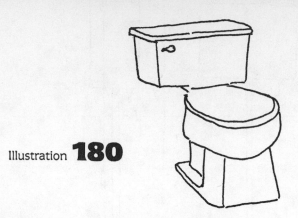

Illustration **180**

## Typical Close-Coupled Toilets

### Removal Of Close-Coupled Toilets

Close-coupled toilets became popular in the late 1930s and early 40s and are the prevalent design of toilet being manufactured today. In this design, the tank is bolted directly to the back of the bowl (see Illus. 180).

Some close-coupled toilets will have the four-bolt foot that we found on the wall-hung tank version. Again, we turn off the angle stop using a *clockwise* direction of rotation on the handle. Then, flush the tank and remove all of the water as possible from *both* the tank and the bowl, as we did for the wall-hung toilet. Again, you might want to read pages 47-55 dealing with angle stops and supplies before doing anything else.

If you have a friend present who can help you transport the toilet out of the house (if you are junking it) or just across the room if you are going to replace a faulty bowl wax, you can then leave the tank coupled to the bowl. If you are doing the job by yourself, you might want to remove the tank from the bowl so that you can handle the heavy components safely.

Tank lids suffer a high mortality rate because they are often lifted and being made of such fragile material, they are subject to breakage. If you have a very old close-coupled toilet which you are replacing with a newer one, the lid to your old toilet might be worth as much as ten dollars to some salvage dealers. So pick up the lid and safely lay it flat, out of the battle zone. Even if you are keeping the same toilet, put the lid safely away for now so you won't have to waste any more time shopping for another one later.

If you are working by yourself, and have removed the supply, put the ⅝ inch box or open end wrench on the tank bolt nuts, underneath the back of the bowl. If the nut is not a ⅝ inch size, use the 6 inch adjustable wrench. Now, with the 16 to 18 inch slotted screwdriver in the slot of the tank bolt (in the bottom of the tank) try turning the screwdriver in a *counterclockwise* direction. If the bolt refuses to turn, hold the screwdriver stationary and move the wrench in a *clockwise* direction of rotation as viewed from *above*. In either case, remove the nut from the bolt on each of the two or three tank bolts.

With all the tank bolt nuts removed, grasp the tank with your two hands, from the bottom sides, and lift it free. I suggest that you carry it right outside for now, or if you are going to reinstall it, put it in a safe place, close by.

With the tank removed, use the 7/16 inch box wrench or the 6 inch adjustable wrench and remove the acorn nuts on each side of the bowl's foot. With the nuts thus removed, you may prepare to lift the bowl. I suggest that you read pages 131 & 132, where we dealt with this procedure for the wall-hung tank design, which is the same as you'll follow for the close-coupled design.

There is still a good quart or more of water inside the toilet's trap and if you tip the bowl too far when moving it, you'll end up with it on the floor.

Now, with the entire toilet removed, read pages 123-126, if you haven't already, which deals with the floor, waste line, closet flange and bowl wax. Also, read pages 47-55 dealing with angle stops and supplies and install a new angle stop right now. Then, read pages 133 through 136, and set your new bowl or reset your old bowl.

If you have purchased a new toilet, you will have two cardboard cartons. Inside the carton containing your new bowl, you will find the closet bolt caps and two flat plastic disks and maybe two spring steel clips. Throw away the two disks and the two little spring clips, but hang onto the caps.

After trimming the long closet bolts to length with the mini-hacksaw, use some DAP or other brand of tub and tile caulk, administered to the bottom edge of the caps, and then set them on top of the closet bolts and gently press down.

You want the trimmed closet bolt to almost touch the top of the cap (inside). Use the depth of the cap as a gauge to mark the closet bolt before trimming. If you cut the bolt off flush with the top of the acorn nut or just a bit higher, and you need to lift the bowl again in the future, you will not be able to reuse these existing closet bolts.

## Installing The Close-Coupled Tank

With the new bowl in place, carefully cut the tank carton top off, which contains the lid, and then cut one side of the remaining carton free to lay upon the bowl. If you are resetting your existing toilet, get any piece of cardboard to lay on the bowl.

Inside the tank, you will find a cellophane or clear plastic bag. This bag will contain the tank bolts, tank bolt nuts, tank bolt washers, both rubber and metal, a round sponge rubber tank gasket and a U-shaped rubber chafing gasket (in the case of AMERICAN STANDARD — see Illus. 181). KOHLER will ship slightly different parts. We will first install the AMERICAN STANDARD tank and then the KOHLER tank.

Now, lay the tank, back side down, flat upon the cardboard covering the bowl. With the 15 or 16 inch slide-jaw pliers, make certain that the plastic lock/mounting nut on the flush valve is tight. Then make certain that the lock/mounting nut on the fill valve is tight (see Illus. 182).

Now, shove the beveled foam rubber gasket over the threads of the flush valve, flat side up against the bottom of the tank. This gasket will completely cover the lock/mounting nut. Now, with the plumber's putty, roll out a little "snake" about ¼ inch in diameter and about 6 inches long.

Make one wrap of putty snake under each flat head of the tank bolts, then shove the rubber washers up the bolts from the bottom. Now, make another wrap of snake under the rubber washers. Following this, apply a good coating of RECTORSEAL/Slic-Tite to the beveled surface of the sponge rubber gasket, already in place on the flush valve. Now, from inside the tank, insert each bolt through the holes in the tank bottom. The tilt-back flush seat of the AMERICAN STANDARD Cadet hides the hole on one side. The tilt-back mechanism will come free, exposing the hole, if you gently spread the mounting legs (see Illus. 175 on page 147).

On the floor at each side of the rear of the toilet, place one brass flat washer and one tank bolt nut. Now, pick up the U-shaped chafing gasket. Next, insert one hand into the bottom of the tank and hold your thumb or finger on one tank bolt head and at the same

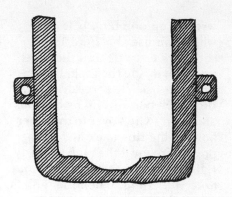

time push the chafing gasket onto each bolt with the bottom of the U-shaped gasket on the back side of the flush valve. You will see a hole for the bolt to pass through on each leg of the chafing gasket (see Illus. 181).

Now, pick up the tank, very carefully, and slowly lower the round rubber tank gasket into the mating hole on the back of the bowl. The tank bolts will find their respective holes with a little wiggling of the tank.

With the tank resting on the bowl, tilt the tank to one side, matters not which, and, keeping a steady hold on the tank, pick up one flat washer and nut that you placed nearby and slide the washer up the tank bolt which is hanging down through the hole in the bowl. Again with your hand inside the tank, push down on the head of the bolt while you loosely thread the brass nut up the bolt. Don't thread the nut up more than three or four revolutions for right now. Then, tilt the tank to the other side and repeat the process. With both nuts still loose, center the tank level upon the bowl, and vertical with the back wall.

Now put the 7/16 inch box wrench or the 6 inch adjustable

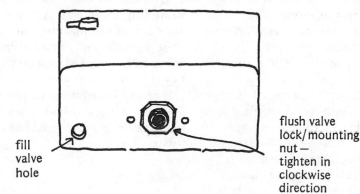

fill valve hole

flush valve lock/mounting nut — tighten in clockwise direction

Illustration **182**

151

wrench on one tank bolt nut while you use the 16 to 18 inch screwdriver to tighten the bolts up, from inside the tank. I suggest that you use the screwdriver to turn each bolt several revolutions and then switch over to the other bolt, doing this back and forth procedure until the tank is nearly rigid on the bowl. *Go slowly and take your time*. When the tank is secured, reinsert the tilt-back mechanism back into the mounting legs. When this is done, read page 146 and reinstall the supply tube.

Since the new toilet has the fill valve already installed, you will have to purchase a ⅜ inch "closet" supply cone washer. Because I want to avoid making a return trip to someone's house to make adjustments to the cheapo fill valves installed in *all* toilets today, I make it a practice to yank out the brand new factory installed fill valve and install a FLUIDMASTER 400A right off the bat. If you choose to do this also, the ⅜ inch closet cone washer is in the box with the new fill valve (read pages 140 & 141).

Now, open the angle stop and fill the tank. You will notice that on the top of the ballcock fill valve (factory installed) there is a hinged, metal (which will probably soon become plastic) triangular float arm bracket held in place by a long machine screw. Under this bracket there is a hexagonal, white plastic nut. If the tank fills very slowly or all of a sudden stops filling, turn off the angle stop.

On an older toilet, the tank bolt might be ⅝ inch in size. Try the ⅝ inch box wrench on the nut. It will work better in the close confines of the back end of the bowl.

Then using the 6 or 8 inch slotted screwdriver, remove the machine screw securing the hinged float arm bracket to the ballcock. Remove the bracket and float arm. With the 8 or 12 inch adjustable wrench, undo the white plastic nut using a *counter-clockwise* rotation as viewed from above. When you have removed the nut, you will see a black rubber diaphragm with two holes on its outside perimeter. Get an empty peanut butter jar or large drinking glass and hold it down over the open top of the ballcock. Now open the angle stop all the way and let the rocketing water carry the diaphragm and the lodged crud up into the jar and down into the tank. Let the water run for a minute and purge the ballcock.

After this, replace the diaphragm back in the top of the ballcock with the white plastic button pointing up. Then, rethread the white plastic nut back into the top of the ballcock using a *clockwise* direction of rotation as viewed from above.

Then, holding the float arm back in position, replace the long machine screw. The front hole in the wings that hold the float arm bracket doesn't have any threads. Only the back wing has a threaded hole. So just wiggle the screw through the first hole and start it in the back threaded hole. Then turn the screw in a *clockwise* direction as viewed from in front.

Now, open the angle stop again and fill the tank. If the water level rises so high that it runs down the overflow tube, bend the float arm down slightly and let enough water out of the tank by tipping the tilt-back mechanism with your fingers to just let enough water out so that the float falls about one or two inches. Then tip the tilt-back mechanism back on its seat and see where the water

line stops. There is a mark on the inside back of the tank for recommended water level.

It has been my experience that these modern, half-baked ballcocks supplied with new toilets do not last very long.

The next title will deal with KOHLER toilets. *All* close-coupled toilets assemble practically the very same way. The only difference between the AMERICAN STANDARD and the KOHLER versions is the number of tank bolts and rubber washers, and the possible number of closet bolts used in the foot.

If your present close-coupled toilet is still in keeping with your aesthetic values, but its performance is unacceptable, first install a new FLUIDMASTER 400A and an AMERICAN STANDARD 3158.078 tilt-back flush valve and AMERICAN STANDARD 3525.011 trip lever (flush handle) before sending it to the "bone pile."

If the toilet is merely sluggish in its duties, check the vent stack (on the roof) for possible bird's nests or other debris. If there was a full obstruction of the vent, the toilet might not even drain. I would suggest that you call your local plumbing suppliers and see who sells a product called CLOROBEN-PT. It's a fantastic degreaser and will ream out a slimed-up toilet trap. You can pour about ½ cup into your tank once a week (for a month) before going to bed and after everyone has finished using the potty. It will really speed up your drains and it removes any bad odors due to bacteria growth, inside the waste pipes.

## KOHLER Close-Coupled Toilet Installation

For those who purchased a KOHLER close-coupled toilet, the bowl setting sequence is the same as for the wall-hung design, as discussed on pages 133-136.

The tank installation is just a little bit different, but not by much. Start again by laying a piece of cardboard over the bowl and then lay the tank back side down, upon the bowl. Again, use the 15 or 16 inch slide-jaw pliers to check the tightness of the lock/mounting nuts on the flush valve and on the fill valve.

Now, inside the plastic bag accompanying the tank, you will find three brass tank bolts, six round rubber washers, three or four little rubber chafing blocks, one round, rubber tank gasket and maybe six metal flat washers.

Roll out a putty snake about ¼ inch in diameter and about 12 inches long, or better yet, two shorter ones equalling the same length.

If three of the rubber washers are larger in diameter than the remaining three, the larger ones go on the inside bottom of the tank and the smaller ones under the back of the bowl.

Now, wrap the snake, once, under the flat head of each tank bolt. If you should find 6 brass flat washers, slide one up each tank bolt now. If you only have three brass washers, then shove up the smaller rubber washer onto each bolt. Next, wrap a snake once, under each of the rubber washers.

Pick up the sponge rubber tank gasket and shove it onto the bottom of the flush valve, flat side up against the bottom of the tank. Then, liberally apply some RECTORSEAL/Slic-Tite to the beveled surface of the tank gasket and the mating depression on the back of the bowl.

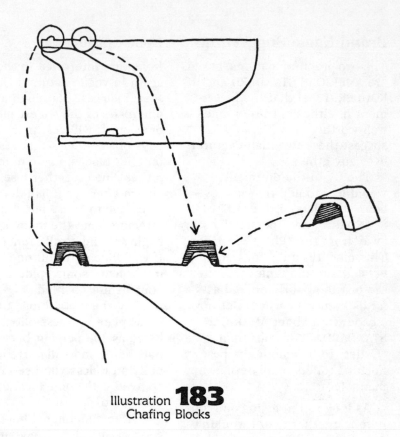

Illustration **183**
Chafing Blocks

Now, place two of the chafing blocks, each near the outside of the front, raised welt on the back of the bowl (see Illus. 183). If you have one chafing block left, it goes in the center of the rear raised welt. If you have two remaining chafing blocks, put one near each edge of the rear welt.

These chafing blocks are U-shaped, and are placed with the legs straddling each side of the welt. Now, insert the three bolts into the three holes in the bottom of the tank. Then, pick up the tank carefully and lower the tank gasket into the mating depression on the back of the bowl. Wiggle the tank a bit to try to get the three tank bolts to drop through the holes in the bowl.

Now with your hand inserted into the bottom of the tank, press down on one tank bolt head and from underneath, slide a rubber washer up each bolt, followed by a flat brass washer. Then thread the brass machine nuts up each tank bolt. The nuts will turn in a *clockwise* direction as viewed from underneath.

With a ⅝ inch wrench or the 6 inch adjustable wrench, hold each tank bolt *nut* stationary from underneath, while you turn the tank bolt from within the tank in a *clockwise* direction using the 16 to 18 inch slotted screwdriver.

With the tank vertical with the wall, tighten each nut several times, going to the next one and back again until the tank is almost rigid, on the bowl.

With this sequence accomplished, read pages 75-77 & 146 and install the new supply. Then open the angle stop and fill the tank. You might have to bend the float arm up or down to achieve the proper water level.

Well, congratulations! Shut the door and be the first one to use it.

## Brand Name Suggestions

The two premium national brands are AMERICAN STANDARD and KOHLER. I feel that the investment in either of these brands is well worth your while and I suggest these two manufacturers over any others.

The fly-in-the-ointment! I would like to add that in close-coupled toilets in the AMERICAN STANDARD line, I personally stay away from the "Plebe" design. This model is a lighter weight version and the tank components are just too poorly crafted as far as I am concerned. But now a good word about AMERICAN STANDARD. I consider their "Cadet" to be among the best flushing toilets of all designs and manufacturers.

As long as I'm giving opinions, here is another one. I wouldn't give you two cents for any "low profile" or "low-boy" or "silent flush" toilet of any manufacture. They are exorbitantly expensive for what you get and often very sluggish in performance, leaving an occasional deposit behind. And, when you go to purchase a seat for one (if the seat is not on the standard bolt pattern) you'll feel like you've just left the proctologist's.

I won't mention the brand name, but one manufacturer not too long ago made a toilet that was also supposed to dispose of the accompanying gas sometimes generated when using such fixtures. This was accomplished by pulling out on the flush handle, before pushing in on the handle to flush the bowl. Well, it was a total bust. The company lost millions and when you lifted the lid, you saw so many hoses and linkages that you'd swear you were looking under the hood of a loaded Lincoln Continental.

## Lost Epidermis

If you are interested in the now-again-in-vogue natural oak toilet seat, I suggest that you purchase one made of the *fewest* pieces of wood. It will cost more but it pays off. The ones that resemble butcher blocks, made of many pieces glued together lose their charm after the finish deteriorates due to "misguided male attempts" and the many pieces begin growing to different heights. If you slide on or off one, you might leave some epidermis of your behind, behind.

Also, the metal hinge tube is brass plated (unless outright listed as 100 percent brass hardware) and will corrode into oblivion unless you keep it sprayed with some form of rust-preventative.

For an economical but fairly good plastic seat, I recommend the BENEKE or BEMIS brands. Their mounting bolts are made of a very sturdy plastic which also drop into the seat hinges from *above*. You merely hold the nut in your fingers from below and with a screwdriver, tighten the bolt from above. When thus tightened, a hinge flap snaps in place hiding the head of the bolt.

Many a toilet bowl is cracked and ruined or just junked because of an impossible task of removing an old, urine-corroded steel bolt, washer or nut holding a seat in place.

## Tile Floors

Many times a bathroom will have its existing linoleum or tile floor laid over the new ceramic tile, *without* the old floor being torn up. Aside from giving the room new radiance, it further raises the toilet bowl anywhere from one inch or more off the old closet flange in the floor.

When the toilet was lifted so that the tile man could do his job, only one bowl wax was required to seal the bowl. Now what happens when the closet bolts are one or more inches too short and the new bowl wax does not even contact the bottom of the bowl?

Even the long closet bolts in most cases won't be long enough to protrude up through the bolt holes in the foot of the toilet so that the acorn nuts can draw the bowl down to the floor.

One method that I have discovered uses four closet bolts (for a two-bolt bowl). Depending upon the waste line diameter, purchase the "No-Seep" type bowl wax and also a standard, sleeveless bowl wax. While at the supplier's, also purchase two additional machine-thread closet bolts, in the standard length, along with two extra, open-domed acorn nuts. (I suggest that you read pages 131-136 also before doing any work.)

Okay, thread the new, open-domed acorn nuts onto the existing closet bolts but only *half-way*. Then, with the mini-hacksaw, cut the flattened heads off the extra machine thread closet bolts. Try gripping the bolts in the jaws of the slide-jaw pliers to steady them as you saw. Then thread the "factory ends" of the closet bolts into the top of the acorn nuts already on the existing closet bolts. Hold the acorn nuts still with one hand as you thread the new bolts in until they bottom-out on the top of the existing bolts.

Now, without any wax rings in place, lift the bowl up and set it down in place over the waste. If the acorn nuts that join the two bolts together are below the holes in the foot of the toilet, you are almost done. If the acorn nuts are in the holes of the bowl's foot or sticking out of the top, we will have to trim the existing bolts

154

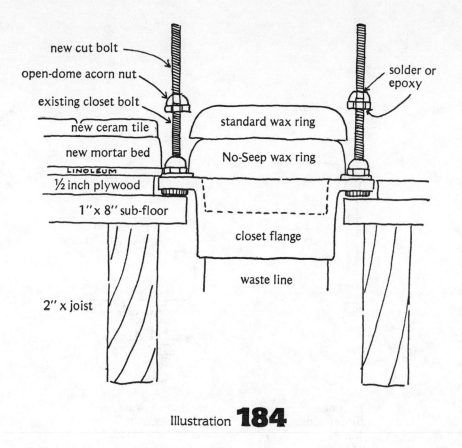

new cut bolt
open-dome acorn nut
existing closet bolt
new ceram tile
new mortar bed
LINOLEUM
½ inch plywood
1" x 8" sub-floor
2" x joist

solder or epoxy
standard wax ring
No-Seep wax ring
closet flange
waste line

Illustration **184**

## Low-Boys

*Low-boys* is a term generally used to describe low-profile, usually one-piece toilets (see Illus. 185). These designs usually have the tank cast as an integral part of the bowl itself, thus the one piece. A few low-profile designs *do* have a separate tank, which is coupled in the same manner as for standard designs.

The low-boy design presents a greater challenge to install (and later to live with) due to their extra weight and bulk. It is not possible, in many instances, to see the closet bolts or the holes in the foot while lifting the toilet onto the closet flange. Some designs also have counter-sunk holes in the foot and you need a 7/16 inch socket wrench to install the acorn nuts.

Another pain-in-the-bum can be fitting up the supply when installing this type in an older home or even in a new home when it will be close to a tub or shower stall or *especially* in an alcove. Because of its width, you will have to lie down on your belly, back and sides in order to reach the fill valve connection. In older homes, the water supply (angle stop) is often too high off

just a little bit. Lift the bowl up again and remove the cut bolts from the acorn nuts. Then, thread the acorn nuts down the existing bolts, about ¾ of an inch below the top of the bolt. Now, with the mini-hacksaw, saw off about ½ to ⅝ of an inch of existing closet bolt and then bring the acorn nut back up so that it is half-way off the top of the bolt. Now, again thread the factory end of the cut bolt into the top of the acorn nut until it bottoms-out on the existing one (see Illus. 184).

If you know how to solder with a propane torch, first sand the top and bottom of the acorn nuts. Then apply flux to both sides and put some inside the nuts. Now, rethread them onto the closet bolts and warm them up with the propane torch. Heat both the nuts and the bolts and use 50/50 solder.

If you cannot solder, I suggest that you purchase a good quality two-part epoxy kit (Plumber's EPOXY-BOND by Atlas Chemical) and apply the mixed compound (the paste form, not putty form) to the threads of both bolts and the inside of the acorn nuts and then reassemble them. Let the epoxy set up until it is real hard.

Both methods will prevent the acorn nut from turning and it will add a good bit of strength to the joints.

Now, place the No-Seep type bowl wax on the waste line (closet flange) and lay the standard bowl wax (without sleeve) on top of the first wax. Center the holes one above the other as best you can. We are now ready to set the bowl for good. Proceed as to the instruction on pages 135 & 136.

Illustration **185**
One-Piece
Low-Boy Toilet

the floor to set one of these toilets. The tank, being so low, is often interfered with by the old angle stop, and the old water line must be chopped out of the wall and lowered. If you have tiled walls or an an outdated color, this situation might rule out the choice of this toilet.

If you wish to replace your present close-coupled or wall-hung tank toilet with a low-boy, you had better measure the height of your present angle stop and compare this measurement with the height of the fill valve connection on your prospective choice.

If the angle stop is as close as 2 inches to the new low-boy connection, there is a *chance* that you can leave the water supply alone by reading the following section: The Inverted Angle Stop.

## The Inverted Angle Stop

If you are removing a wall-hung tank toilet to install a close-coupled or low-boy toilet, you might find that the height of the angle stop is too close to the bottom of the tank and that you cannot bend the new supply to fit without seriously kinking it, or it might simply be impossible to bend the supply to the proper shape.

There is a way out of this predicament . . . sometimes. When installing the new ½ inch IPS by ⅜ brass ferrule compression angle stop, leave the threaded sleeve pointing *down* instead of up. Then, on this *one* installation, I am going to recommend the use of the spirally grooved closet supply with *rubber cone washer* top, *not* the flat brim type.

I can recommend the spirally grooved supply for this situation because you will have to bend the supply in a real tight radius

existing wall-hung tank

new close-coupled or low-boy toilet tank

existing rubber cone washer angle stop

new brass ferrule compression angle stop and spirally grooved supply

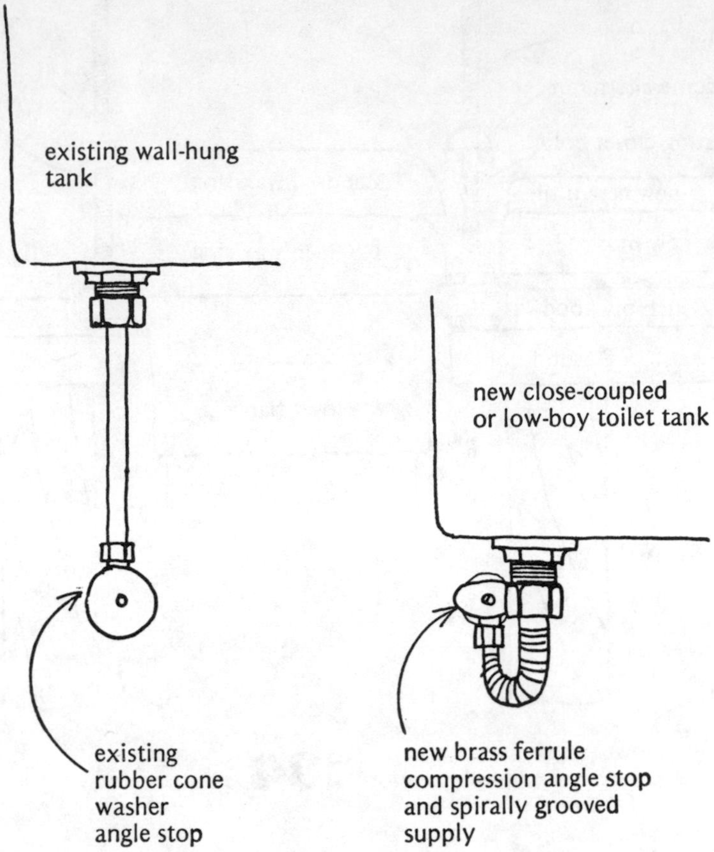

Illustration **186**
Angle Stop for Low-Boy Toilet

(U-shape) that you cannot make with your hands or even with a spring tubing bender. It would require a professional, expensive tubing bender and the expertise to operate one in order to use the smooth, ⅜ inch supply.

You will be able to bend the spirally grooved supply with merely your hands. However, I suggest that you use a piece of rope or wire and bend it to the appropriate shape required to connect the tank and the angle stop. Then, measure the length. In this way, you will purchase the supply closest to the proper length (see Illus. 186).

## The True Wall-Hung Toilet

The true wall-hung toilet (Illus. 187) is hung entirely on the wall, off the floor. For those of you building new homes or a new bath addition, you might consider this design. Of all the toilet designs, the true wall-hung is the nicest to live with. Scunge does not collect around a base on the floor; you can drag a mop across the floor underneath and have a nice area rug below rather than the usual, ugly, "wrap-around-the-bowl, electrified cotton candy jobs."

The true wall-hung is held in place by more than an act of God.

It is held there by what is called a "carrier," which is a heavy metal bracket that is screwed, nailed and/or bolted to the inside of the wall. *Hopefully not a standard 2 inch by 4 inch stud wall.*

The minimum wall thickness that I will install a true wall-hung toilet on is *8 inch studs, on 12 inch centers* for *four feet either side of the carrier*. And, I prefer to see a 2 by 10 or 12 inch wall for this application. The waste line and the vent stack are both inside the wall, leaving little room for standard 2 by 4 inch blocking.

As you might expect, the cost of building the wall and the extra plumber's time are both considerable, but well worth the investment. Since this installation is a bit involved, I am not going to send you to the wolves on this one. Get in touch with your plumber if you are interested in the possibilities of the true wall-hung or if you must deal with a leaking one.

This design is not the latest *flush in a pan*. Thomas C. Crapper had one on the market back in 1888!

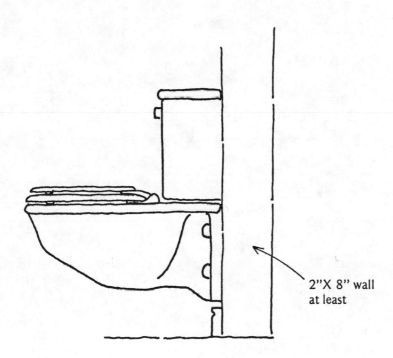

2"X 8" wall
at least

Illustration **187**
True Wall-hung Toilet

# GLOSSARY

**Acorn Nut:** The nut, having an acorn shape, which is used in conjunction with closet bolts to hold the toilet bowl to the floor.

**Angle Stop:** Valve in a 90 degree configuration that controls and shuts off the water service to the valves (faucets) and toilet tanks above.

**Ballcock:** One form of fill valve used to introduce water to the toilet tank.

**Bonnet Nut:** The nut, resembling a bonnet, that secures the valve stem in the valve, whether it be cock, 4 inch center set, widespread or wall-hung kitchen sink faucet or tub and shower valve.

**Bowl Wax:** The round, highly viscous seal that is sandwiched between the horn of the toilet bowl and the closet flange or lead bend, at the floor. Also referred to as "wax ring".

**Closet:** In the vernacular of the trade, a word used in place of toilet.

**Closet Bolts:** The bolts used to secure the toilet to the floor or closet flange.

**Closet Flange:** If you have one, it is a flat flange secured to the top of the toilet waste line, level to the floor, which holds the machine type closet bolts and holds the toilet down tightly to the floor.

**Cock:** A single valve installed on a sink or counter, on the bottom of a water heater or a male fitting such as the tubing connection on the Fluidmaster 400A fill valve.

**Cone Washer:** A rubber, beveled washer used in conjunction with supply tubes on angle stops and faucet connections.

**Continuous Waste:** Those tubular plumbing parts attached to one lavatory or kitchen sink tailpiece which carries the waste water over to the other tailpiece or disposer el and down to the trap.

**Diverter Valve:** The center valve on a tub and shower valve which sends the water to either the shower head or the tub spout.

**Eccentric:** The offset water connections that fasten the wall-hung kitchen sink faucet body to the nipples in the wall.

**Escutcheon:** The coned or flattened round object made of porcelain or chromed metal which is used to hide whatever is behind or underneath it.

**Escutcheon Nut:** The little round nut that holds a faucet valve escutcheon to the valve underneath.

**Fill Valve:** The valve that controls the inlet water to the toilet tank, such as a ballcock or Fluidmaster 400A fill valve.

**FIP:** The abbreviation for Female Iron Pipe.

**Float Arm:** The arm that connects the float ball to the valve on a ballcock.

**Fluidmaster 400A:** My choice of fill valves.

**Flushball:** The rubber ball that rests on the flush valve seat on a flushball flush valve.

**Flush Elbow:** The tubular brass pipe that delivers water to the toilet bowl from the toilet tank on a wall-hung tank toilet.

**Flush Valve:** The valve in the bottom of the toilet tank that lets water from the toilet tank into the bowl, thus flushing the bowl of its contents.

**Friction Ring:** A flat brass washer used in some slip joint connections such as at faucet connections and sometimes toilet flush elbow connections.

**Horn:** A raised, round exit hole on the bottom of a toilet bowl. This horn nests in a bowl wax or wax ring when the bowl is set in place.

**Jam Nut:** A nut used to retain some old styles of cross-shaped handles to valve stems.

**Lift Spout:** A tub spout which has a lift knob to send water which would issue out the spout up to the shower head.

**Manifold:** The portion of valve where hot and cold water are mixed, after leaving the valves themselves but before exiting the spout.

**Mixing Valve:** A valve which is served with hot and cold supplies where the water is mixed to the desired temperature BEFORE exiting the spout.

**Nipples:** Pieces of pipe, from 1 inch to 12 inches in length, with male threads on each end.

**Packing Nut:** A nut which maintains pressure on valve packings to prevent leakage from around the stem.

**Running Thread:** A hollow brass or plastic tube with fine threads running down its entire length.

(continued)

159

One end threads into the packing nut and the other end threads into an escutcheon nut or escutcheon, thus securing the escutcheon in place.

**Setting:** A term in the vernacular meaning installing. Would be used in reference to faucet valves, toilets, etc.

**Slip Nut:** The nut used in slip joint connections. It applies pressure to the rubber slip nut washer.

**Spud:** The brass fitting in the wall-hung toilet bowl which secures the flush elbow to the bowl.

**Supply Tube:** The round piece of tubing that delivers water from the angle stop to the faucet or fill valve above.

**Tailpiece:** On bathroom sinks it is the 1¼ inch diameter section of tubular brass that connects the waste to the trap. On kitchen sinks, it is the 1½ inch diameter section of tubular brass that connects the basket strainer to the trap or continuous waste.

**Trap:** The piping that attaches to a tailpiece and through two 90 degree bends (P-trap) carries waste water to the drain in the wall without letting dangerous sewer gas exit the fixture (sink, tub or shower pan—the toilet has one which is an integral part of the bowl).

**Trap Arm:** That portion of a P-trap that lies horizontal and connects to the wall nipple.

**Trip Lever:** In the vernacular of the trade, the term meaning the toilet tank's flush handle mechanism.

**Valve:** A mechanical device which controls the flow of water, or other medium.

**Valve Stem:** A round, metal dowel onto which the valve handle/handles are attached and by which the valve is actuated.

**Washer:** STEM—A rubber disk which fastens to the end of a faucet stem to prevent water from flowing through the valve. FLAT—A brass or steel circle with a hole in the center used to evenly apply a compression force.

**Waste:** Those plumbing parts installed in the hole of the sink bottom which carry waste water to the trap.

**Wax Ring:** Same as bowl wax, on first page of glossary.

# About The Author

Peter Hemp is a big, friendly man—father of three young children—who lives with his wife and kids in the house in Albany that he grew up in. Peter learned plumbing from watching his father, Homer, and later, on the job. He spent some time on his grandfather's dairy farm in Waukau, Wisconsin, where he observed Homer tinkering and inventing. "If he were alive today, he could fix a 747 with a rubber hose, a hat pin and a rawhide boot strap," Peter asserts.

Peter's father enjoyed remodeling the family houses and plumbed and wired them. Now Peter, 39, specializes in plumbing. "I've done it all," he says, "I was a foreman on a big sewage job for the State; did some steam plumbing on some experimental steam vehicles; and for the last 10 years I've been on my own. My work now is strictly on residential and commercial property. I love to work for restaurants that enjoy feeding me."

Among his fellow plumbers, Peter is known as a maverick—a turncoat who insists that homeowners can do some of their own plumbing repairs if they get "The Straight Poop." Speaking of the right stuff, it was written to help even the most INEXPERIENCED and TIMID homeowners save lots of money on their plumbing bills.